Learning Toward an Ecological Consciousness

Learning Toward an Ecological Consciousness: Selected Transformative Practices

Edited by

Edmund V. O'Sullivan
and Marilyn M. Taylor

First published 2004 by
Palgrave Macmillan™
175 Fifth Avenue, New York, N.Y. 10010 and
Houndmills, Basingstoke, Hampshire, England RG21 6XS
Companies and representatives throughout the world

Palgrave Macmillan is the global academic imprint of the Palgrave Macmillan division of St. Martin's Press, LLC and of Palgrave Macmillan Ltd. Macmillan® is a registered trademark in the United States, United Kingdom and other countries. Palgrave is a registered trademark in the European Union and other countries.

ISBN 1–4039–6304–5 hardback
ISBN 978–1–4039–6305–5   ISBN 1-4039-6305-3 paperback

Library of Congress Cataloging-in-Publication Data
    Learning toward an ecological consciousness : selected transformative practices / edited by Edmund V. O'Sullivan and Marilyn M. Taylor.
        p. cm.
    Includes bibliographical references and index.
    ISBN 1–4039–6304–5 (cloth)—ISBN 1–4039–6305–3 (pbk.)
    1. Environmental psychology. 2. Environmental education. I. O'Sullivan, Edmund, 1938– II. Taylor, Marilyn M.

    BF353.L42 2003
    304.2—dc21   2003053270

A catalogue record for this book is available from the British Library.

Design by Newgen Imaging Systems (P) Ltd., Chennai, India.

First edition: January, 2004
10 9 8 7 6 5 4 3 2 1

Transferred to digital printing in 2008.

Contents

**Part 3   The Dynamic Relation of Personal
          Agency in Community Context**

INTRODUCTION

Conundrum, Challenge, and Choice

We live in a time of great possibilities and also of grave dangers; both arising from the same capability of our species to pursue effectively, single-mindedly, its goals. Three hundred years of technological advance and extension of our basic physical abilities has resulted in our ability to reach most parts of the planet within 24 hours, communicate instantly through cyberspace to anywhere on the globe, visually apprehend events as they occur around the world within minutes, launch disaster relief in one part of the world from any other part of the world within a day, walk on the moon and maneuver in space, provide every child on earth with vaccines and other medicine that eliminate most life-threatening and debilitating childhood diseases, and produce food on a scale that can now eliminate starvation. And the list of benefits goes on.

At the same time, we are also able to lay waste vast portions of the earth and entire populations with nuclear arms delivered with laser precision from unmanned craft on earth and from space. On a daily basis manifold manufacturing and refining processes around the globe also generate toxic wastes that pollute the earth, water, and air, threatening all species of life on earth including our own. We are creating more garbage than we can dispose of safely. Vast processes of destructive environmental change precipitated by industry and hydrocarbon combustion–based transportation are progressing at a rate perceptible to everyone.

Our decisions and priorities do not reflect an intention toward life. We are not using our knowledge and technical ability to reverse the dangerous course we seem to be on. The pattern of choices with respect to how we use our technical expertise for what and for who is creating deep dissention, resentment, and rage that translates into continuous war and terrorism. The capability to produce wealth and material necessities that should improve the human condition are instead creating rapidly widening gaps between the rich minority and the poverty-stricken majority. Clearly, traditional science and its applications, the flagship of our modernist civilization, have had a mixed impact on the health and well-being of the earth.

We believe a key element in the conundrum is that in generating and sustaining the scientific technological enterprise, we have positioned ourselves outside the world we are acting upon. Here, we use the term "instrumental consciousness" to refer to this modernist mode of thinking and acting. Everything becomes a means. Being enraptured by our own inventions, our goals are often material in nature. We have, possibly unwittingly, transformed ourselves into achievers and users. These "careers" are endless activities that do not seem to bring an enduring sense of fulfillment. And they create myopia—a fixation on what we are doing and preoccupation with doing more of it. Paradoxically, from beginning as a detached agent acting on the world, we are unconsciously drawn completely inside it. We lose awareness of our place in the broader context and the impact of our endeavors. Importantly, as the consequences of our civilization are emerging, we resist facing the overwhelming implications. The same instrumental consciousness enables us to distance ourselves from the painful consequences (Macy, 1998).

How are we to break out of this destructive spiral? One option has been to deconstruct modernist assumptions through rigorous intellectual analysis. This includes resisting the substitution of any other synthesis or overarching perspective and refusing to prioritize any perspective over others. Taken to its conclusion, deconstructive postmodernism, indeed antimodernism, leaves us nowhere to stand and no avenue into a different future (Kegan, 1994). We are still positioned outside the world. To act, we must step into the world, select a direction, and invest in it our energy and confidence, at least temporarily.

So this book is about practices that situate us *within* a journey, reentering the world we are acting on and opening up ourselves at the deepest levels to learning—the transformation of our fundamental assumptions and beliefs about ourselves and our relationship to our environment. We think that approaching these challenges in the familiar way, as heroes fixing problems, is to vastly underestimate and even to exacerbate threatening conditions. And to infuse our world with skepticism is to paralyze ourselves. We seek a systemic awareness and the courage to engage wholeheartedly as some of many participants. This demands basic reorientation of how we understand ourselves how we lead, how we organize ourselves, how we learn, and what we appreciate as knowledge. As Albert Einstein is often quoted to have said, we are not likely to solve problems from the same perspective within which they were created.

Through *mindful practice* we are *learning our way into* seeing, acting, and understanding that which is now outside our current consciousness. Edmund O'Sullivan et al. (2002) speaks of transformative learning as comprising survival, critique, and creation. We think these components are co-occurring elements with each having a sequential emphasis. We must survive the despair of our current condition once we have opened ourselves to it. We must become aware of the ontology that underlies our current course and recognize our immersion in it (critique). And we must create an expansive, life-giving vision that has sufficient depth of meaning to engage the human spirit. This order of learning derives from active engagement in practices that embody ecological values—connection, openness, generosity, appreciation, partnership, inquiry, dialogue, and celebration. Learning beyond the limitations of an instrumental, modernist consciousness requires what Macmurray (1957) identified as the primacy of practice—concepts are generated from and illuminate practice. For practice to be mindful, it demands not only reflection but also dialogue. We engage collaboratively with others and their different perspectives in reconstructing an understanding of ourselves and our world.

As contributors to this volume illustrate in their diverse practices, the notion of "educator" is expanded well beyond conventional conceptions. In the first place, as educators we are at work in all corners of life—in the workplace, the community, communities of practice, and relationship networks. Second, as educators we are not purveyors of knowledge. We are designers and participants in environments and processes through which people are able to learn toward an ecological perspective. We are jesters, exemplars, caring colleagues, and midwives to transformative change in ourselves and others. We challenge, confront, console, accompany, affirm, and enquire. Above all, we ourselves learn.

The wide-ranging selection of transformative practices presented here offer avenues toward an emerging ecological consciousness that reshapes us, our actions, and our understanding. These practices, as a collection, are an expression of the principle of equifinality, that is, that there are many paths to a destination. A corollary is that we begin where we are and in a way in which we are moved and able to begin. The contributors and those whose experience and reflections are represented (where identified) in the chapters begin in multiple cultures, at least three indigenous, on at least four continents, in at least eight countries. They are men and women who speak through a gendered experience implicitly if not explicitly. Signifying transformation through connection in multiple ways, the practices cross layers and domains of the social and natural world—the personal, interpersonal and primary groups, cultural and other communities, the workplace, educational institutions and the wider society, and natural environments. Some begin at a micro-level moving out to a wider world; some begin in the wider world that leads to a personal practice; others highlight resonance among experience on many planes simultaneously. The contributors and those represented in their chapters have arrived at their work from many walks of life, including: educators (ecological, adult, and leadership), community and environmental activists, organizational change interveners, psychotherapists, researchers, and writers. The book comprises many different disciplines, literatures, and discourses. What they all share is concern and dedication toward enhancing our human experience and our earthly home.

The chapters elaborating specific practices are introduced in more detail in the prologues to each of the three sections of this book.

References

Kegan, R. (1994). *In Over Our Heads: The Mental Demands of Modern Life.* Cambridge, MA: Harvard University Press.

Macy, J. (1998). *Coming Back to Life: Practices to Reconnect Our Lives, Our World.* Gabriola Island, BC: New Society Publishers.

Macmurray, J. (1957). *The Self as Agent.* London: Faber and Faber.

O'Sullivan, E., Morell, A., and O'Connor, M. A. (2002). *Expanding the Boundaries of Transformative Learning: Essays on Theory and Praxis.* New York: Palgrave.

CHAPTER 1

Glimpses of an Ecological Consciousness

Edmund V. O'Sullivan and Marilyn M. Taylor

A New Understanding of Consciousness

Recognition of the role of consciousness in shaping our experience, our perceptions, our expectations, and, ultimately, our actions is one of the most powerful themes to emerge in Western societies during the twentieth century, another Copernican revolution according to Willis Harman (1988). He notes Nobel neurological scientist, Roger Sperry's observation: "Current concepts of the mind–brain relation involve a direct break with long-established materialist and behaviorist doctrine that has dominated neuroscience for many decades. Instead of renouncing or ignoring consciousness, the new interpretation gives full recognition to the primacy of inner conscious awareness as a causal reality" (Harman, 1988, p. 11). How we think, how we interpret what we see, indeed, what we see and experience is recognized as critical in the unfolding of our history and our lives. Humberto Maturana and Francisco Varela (1987), Chilean biologists of cognition and consciousness, assert that we "bring forth a world." Fritjof Capra (2002) has summarized their cognitive theory another way, "The process of knowing is the process of life.... The organizing activity of living systems, at all levels of life, is mental activity" (p. 34).

Further, at a biological level, cognition of organisms is now seen to be "structurally coupled" (Maturana and Varela, 1987) with its environment. That is, environmental disturbances prompt organisms to restructure themselves and, on that basis, behave differently. Robert Kegan (1994) makes

a similar observation concerning the role of our social and cultural environments as influences in constructing and reconstructing our consciousness.
He names these demands that call forth consciousness development, "the
hidden curriculum." These developmental themes illuminate the profound
co-constitutive relationship between ourselves and our world.

With consciousness as the source of our action, we examine the predom-
inant perspective of our age, that is, what we have termed the "instrumental
consciousness" of the modern era. As a backdrop for the array of transformative practices in the three sections of this book, we contrast instrumental
consciousness and an emerging ecological consciousness in the three
domains: conceptions of knowledge and education; social configurations
(organizations, communities, and institutions) and leadership; and conceptions of ourselves.

What is Meant by "Consciousness"?

Fritjof Capra (2002) makes an important distinction between the primary
consciousness (basic cognitive, perceptual, sensory, and emotional processes
that we share with mammals and other vertebrates) and reflective consciousness, "a level of cognitive abstraction that includes the ability to hold mental
images, which allows us to formulate values, beliefs, goals and strategies"
(p. 39). For the moment, we will focus on reflective consciousness.

What we mean here by "consciousness" is the "frames" or mental structures through which we interpret our world, understand ourselves, and find
meaning. It is our ontology—our reality. Kegan (1994) speaks of our "ways
of organizing experience" (p. 9). Harman (1988) alludes to the pervasiveness
of consciousness: "The person's total belief system is an organization of
beliefs and expectancies that the person accepts as true of the world he or she
lives in—verbal and nonverbal, implicit and explicit, conscious and unconscious" (p. 15). Ken Wilber (2000) reminds us of Clare Graves's notion of
consciousness as "levels or waves of existence." Charles Taylor (1989) speaks
of our "inescapable operational frameworks" about which we have a "strong
evaluation" arising from powerfully tacit standards that precede logic. "To
think, feel, judge within such a framework is to function with a sense that
some action, or mode of life, or mode of feeling is incomparably higher than
others which are more readily available to us" (Taylor, 1989, p. 20). Robert
Marshak and Judith Katz (1998) speak of our tacit perspective, comprising
our beliefs, assumptions, values, theoretical constructs, expectations, and
lessons learned, as a prism that filters and shapes our perceptions and
responses. We act necessarily out of what we take to be reality as we have

apprehended it. We cocreate our experience. Our consciousness is, in this sense, a causal dimension through our interaction and action.

As an attribute of a person, consciousness is mental structure; as an attribute of a human system, consciousness is its culture. Cultural consciousness is the taken-for-granted beliefs, assumptions, rules, and values that constituent members of the culture share as reality.

> Every society ever known rests on some set of largely tacit basic assumptions about who we are, in what kind of universe we find ourselves, and what is ultimately important to us. Some such set of assumptions can be found to underlie the institutions and mores, patterns of thought and systems of value that characterize society. (Harman, 1988, p. 10)

Taylor (1989) reminds us that there is a cost to diverging from the cultural synthesis. In premodern societies where cultural consciousness "stands unquestioned," dissenters are threatened with condemnation. In modern societies, while commonly shared frameworks are made problematic, a sense of alienation or meaninglessness awaits those who are unable to find their own personal sense of purpose and meaning. As we move to the edge of the modern context, the grip of the culture on constituents' consciousnesses is loosening or perhaps shifting to a more complex demand, that of personal authority, "a self-authorship that can coordinate, integrate, act upon, or invent values, beliefs, convictions, generalizations, ideals, abstractions, interpersonal loyalties, and intrapersonal states" (Kegan, 1994, p. 185). We turn now to the modern era and its consequences for consciousness and environment.

The Instrumental Consciousness—Subjectivity, Process, and Relation Eclipsed

Through the Age of Enlightenment and the Industrial Age, the Western world has sojourned for 300 years in the benefits, consequences, and limitations of what has come to be known as the modern era. Empirical science challenged and defeated the Church for legitimacy of its grounds for Truth. Through systematic observation and analysis, Copernicus dislocated the earth as the center of the solar system. Newton defined explanatory laws of physics—dynamics of the material world. Descartes dissociated mind from matter and observer from observed and Darwin replaced the creation story with discernable patterns of biological evolution as the origin of the human race (O'Sullivan, 1999). The momentum of empirical science drove application resulting in the invention of a wide variety of machines that vastly increased production of goods, extraction of natural resources, production of food, and ultimately transportation and communication. The industrial age emerged and flourished. It amplified and justified the confidence of Western culture in its conviction of continuous progress. Modernity is characterized by "... belief in the value of the past; conviction of the nobility, even superiority, of Western civilization; acceptance of the worth of economic and technological growth; faith in reason and in the kind of scientific and scholarly knowledge that can come from reason alone ... " (Nisbet, 1980, p. 317).

The mechanistic images of Newtonian science and technology have shaped our understanding of ourselves, our purposes, our relations with each other, and our relation to our environment. They have emphasized a focus on tools and tasks. We are what we can accomplish; it has become our highest purpose. We acquired a predominantly, "instrumental consciousness."

> Three centuries ago, when the world was seen as an exquisite machine set in motion by God—a closed system with a watchmaker father who then left the shop—the concept of entropy entered our collective consciousness. Machines wear down; they eventually stop . . . . This is a universe, we feel, that cannot be trusted with growth, rejuvenation, process. If we want progress, then we must provide the energy, the momentum, to reverse decay. By sheer force of will, because we are the planet's consciousness, we will make the world hang together. We will resist death. (Wheatley, 1992, p. 17)

Instrumental Epistemology and Education

Knowledge became synonymous with science: abstract constructs, and theory derived from empirical observation, logical analysis, and hypothetico-deductive experimental methodology. The etymology of science, "*scientia*" meaning "knowledge" in a much broader sense, was more narrowly conceptualized. Allegiance to analysis led to compartmentalization of "knowledge" itself. Stephen Toulmin (1985) observes that for the past 300 years only rarely would scientists and scholars cross the boundaries of their clearly delineated discipline.

Edmund O'Sullivan (1999) notes that the wholeness of creation apprehended through premodern cosmologies is entirely eclipsed by the modernist perspective. Within Western culture, practice-based sources of learning, knowledge creation, and expertise have been devalued though they are essential to daily living. Those whose professions and life work contributed necessarily through practical expertise and wisdom are also discounted—women, working class, artisans, and people working on the land and sea. In non-Western countries and among indigenous peoples of the "new world" such as North America, modernist values of Western culture rendered invisible whole ways of life. Vandana Shiva (2000) highlights examples of both "piracy" of indigenous knowledge by modernist commercial interests and disregard of basic indigenous wisdom that protects biodiversity and sustainable life.

"Education" in a modernist world has been understood primarily as the conventional dissemination of knowledge that has been generated through formal research and scholarship. Again, the etymology of the word, "to lead or draw out" implying attention to the learner is replaced by a focus on the subject matter and cognitive processes that must be mastered. The powerful image of the learner as Locke's "tabula rasa" combined with the highly compartmentalized structuring of knowledge has led to the bureaucratization of educational organizations and processes. With few exceptions, schools and universities are configured for individual students in every field and profession to receive knowledge as packages assembled and delivered by individual teachers in increasingly large educational institutions. Knowledge as a disembodied commodity takes on new life in an electronic age with its Internet possibilities for distributing packaged knowledge across the globe.

Instrumental Configuration of the Social World and Leadership Practice

The instrumental imagination has patterned how we conduct our lives and how we structure ourselves to achieve our largely material purposes. The social theories of Enlightenment philosophers, John Locke and Thomas Hobbes, greatly influenced the structuring governments, especially the then emerging republics like the United States of America. The assumptions about the social world were patterned after the natural science of the day. Capra (1983) notes, "... the function of government was not to impose laws on people, but rather to discover and enforce the natural laws that existed before any state was formed. According to Locke, these natural laws included the freedom and equality of all individuals as well as the right to property, which represented the fruits of one's labour" (p. 69). These were laudable goals but when disassociated from inherent interdependencies set the stage for laissez-faire economics—single-minded material-wealth producing endeavors. As elaborated in the following, O'Sullivan (1999) notes that social configurations, including societies, were conceptualized as contractual arrangements among separate individual entities, in Hobbes's words, social atoms.

Community-based structures of premodern productivity were gradually replaced by industrial work organizations modeled after machines. Workers were trained to perform repetitive, specialized functions with no relation or awareness of the nature of the whole production process to which their efforts contributed. Work became disconnected from its origins or its outcomes. Motivation to work that provided food, shelter, and quality of life shifted to that of compliance for compensation (Bergquist, 1993). Techniques to ensure compliance were introduced to discipline workers in line with the production and productivity priorities of factory owners (Morgan, 1998).

Fredrick Taylor, recognized as the originator of scientific management, refined earlier methods of fashioning work organizations as efficient machines, configuring separate parts into efficient operation through command and control structures (Kanigel, 1997). For Taylor, it was the managers' responsibility to do the thinking and organizing, selection, training, and monitoring of workers while the workers' responsibility was to know their particular job and comply with managers' instructions. While the technical advantages of efficiency, standardization, mass production, and the creation of wealth have been obvious so too have been the costs of dehumanizing the workforce and the cumulative degradation of the environment.

Mechanistic organizational forms—classic bureaucracy—not only shape private enterprises but also public service organizations. Citizens are recipients of standardized services and sources of revenue, and are compliant to laws and regulations. In the health sector, health knowledge is based on a mechanistic perspective of the human body (Merchant, 1990) and the health care system has evolved into an elaborate bureaucracy. Patients are the recipients of treatment based on highly specialized scientific knowledge and technology.

An important dimension of modernism is the elevation of a small number of the few over the many as authorities in hierarchical bureaucracies and/or as authorities in scientific professions. Responsibility for all aspects of life is shifted to organizational authorities and specialized experts. Merrelyn Emery (1999) observes, "... critical feature is that responsibility is located at least one level above where a particular activity is being performed.... Everyone, except the person at the top, is licensed to be irresponsible" (p. xv). In this conception, the leaders are perceived as heroes, the ones who look after the vulnerable, the unable. In basic human terms this one-up-one-down relationship is often destructive and is most certainly dysfunctional and stressful for those who lead. For those who are led, it is disempowering, discouraging, and dissatisfying. Dependency and counter-dependency are accompanied by insecurity and anger leading to avoidance and aggression

(Bion, 1962). This pattern is one of many unconscious processes that can grip an organization and its constituents if the only legitimate discourse is circumscribed by technical tasks, strategy, logic, and inputs/outputs, while suppressing or repressing the so-called less tidy and irrational aspects of the human experience.

In the shadow of the rationally based bureaucracy, we find key nonrational dimensions: persons struggling to surface and to find expression. Sociologist Max Weber (1958) noted that the more the bureaucratic form of organization advances, the more perfectly it succeeds in eliminating all human qualities that escape technical calculation. However, Carl Jung (1953) suggests that irrational qualities never accept their banishment idly and are always looking for a way to make an impact. We see this in much of the unofficial politicking that shapes organizational life and also in factors such as stress, lying, cheating, depression, and acts of sabotage (Morgan, 1998).

As citizens of the industrialized cultures, we are immersed in and surrounded by the mechanistic metaphor that strongly invites us into an instrumental consciousness at work, in our communities and in schools. Kegan (1994) suggests that most of us tend to accept the given cultural assumptions embedded in social configurations uncritically as reality; we are obedient to them. Most of us "internalize and identify with the values and beliefs of our social 'surround'—as these may be communicated by family, peer group, state, religion, ethnic clan, geographic region, or social position..." (Kegan, 1994, p. 76) and carry them throughout adulthood. To this extent, mechanistic forms of social organization have a tenacious grip on our consciousness. Reconfiguration of our social world—organizations, institutions, communities, relationships—is, therefore, a critical transformative practice *in learning our way toward an ecological consciousness.*

Instrumental Consciousness and "the Minimal Self"

Paradoxically, as we place ourselves at the apex of creation, we simultaneously reject or disregard elements of our humanity that are self-affirming and life-sustaining—the quality of our relationships to each other and to our context, our inherent capacities to heal, renew, and evolve, and our worthiness simply to sojourn as an integral inhabitant of the earth. We have fostered "the minimal self" (Lasch, 1978). O'Sullivan (1999) speaks of the nihilist self-encapsulation: a deeply truncated sense of the self that has caused great suffering, alienation, and fragmentation in our century.

While we have inherited continual technological benefits that deliver and hold promise for increasing our life span, reducing mindless labor, enhancing mobility and communication, and the like, the accompanying instrumental consciousness seems to have "sapped" our lives of the meaning that sustains the human spirit. There is no place in the world economy governed by the profit motive for the cultivation and nourishment of the spiritual life. Leisure, contemplation, and silence have no value in this system because none of these activities are governed by the motivation of material profit. Spiritual concerns and activities are met with modernist "tolerance" and/or skepticism. Our world economy is driven by material wants and needs and makes invisible the hunger of the spirit.

Transforming the minimal self is critical for two reasons. The first is that as we treat ourselves, so do we treat others and our planet (Roszak, 1992). The inability to appreciate inherent value is a way of seeing. Instrumental consciousness apprehends only instrumental value. My self and my life are significant on the basis of what I produce. Our environment is valued as it can be used for instrumental human purposes.

The second is that the human spirit is required for the momentous project of reversing the destructive trends across our world. We must be gripped by the inherent worth of ourselves, of others, and of our world in order to sustain our commitment to what is likely to be a very long journey out of the wasteland. Faith not knowledge will be the source of renewing energy.

The Failure of Modernism and Instrumental Consciousness

The growing environmental movement has brought our attention to the worldwide complex negative impact of the Modernist project, which is accelerating with globalization. Rainforest devastation, global warming, human rights violations seem to follow the market along with and, perhaps, more than any of its proclaimed positive effects. In terms of wealth distribution, our world today is at its highest level of inequities. The laundry list is long and ominous as illustrated in the 2003 *State of the World* Report (Starke, 2003). It includes ozone layer depletion, loss of biodiversity, climate change, starvation and food security, and increasing toxic waste. Although the global market rhetoric still boasts of a trickle down distribution of wealth from rich to poor, the facts indicate the contrary, even by World Bank accounts. In a wide-ranging study covering 85 percent of the world's population from 91 countries, Branco Milanovic (2002) (a senior World Bank economist) found that the richest 1 percent of the world have income equivalent to the poorest 57 percent. Four-fifths of the world's population lives below what populations in North America and Europe consider their poverty line (Milanovic, 2002). Wealth has moved consistently upward to a smaller and smaller elite group while leaving the vast majority of peoples of the world increasingly destitute. Additionally, evidence indicates that employment in the global market is not a good employer. The ratio of unemployed to employed is increasing to astronomical levels in our world today. The UN agency for labor has said that there are 160 million people without work around the world as of 2001, 20 million more than three years ago (Doole, 2001).

Ecological Consciousness—Recovering Subjectivity, Relation, and Process

As the grip of modernism loosens, we are invited and challenged by new possibilities, to re-imagine our world and ourselves. We now touch on some of the shifts in perspective occurring in the twentieth century that we see as holding promise for enabling us to face the enormous challenge we face in reversing environmental degradation, global inequities, and our sense of alienation in the new millennium.

The Ecological Self

In an ecological perspective, there is no sense of the person without the sense of community. The philosopher John Macmurray (1961) maintains that the development of the person involves a type of reciprocity where the person is at once subject and object, encompassing both modes simultaneously. This is the notion of the personal self in co-constituted relationships (Sullivan, 1990).

We seem to have a deep primordial need for reciprocal acknowledgment and in its absence in early stages of development or for prolonged periods of time, there is the likelihood of breakdown (Sullivan, 1990; O'Sullivan, 1999). It would seem that inherent in what it means to be human is the sharing of conscious understanding and the lived experience including emotions as intimately as possible. Intimacy here means a presence to one another at our deepest levels of subjectivity. It is clear that each species carries with it an "emerging imperative" for the enhancement of its own life processes.

At the same time, we are also very clearly aware that there is an interspecies awareness that from our very beginnings is opening us up to a wider world. This wider sense of connection with all the powers of the world is a primary matrix for all our subsequent development. Our personal world is not simply connected to the human community. We are creatures of the wider earth community and the very universe itself. We would characterize this as our original birthright or innocence where the powers of the universe stand poised to join us on this wonderful journey that we call the gift of life. In the modern world we have limited our vision of the deep relational quality of all reality to what indigenous peoples call "all my relations." Even though the human family, in its many manifestations, provides the initial

Figure 1.1 Nested World Contexts of Life in the Universe.

primary matrix for the protection and development of human life, we are aware of what Chellis Glendinning (1995) calls the initial primary or primal matrix, which embeds us both in the depth and width of our planet and universe. Eimear O'Neill (2003) depicts this wider matrix as nested world contexts, illustrating them in figure 1.1.

> In the context of the universe lies earth, in the context of that, various land/based nations, and within those, peoples, communities and families. The personal self is human-centered within the larger biosphere of earthed community. These circles are holons, coherent and metaphorically membraned off from each other, as well as overlapping in their depths with others peoples, communities, families and selves in co-constituting ways. (O'Neill, 2003, pp. 9–10)

O'Neill's images of our wider connectedness are similar to the recent representations of the interconnectedness of life at the micro-level. Capra

(2002) notes the breakthrough work of microbiologists such as Harold Morowitz who has illuminated life at the cellular level; its origin, development, and maintenance, is contingent on relationship. Neurobiologists and cognitive scientists are also reframing mind and matter as inextricably intertwined, elaborating the detailed meaning of embodied consciousness.

> When cognitive scientists say that the mind is embodied, they mean far more than the obvious fact that we need a brain in order to think. Recent studies in the new field of cognitive linguistics indicate strongly that human reason does not transcend the body, as much as Western philosophy held, but is shaped crucially by our physical nature and our bodily experience. It is in that sense that the human mind is fundamentally embodied. (Capra, 2002, p. 61)

In that the history of our development is represented in the structures of our consciousness and our physical beings, the minimal self is replaced by a more expansive self across both space and time.

Warwick Fox (1990) contends that an ecological self is achieved through a complex process of identifications, that is, with a notion of the ecological self as the process of ever-widening identifications. Fox suggests that there are three general kinds of bases for the experience of communality that may be referred to in ecological identification, specifically, the personal, the ontological, and the cosmological.

Personally based identification is the experiences of community with others brought about through the process of personal involvement. Personal identification refers not only to friends, parents, relations, pets, and so on, but also to more abstract entities such as schools, clubs, nation, and continent. All of these are part of our personal identity in that any assault upon the integrity of this identification is perceived as a personal assault upon us.

In contrast to personally based identity, ontological and cosmological identification is transpersonal. Ontological identification as transpersonal identification refers to experiences of communion and commonality with all that is and that are brought about through the deep-seated realization of the fact that things just are. It is the profound realization that our existence and all that exists seems to stand out as foreground from a background of nonexistence, voidness, or emptiness. This sense of the specialness or privileged nature of all that exists means that "the environment" or "the world at large" is experienced not as a mere backdrop, but rather as Being. We have perhaps all experienced this state of being, this sense of communality with all that is, simply by virtue of the fact that it is, at certain moments, glimpses of the full significance that "Things are!" There is something rather than nothing! Amazing (Fox, 1990)! Ontological identification on a consistent and ongoing basis involves a radical openness to all of existence.

Finally, Fox articulates the notion of cosmological identification in referring to experiences of communion and communality that arise from the profound realization of the fact that we and all other manifestations of existence come into being from a single unfolding reality. This type of realization or identification can be achieved through an empathic incorporation of mythological, religious, or scientific cosmologies. Pierre Teilhard de Chardin (1959) referred to this cosmic identification as an unending generative process:

> The farther and more deeply we penetrate into matter, by means of increasingly powerful methods, the more we are confounded by the interdependence of its parts. Each element of the cosmos is positively woven from all the others: from beneath itself by the mysterious phenomenon of "composition," which makes it subsistent through the apex of an organized whole; and from above through the influence of unities of a higher order which incorporate it and dominate it for its own ends. (p. 256)

There are varying accounts of this deep-seated realization of the processes of the universe and our identification with the unfolding process. This rootedness in the entire cosmic process is the source of an embodied orientation and enormous energy.

Cosmological identification is illustrated in most indigenous cultures, ancient religious traditions as well as modern evolutionary perspectives (see O'Sullivan, 1999).

There are indeed great difficulties in identifying just how to establish a viable context for a flourishing and sustainable human mode of being. Of one thing we can be sure, however. Our own future is inseparable from the future of the larger life community that brought us into being and sustains us in every expression of our human quality of life: in our aesthetic and emotional sensitivities, in our intellectual perceptions, in our sense of the sacred as well as in our physical nourishment and our bodily healing.

Ecology and Configurations of the Social World

As we have seen, social configurations draw forth (in that sense, educate) and reflect a consciousness. We now explore social configurations that reflect an ecological consciousness, but also, more critically at this moment of history, foster our learning toward an ecological consciousness. Just as social organizations and cultural institutions impact constituent members with their consciousness demands, so too, do wider environments impact social organizations and institutions, calling forth fundamental structural and normative shifts. Over several decades organizational scholars and practitioners have recognized that the context of organizations has changed. Richard Beckhard and Wendy Pritchard (1992) stated: "Although the elements are the same, the pace and complexity of changes to new forms, ways of living, and values are of an order of magnitude never before experienced" (p. 1).

In recent decades we see emergent organizational forms having the following six qualities. First, they are fluid systems. Second, they form and re-form according to their evolving purposes and the realities of their environments. Third, communication is multidirectional. Fourth, responsibility and authority are diffused throughout. Fifth, diversity is valued. Sixth, learning is central.

The demands of a turbulent environment are, remarkably, some of the same social configuration qualities we believe key to the ecological consciousness challenge. Organizations require an acute environmental awareness and extraordinary internal coherence and flexibility. They need to be self-renewing, not as a one-time event but as an ongoing process. Organizational flexibility and self-organization implies intelligence and judgment to be distributed throughout the system. No one person or subset of persons can apprehend, interpret, or respond to the range and amount of information that is presented to the system from its environment. Coherence is achieved on the basis of common values and maintained through an extraordinary fluidity of communication based on practicality. Coherence cannot be static. Diversity of perspective and orientation is vital since the dynamic environment demands different organizational responses on a continual basis.

In what seems to be the close of the modern era, the pace of change is driving organizational innovation. William Bergquist (1993) characterizes the postmodern organization compared to the modern as oriented by intention instead of outcome, loosely rather than firmly bounded, networked rather than formally structured communication, formation on the basis of function rather than on economy of scale, variably structured with hybrid and complex forms rather than uniform and simple. We see these themes beginning to emerge in organizational life. Decentralization and the generation of self-organizing teams have been key themes in the theory and practice of leading-edge management over the past several decades. Vision, mission, and values have become pervasive themes in both organizational practices and rhetoric. Capra (2002) observes:

> Understanding organizations as living systems . . . will help us to deal with complexities of today's business environment . . . [and] design business organizations that are ecologically sustainable, since the principles of organization of ecosystems, which are the basis of sustainability, are identical to the principles of all living systems. (p. 100)

The fundamental elements in organizational redesign approaches that have been emerging over several decades exemplify these ecologically oriented organizational forms. We will highlight two of these that are carefully constructed with our environment as a central element. The one with the longest history in practice and extensively theoretically elaborated is based on an open systems theory growing out of the socio-technical systems design of Fred Emery and Eric Trist (1972). Fred and Merrelyn Emery evolved intervention methods that ". . . put . . . our recent misadventures with mechanistic assumptions and ways, bureaucratic structures and the strong trends toward dissociation which they created . . . behind us" (Emery, 1999).

> While the social environment is currently out of control, we can tame it. We can restore at all levels, a more appropriate culture, one in which people have knowledge of a respect for their environment in the broadest sense. Its basic unit is "people-in-environment" who proactively and creatively make adaptive changes as a matter of course. The resulting culture is associative, joyful and wise. It is the expression of a "participative democracy." (Emery, 1999, p. xv)

All elements of the Emerys' practice are fundamentally distinct from those of modernist organizations.

The Emerys developed organizational change processes through which people can either create or redesign their organizations or communities and systems of governance to be actively adaptive through wide participation in "an open responsible system." They distinguish the underlying assumptions behind these organizational forms, "design principle two" (DP2), from those of bureaucratic organizational forms, "design principle one" (DP1), as follows:

> People are taken to be purposeful, potentially ideal seeking systems (Ackoff and Emery, 1972), simultaneously pursuing autonomy, belongingness and meaning. . . . Human behavior and environments can be

recognized as mutually determining.... DP2 structures provide an environment within which we may rise above everyday purposes, to seek ideals. (Emery, 1999, pp. xv–xvi)

Active adaptation is for the Emerys, "ecological learning," which "... comes from our inbuilt adaptation to our world and our ability to immediately and directly extract meaningful knowledge of it..." (Emery, 1999, p. xvi). Through Search Conferences and Participative Design Workshops, members of a human system work together to construct a common understanding of their world and the nature and significance of their work in the context of that wider environment. The Participative Design Workshop provides a process of data gathering, analysis, and decision-making through which members of an organization structure and manage their work. Tuning into the environment and participative organizational design are ongoing processes for an actively adaptive system. The Emerys envisage and apply these processes creating "econiches" that elicit positive human ideals, joyfulness, and energy through which broader societal change is fostered.

The second example of fluid and participative organizational design approach is the "chaordic" perspective characterized by Dee Hock (1999). "Chaord" comes from the combination of chaos and order. It represents, in complexity theory, the "place," the juncture or edge between chaos and order where living systems arise and thrive. Hock was confronted with the challenge of creating an organizational structure that would deal with what he viewed as the chaos of the credit card industry. The challenge provoked him to examine assumptions about "organization." "Our current forms of organization are almost universally based on compelled behavior.... The organization of the future will be the embodiment of *community* based on *shared purpose* calling to the *higher aspirations of people*" (Hock, 1999a, p. 6).

Hock and his colleagues traced information processing structures in diverse living systems and by analogy derived the following principles of organization. First, power is distributed to the greatest extent possible, that is, power is "pushed" as far as possible to the periphery of the organization. Second, the system is self-organizing, that is, participants self-govern. Third, governance is also maximally distributed throughout the system, no one part being allowed to dominate another. Fourth, the system functions with a blend of cooperation and competition, that is, each part must be permitted to compete innovatively but within a perspective that subordinates self-interest to the good of the whole. Fifth, the organization must be both malleable and durable, that is, constant change in form and function around enduring basic purpose and principles. Hock attributes the success of the

VISA corporation to adherence to these chaordic organizational principles (Hock, 1999a).

Hock and others interested in the fundamental transformation of organizations and institutions have formed a non-profit entity, The Chaordic Alliance, dedicated to fostering "chaordic institutional change." A chaordic design process undertaken by representative team of people has been developed and elaborated. The process that is iterative begins with the derivation of shared purpose based on deep and meaningful convictions and a set of commonly understood principles describing how members will conduct themselves. The subsequent elements are: identifying all relevant participants; creating an organizational concept that generates trust, justice, equity, and effectiveness; drafting a constitution, an elaboration of the rights and responsibilities of members; and envisaging innovative practices. These design principles have generated organizations like the United Religious Initiative whose purpose is "to promote enduring, daily interfaith cooperation, end religiously-motivated violence and create cultures of peace, justice and healing for the Earth and all living beings" and the Northwest Atlantic Marine Alliance whose purpose is "to restore and enhance an enduring Northwest Atlantic Marine System supporting a healthy diversity and abundance of marine life and human uses through a self-organizing and self-governing organization" (1990b).

In an ecological perspective of social organization, the orientation of leadership is simultaneously transformed. In a social configuration that, as a fluid and ever-changing entity, has human responsibility, thought, and decision distributed throughout, leadership is not properly conceived as the source of direction from the "top." Rather, it is a shared and functionally based partnership activity that benefits the entire human system. On the basis of experience, leadership is also educative, that is, it fosters maximal learning among others and within the system as a whole. Hock's (1999a) summary of the responsibilities of management are: first, to manage one's self (integrity, character, wisdom, knowledge, time temperament, words, and acts); second, to manage relationships with those who have authority in the system; third, to manage one's relationships with associates; and fourth, enable all other people to do the same.

Leadership also takes the form of learning the organization's context, generating knowledge of environmental demands and conditions, and conveying this knowledge throughout the organization as a basis for decisions that orient the organization's direction. Leadership is replicated and rotates among members of a human system who are deeply committed to a common purpose and shared basic operating principles but who may generate a diverse range of activities and means of accomplishing the common purpose. In resilient organizations, all members have knowledge of the whole and its context as well as their own particular technical expertise that is often widely distributed.

Studying Arie de Geus (1977) and his construct of the "living company" and Etienne Wenger's (1998) concept with "communities of practice," Capra (2002) highlights elements of organizations as living systems and the nature of the leadership that fosters living processes.

> We are dealing here with a crucial difference between a living system and a machine. A machine can be controlled; a living system, according to a systemic understanding of life, can only be disturbed. In other words, organizations cannot be controlled through direct interventions, but they can be influenced by giving impulses rather than instructions. To change the conventional style of management requires a shift of perception that is anything but easy, but it also brings great rewards. Working with processes inherent in living systems means that we do not need to spend a lot of energy to move an organization. Force energy is not the issue; the issue is meaning. Meaningful disturbances will get the organization's attention and will trigger structural changes. (p. 112)

Ecologically Oriented Epistemology and Education

Knowledge in an ecological perspective is firmly imbedded in the practical world. Common knowledge is not based in ideological allegiances but rather is a shared human experience with all its challenges, dimensionality, and richness. It is based in a common context on which we depend for understanding and survival. We generate knowledge from the practice of living and working—action, reflection, commonsense-making, social construction. That is, knowledge is not individually derived and held, but rather generated within relationships with others.

The dualism of the modernist synthesis evaporates when we begin with practice instead of abstractions and as we generate conceptual maps of our experience—insights, awareness, coherent perspectives, and narratives that are ever-changing in relation to our ever-evolving experience. There is a firm, yet fluid ground for human communication and connection to others. There is a continuous connection to other living beings, to our wider environment, and to our time in the history of the earth and beyond. Like the premodernists we live a connected existence; unlike the premodernists, we understand ourselves to be in an open system in which there is no grand narrative, only an unfolding indeterminate story that we are cocreating as we make our choices and create social configurations and use technologies.

As such education is understood to be an ongoing process of learning and knowledge as temporary syntheses in ongoing change. While we know how to foster and catalyze learning, it is pandemic, not something confined to formal educational institutions. Learning, meta-level learning, indeed, transformative learning, occurs in all dimensions of life. Educators are those who enable our learning—colleagues, friends, neighbors, parents, children, organizational leaders, spiritual leaders, artists, researchers, teachers, mentors—especially those who enable us to *learn* as we live and work and inspire us to a life of inquiry—openness and discernment.

In the chapters that follow, we see exemplified the myriad of educational acts that occur in relationships among people in a vast range of learning settings. We see the erosion of dualisms between knowledge and action, mind and body, material and spirit, reason and emotion, school and community, work and learning, as people are inspired to reach beyond an instrumental consciousness into uncharted territory to confront our serious ecological challenges and create new possibilities in our critical historical moment.

References

Beckhard, R. and Pritchard, W. (1992). *Changing the Essence: The Art of Creating and Leading Fundamental Change in Organizations*. San Francisco: Jossey-Bass.

Bergquist, W. (1993). *The Postmodern Organization*. San Francisco: Jossey-Bass.

Bion, W. R. (1962). *Experiences in Groups and Other Papers*. New York: Basic Books.

Capra, F. (2002). *The Hidden Connections*. New York: Doubleday.

de Chardin, P. T. (1959). *The Phenomenon of Man*. New York: Harper Torchbacks.

de Geus, Arie. (1977). *The Living Company*. Boston: Harvard Business School Press.

Doole, C. (2001, January 24). *World Unemployment Rises*. London: BBC World Service News.

Emery, F. and Trist, E. (1972). *Towards a Social Ecology*. New York: Plenum Press.

Emery, M. (1999). *Searching: The Theory and Practice of Making Cultural Change*. Amsterdam: John Benjamins Publishing.

Fox, W. (1990). *Toward Transpersonal Ecology*. Boston: Shambala Press.

Glendinning, C. (1995). *My Name is Chellis and I'm Recovering from Western Civilization*. Boston: Shambhala.

Harman, W. (1988). *Global Mind Change: The Promise of the Last Years of the Twentieth Century*. Indianapolis, IN: Knowledge Systems.

Hock, D. (1999a). *The Birth of the Chaordic Age*. New York: Wm. C. Brown.

Hock, D. (1999b). The Birth of the Chaordic Organization: Human Resources and Resourceful Humans? An address to KPMG, Boca Raton, Florida, September 27, 1999. On-line: www.chaordic.org.

Jung, Carl. (1953). *Collected works. Vol. 7: Two essays on analytical psychology*. Trans. R. F. C. Hull. New York: Bollingen Foundation.

Kanigel, R. (1997). *The One Best Way: Frederick Winslow Taylor and the Enigma of Efficiency*. New York: Hudson.

Kegan, R. (1994). *In Over Our Heads: The Mental Demands of Modern Life*. Cambridge, MA: Harvard University Press.

Lasch, C. (1978). *The Culture of Narcissism: American Life in an Age of Diminishing Expectations*. New York: W. W. Norton.

Macmurray, J. (1961). *Persons in Relation*. London: Faber and Faber.

Macy, J. (1998). *Coming Back to Life: Practices to Reconnect Our Lives, Our World*. Gabriola Island, BC: New Society Publishers.

Marshak, R. and Katz, J. (1998). *The Covert Processes Workbook: Dealing with the Hidden Dimensions of Individuals, Groups and Organizations*. Bethel, ME: NTL.

Maturana, H. and Varela, F. (1987). *The Tree of Knowledge*. Boston, MA: Shambhala.

Merchant, C. (1990). *The Death of Nature: Women, Ecology, and the Scientific Revolution*. New York: Harper and Row.

Milanovic, B. (2002). World Bank Website. On-line: www.worldbank.org/research/inequality/.

Morgan, G. (1998). *Images of Organization: The Executive Edition*. San Francisco: Berrett-Koehler.

Nisbet, R. (1980). *History of the Idea of Progress*. New York: Basic Books.

O'Neill, E. (2003). *Holding Flames: Women Illuminating Knowledge of s/Self*. Doctoral Dissertation, Ontario Institute for Studies in Education of the University of Toronto.

O'Sullivan, E. (1999). *Transformative Learning: Educational vision for the 21st century*. Toronto: University of Toronto Press.

Roszak, T. (1992). *The Voice of the Earth: An Exploration of Ecopsychology*. New York: Simon & Schuster.

Shiva, V. (2000). "Forward: Cultural Diversity and the Politics of Knowledge." In George Dei et al. (Eds.), *Indigenous Knowledges in Global Contexts: Multiple Readings on Our World*. Toronto: University of Toronto Press.

Starke, L. (Ed.) (2003). *State of the World: A Year in Review*. New York: W. W. Norton.

Sullivan, E. (1990). *Critical Psychology and Pedagogy: An Interpretation of the Personal World*. Toronto: OISE Press.

Toulmin, S. (1985). *The Return to Cosmology: Postmodern Science and the Theology of Nature*. Berkeley, CA: University of California Press.

Taylor, C. (1989) "Inescapable Frameworks." *Sources of the Self: The Making of the Modern Identity*. Cambridge, MA: Harvard University Press.

Weber, M. (1958). *The Spirit of Capitalism and the Protestant Ethic*. New York: Charles Scribner and Sons.

Wenger, Etienne. (1998). *Communities of Practice: Learning, Meaning and Identity*. Cambridge: Cambridge University Press.

Wheatley, M. (1992). *Leadership and the New Science*. San Francisco: Barrett-Koehler Publishers.

Wilber, K. (2000). *A Theory of Everything: An Integral Vision for Business, Political Science, and Spirituality*. Boston, MA: Shambala Publications, Inc.

PART 1

Educational Forms and Processes
Toward Ecological Consciousness
Prologue

> The universe is one whole, as it were, and is in some sense unbroken.
> Of course, only under very refined observation does this show up.
>
> David Bohm
> *Wholeness and the Implicate Order* (1980)

While processes of education and learning are integral in all practices featured in this book, part I of the book comprises *practices of gathering people together with the dedicated purpose of illuminating the connectedness of our world*, our belonging *within* it, and relational ways of being and acting.

Each of the four educational practices featured in this section are oriented toward transformative learning for relational awareness and action. As such they invoke a focus and engagement with the world whose complexity and dimensionality necessarily transcend the boundaries of traditional disciplines. All four create nontraditional environments that foster connections among learners and educators in challenging new experiences through which they learn not only "what" but also the transformative "how" and "why." Each creates opportunities for comprehending how relationship and consciousness interweave in the search for understanding. All practices engage the learners as whole persons—passion as well as reason, action as well as reflection and thought. All recognize that their educational practices are emergent, evolving as they are enacted. There are also different "paths" represented. The section opens with chapters 2 and 3 that place the natural world centrally in the educational practice, while chapters 4 and 5 are oriented to systems thinking and dialogical practice within layers of social organization fostering contextual and relational consciousness. Larry Daloz's practice (chapter 2) is situated in a natural setting in the United States outside formal educational structures, while chapters 3 to 5 highlight practices within formal institutional educational settings (all observing the difficulties that the conventional university setting generates)—one in a school-wide undergraduate innovation in Australia, and in Canada, first an entire graduate leadership program and the other within a course in a graduate education program.

Larry Daloz opens this section with a penetrating consideration of the meanings of interdependence and a thoughtful elaboration of five essential dimensions of education and learning for an ecological consciousness. The essay is based on his practice at the Whidbey Institute, a learning center for retreats and programs, situated in the forests and meadows of Whidbey Island in the Puget Sound. From his experience of a program that he and his colleagues offer for adults in leadership for bioregional citizenship, Daloz has identified and sets out seven fundamental elements critical in the creation of environments for this kind of learning.

Stuart Hill, Steve Wilson, and Kevin Watson (chapter 3) set out the concept of *learning ecology* and elaborate its bold practice through the innovative School for Social Ecology and Lifelong Learning in undergraduate studies and in a residential program for graduates of the school. Their perspective and practice integrate a focus on natural ecology and its constructs throughout the school's curriculum. But importantly it is a "meta-framework" that highlights educational choices and their consequences, diversity in approaches to and styles of learning, and different contexts and social roles in learning. The authors illustrate their innovations in curriculum, course structures, and practices and assignments that foster shifts in learners' perspectives and values toward meaning, peace, justice, and ecological respect.

Don de Guerre and Marilyn Taylor (chapter 4) carefully elaborate the design and challenges of graduate leadership education that is based on a socio-ecological systems perspective. The approach involves learners and teachers becoming participants in a temporary organization, a learning system that serves as a practical context that generates as well as uses knowledge. They first elaborate the rationale and principles of a systemic leadership education program and contrast its key design features to those of conventional education. Then, observing that educational innovations fostering relational perspectives endure only with great difficulty in modernist institutional settings, they explore qualities of an econiche that can adequately support transformative graduate leadership education.

Marilyn Laiken (chapter 5) discusses and works with the challenge of creating spaces for reflection in the workplace, a critical element of transformative learning. Working with learners whose interest is in becoming effective agents of change, she describes her practice of designing and teaching a graduate course on the theory and practice of high performing teams within a Workplace Learning and Change program. She provides a thoughtful account of fostering direct experience, dialogic communication, moments of reflection, and processes of discovery. A central goal of the practice is to foster the value of reflective practice for the workplace as well as the classroom.

CHAPTER 2

Transformative Learning for Bioregional Citizenship

Laurent A. Parks Daloz

We stand at a critical moment in Earth's history, a time when
humanity must choose its future...

Earth Charter

The Call for Transformation

I t is a premise of this volume that we are living in extraordinary times. As
Edmund O'Sullivan (2002) reminds us, we are not merely at a turning
point in human history, but "a turning point in the very history of the
earth itself" (p. 2). We are already in the midst of the most rapid mass extinction of species in 65 million years[1] and if present patterns of resource use and
greenhouse gas production continue, a six-degree rise in global temperature
within our grandchildren's lives will dramatically decrease the human population as well (Harvell et al., 2002).

And yet despite a brisk gust of warnings from scientists, NGOs, and some
sectors of the religious community, on the whole we remain remarkably
oblivious to the danger. It is as if as a species we are autistic, says the cultural
historian Thomas Berry (1999). Our very mode of consciousness has established "a radical discontinuity between the human and other modes of
being..." (p. 4). We seem afflicted with an incapacity to see beyond our own
narrow and self-serving needs or to take the perspective even of the more
vulnerable of our own, much less of other species. Still less are we able to
recognize that *our* survival rests directly on *theirs*.

It is also a premise of this volume that responsible global citizenship requires not only a new social and ecological imagination but a shift in consciousness itself—a transformed way of understanding and construing "reality." As Einstein famously observed, you cannot fix a problem with the same consciousness that caused it in the first place. We have to change our minds—as individuals and as a culture. Indeed, such thoughtful critics as Mary Evelyn Tucker (2002) and Brian Swimme (1996) have even declared that we must do no less than "re-invent ourselves at the species level."

As human beings increasingly dominate the planet and technology continues to shrink it, the world of the average person—whether a Rai villager in Nepal or a coffee-sipping Microsoftie in Seattle—grows steadily more diverse, complex, and morally ambiguous. In *Common Fire* (Daloz, Keen, Keen and Parks, 1997), we spelled out the prevailing "habits of mind" of people committed to the common good over the long haul—the capacities that enabled them to work effectively under complex and challenging conditions. It was clear to us that they were not simply born that way. Rather, the people we studied had developed as they had in response to a complex of influences throughout their lifetimes, influences that had prepared them for a series of transformations that brought them to where they were. Understood as fundamental shifts in meaning-making capacity, these transformations were neither random nor simply cumulative. They were the result of particular life experiences in the context of a developmental sequence (Daloz, 2000).

Robert Kegan (1994) has offered a clear map of the sequence during adulthood, describing a great dialectical movement from a late adolescent orientation framed in an interpersonal lens ("Third order consciousness"), through a counter movement toward a self-authoring stance ("Fourth order consciousness"), to a new "trans-system" position holding the strengths of each but transcending both ("Fifth order consciousness"). This movement characteristically spans most of our adult lives. Progress from one to the next "order" is not inevitable, however, and may or may not occur depending on a wide variety of lifespan circumstances.

Most of those we interviewed in *Common Fire* (Daloz et al., 1997) showed many of the characteristics of Kegan's (1994) fifth order. They demonstrate an orientation that Parks (2000) described in part as "interdependence"—an achieved synthesis of the prior "dependent" and subsequent "inner-dependent" stages that she observed in young adults as they made their way toward moral and religious maturity.

Toward a Consciousness of Interdependence

Increasingly familiar these days, the term "interdependence" seems to be used in at least three ways: to identify a new global phenomenon brought on by technological developments; to make a phenomenological assertion about the nature of reality; and to describe a highly developed way of making meaning.

"As the world becomes increasingly interdependent and fragile," says the *Earth Charter*, "the future at once holds great peril and great promise."[2] In this first sense, interdependence seems to be a new phenomenon, growing with the fragility of the planet. The implication is that technology has brought us together in ways that require us to replace a less tightly inter-woven past with a new awareness of our interconnectedness.

In the second sense, modern science, especially quantum mechanics and molecular biology, has revealed the *intrinsic* interdependence of life and the universe in profound and dramatic ways. Indeed, a tacit awareness of this interdependence has been with us from at least the early Chinese and Indian civilizations and probably in preliterate societies long before that. For as long as humankind has lived in close proximity with the natural world—which is to say our entire evolutionary history—we have known in some sense that all things are connected. It would be truer to note, in fact, that it is only in very recent times that we have lost this awareness, that we have developed the conceit that we are separate from the rest of the living planet, a conceit that has nearly brought the planet and us to our knees. In this sense interdependence is a fact of existence. Our job is to learn it again, or really, in a new way, ade-quate to the particular configuration that it has taken in our time.

And in a third sense the term refers to a way of being in the world, a way of making meaning. Thus, to grasp a sense of interdependence means some-thing more than simply acquiring it as knowledge, though that is a start. To learn interdependence in our bones requires a new consciousness, a develop-mental transformation; we must reinhabit it so that we know and live it in our very being.

To grasp a tangible sense of this rather abstract idea, imagine a fallen log on the floor of the Pacific Northwest rainforest. Half-rotted, green with moss, and sprouting shrubs and saplings, it lies in a moist pocket, brushed by occasional light filtered through gently undulating branches overhead. In the Northwest they call it a "nurse log."

For a nurse log, the line between life and death is very thin indeed. It is vir-tually impossible to tell where one begins and the other ends. Life moves through it like wind through the forest or light through a mountain stream.

This log was born into its present life some two centuries ago—about the time that Lewis and Clark were making their way down the Columbia River. A red-cedar, it blew down perhaps 40 years back and remained alive on the ground for several years before the tree-life flickered out. It has only begun to transform.

By then, a host of bark borers, ambrosia beetles, and carpenter ants had begun their work, drilling through the protective bark, devouring the tender cambium, clearing dark tunnels through the wood, making a dwelling place for fungi, bacteria, and uncounted microbes to decompose the cellulose, blurring the line between one form of life and the next.

Whole worlds of new life flourished inside, while on the surface, a dozen different mosses—leafy Mnium, stately Tree Moss, electric green Broom Moss, elegant Feather Moss—a half dozen lichens of indescribable shapes, a couple of humble liverworts, and maybe even a slime mold made a bed for the tiny, vulnerable seeds of evergreen huckleberry, cedar, and hemlock.

There is more life in this log now, in far more forms, than ever before in its history. The soil it will leave behind when it has finally rotted, taking almost the same amount of time it took to grow in the first place, will be three times richer than before in nitrogen and phosphorus. A single handful of that soil will hold more living individuals than there are humans on the entire planet and enough miles of fungal threads to span the continent. Those threads, called "mycorrhizae," may link the fir towering over your head with a mushroom at your foot with a nearby rhododendron, with a distant alder in a clearing. The entire mat of soil beneath you is an intricately woven web laced through with life.

Stepping back now, notice that this particular log, in fact each patch of forest floor, is an utterly unique reflection of its particular place. The compact cushion of electric green moss along the crest of the log yields to an elegant golden "feather moss" in a shadier section, which gives way in turn to a large, leafy moss clinging to the darker, damp sides. Each plant in its particular configuration varies with the pattern of shifting light overhead, the moisture available, the substrate beneath. As the branch above grows and extends its shade, available light decreases, moisture increases, and a more shade-tolerant and moisture-loving moss follows the shadow. The life of this log shifts and shifts again in a perfect dance with its known universe. This is the one place, the one time in the entire cosmos that it could be what it is here, now.

The story of the nurse log is the story of a perfect dance, a transformative community—a place of rebirth over and over and over again. Surrounded by this living, green miracle, how can we help but be reminded again and again that all Creation is an interdependent dance? How can we forget what John Muir told us, "If you try to pull out any one part of Nature, you find it's hitched to everything else in the Universe."

In a wonderful essay, David Selby (2002) suggests that the metaphor of a dance may be more adequate than that of a web, for it is not the separate objects or even the connections among them alone that must attract our attention, but the *dynamic relationships* among them that are primary to a model of radical interdependence. While the metaphor of a web is still useful, he suggests that "Global and environmental educators need to embrace the metaphor of dance and the level of presence of unbroken wholeness it represents..." (p. 83).

What are some of the ways of being that might move us toward an interdependent consciousness? Here is a first run at five such forms. Exploratory at best, they are not intended to be comprehensive. They are derived in part from the *Common Fire* (Daloz et al., 1997) study, in part from a series of conferences at the Whidbey Institute among a group of scientists and scientifically informed religious scholars,[3] and in part from five years of recent experience and reflection on our work at the Institute.

Enhancing Systemic Awareness

What, then, are some of the moves in the dance of radical interdependence, ways of being that might move us toward an interdependent consciousness?

While the term, "systemic awareness" implies a knowledge of general systems theory,[4] what interests us here is the ability to *think systemically*, to step away from the immediate context and view it in terms of its parts and the connections among them that make it a whole. This capacity presupposes the development of critical thought—the ability to recognize, question, and articulate the assumptions underlying one's own as well as others' thought and actions (Brookfield, 1987)—and entails the achievement of what constructive developmentalists call "contextual relativism" (see Belenky et al., 1986; Perry, 1999).

Although this capacity should be at the heart of higher education, it is not always found there. When Sharon Daloz Parks was interviewing incoming students at a prestigious business school, she would ask, "During your future career, whom do you think you might harm?" She was struck by how often the student would fall silent, look puzzled, and then stammer: "Well, nobody, I hope." And then after more thought, "Maybe I might have to fire somebody..." It was apparent that in their moral imagination, they were sitting at a desk face-to-face with someone they had to fire. What was missing was the recognition that as they moved into the kind of power they all sought, they would be making decisions that would affect thousands of lives with the stroke of a pen (Piper et al., 1993, p. 52). This distinction between interpersonal, face-to-face morality and a systemically informed ethic casts valuable light on a number of knotty public discussions.

Consider, for example, an argument between Mark, an opponent of gun control, and Sam, an advocate. Both agree that there is too much violence but disagree about the role that guns play in it. "If a law-abiding citizen like me can't buy a gun to protect himself and his family," says Mark, "then violence will be worse because if you take away our guns, we will be helpless before criminals who will get guns anyway."

"I don't think so," replies Sam. "Violence only begets more violence. To reduce the violence, restrict everyone's access to guns because when everyone has a gun, no one is safe." We all know the debate.

Laying aside the specifics of the argument for a moment, consider where each is located imaginatively when making his case. When Mark thinks of the violence in society, he imagines an armed enemy "out there" in front of him, himself behind his gun, and his family behind him. His is essentially an interpersonal imagination from which it makes sense to protect your family and tribe with a gun of your own. He is looking at the problem from a kind of ground-level perspective in which tribes of good and bad gun-owners war with one another. He is not particularly interested in asking what kind of a society would emerge from this imagination.

Sam, on the other hand, is asking precisely that question. Seeing systemically, he regards the problem from above, in a sense, and recognizes a larger context, seeing both sides *and the system* within which multiple and dangerous conflicts are occurring. From there he is able to discern the larger pattern that Mark misses, and thus calls into question the whole drama of "us" versus "them." Moreover, he is likely to make other connections as well, perhaps noting our historic legacy of a frontier mentality and the way it is playing out in an urban and suburban society, the active promotion of firearms markets, the horrific media diet of violence in which guns become both commonplace and glamorous, or the symbolic relationship between guns and machismo in American society. This more complex awareness and analysis is generated by a recognition of the larger context made possible by systemic thought.

In constructive developmental theory this shift in perspective entails an actual developmental transformation. At the level of interpersonal morality, we tend to make judgments primarily on the basis of their face-to-face impact, a form of meaning-making that comes into being with adolescence. It is *tribal* in that it rests on primary affiliation with those who are "like us." Thus, we vote for a president with a personality we like rather than positions on issues we value; we make decisions based on what is good for ourselves or our tribe rather than the larger whole; we favor the short term and immediate over the longer view. Rather than work to create a safer world for all, we tend simply to shoot back, assuming that if *we* are safer, that's all that matters.

While once highly adaptive, this form of meaning-making has obvious limitations in today's world. The future of our planet increasingly rests on our ability to see that none of us is finally safe until the system itself is a safe place for all.

Cultivating a Sense of Place

"Among the greatest of all gifts is to know our place," says Barbara Kingsolver (2002, p. 40). Although a shibboleth among poets and environmentalists, this aspect of consciousness is new to many of us in education. I have been somewhat slow, myself, to come to recognize the power of place, despite my abiding attachments to northern New England and the Pacific Northwest. Indeed, it has been chiefly since moving to the Cascadia bioregion that I have come to realize how much of a New Englander I am. The Green and White mountains of northern New England are my "soul's landscape," and it's to the echoes of that special ecology that I resonate when I hike through the green-gold misty mosslands and ancient trees of the Olympic Peninsula. But it is only recently that I have come to understand why it matters for us to know our soul's landscape, our *place*.

Parks (1989) first brought it to my attention in a graceful essay called "Home and Pilgrimage" in which she noted that when the metaphor of *journey* becomes a total analogue for one's life, when it is sheared off from its "companion metaphor" of *home*, we lose our compass, our deep sense of purpose, the very reason for our pilgrimage. The circularity of life is a deeper truth than its linearity and, however necessary it may be for our own growth to leave home, the end of the journey—at least in a metaphorical and spiritual sense—must finally be to return home and, as T. S. Eliot (1958) said, "know the place for the first time."

We are moving well into a global era in which the balance between home and pilgrimage is severely skewed. While a commitment to the ideal of individual freedom may properly be counted as a mark of true progress, the ideology of unlimited freedom with its corresponding disregard for the value of limits threatens to destroy the home that gave it birth. Translated to the economic sphere, the companion ideology of the "free market" moves human beings around the planet as disembodied "labor," strips and levels mountains for "resources," and poisons the water and air of our global commons in the name of unconstrained "growth." ("Anyone who thinks you can have infinite growth on a finite planet is either a madman or an economist," cracked Kenneth Boulding.) And the fawning ideology of "technological progress" promises a future increasingly devoid of relationship with the immediate, the particular, the intimate, as technophiles dream of an electronically driven "global brain," of instantaneous planetary communications out of all sync with human time and grotesquely devoid of any semblance to a human body.

"I don't know exactly what a prayer is," sings poet Mary Oliver (1992), "but I do know how to pay attention..." (p. 94). There is something sacred about the capacity to be truly present in the tangible world. My friend, Kurt

Hoelting, a Zen practitioner who leads meditative kayak trips in the Alaska wilderness, has reminded me that for traditional peoples, to know one's place was both a form of worship and a matter of sheer survival. To know the properties of local plants, the habits of animals, the dangers and secret pathways of the forest, the pools and rapids of the river, was essential knowledge. One could die for lack of it. The development of such intimate knowledge of place requires close observation, deep listening, and a will to withhold judgment and to experience what is simply present. This takes time. You have to be there long enough for the mud to settle and the water to clear (Mitchell, 1988).[5]

While clearly our survival no longer depends in quite the same way on such knowledge, in the long run, it very well might. In a world of multi-tasking and genetically engineered apples from Chile, we are ineluctably losing contact with what is immediate, tangible, and nourishing. By denying the pain of this loss—or simply failing to notice it at all—we are able to objectify and treat as a mere commodity for exploitation the land that has shaped our consciousness and taught us who we are (Abram, 1996).

Times like these call us with more urgency than ever to know our place, to learn its history, to engage with its material reality, to love and protect it. This does not require that we never travel, nor that we live in one particular place for the rest of our lives. But it does require that we ask ourselves "Where is my soul's landscape?" and that we wonder hard to ourselves what it would actually mean to make a commitment to be in that place, to come to know its outlines—its smells, its history, its plants and animals, its people, its geography, its special magic—and ultimately to commit to its preservation and flowering. We must risk actually *loving* that place enough to preserve it.

Nourishing a Semi-Permeable Self

Each of us thinks of ourselves as unique—as "possessing" something we call a "self." That "self," we tell ourselves, is relatively stable across time. And yet, as Mary Catherine Bateson reminds us, "the self fluctuates through a lifetime and even through the day, altered from without by changing relationships and from within by spiritual and even biochemical changes. Clarity about the self dims and brightens like a lamp in a thunderstorm . . . but all our learning and adapting is devoted to keeping it alight" (Bateson, 1994, p. 66).

It is not my intention at this point to enter into a lengthy discussion of the extent to which that "self" is grounded in some innate biological structure or is purely constructed out of the social matrix in which we find ourselves. But I would like to recognize that as with all growing things, the self feeds on what it finds in the environment—transforms and is transformed by it. We shape and are profoundly shaped by those who surround us, especially those who matter to us. "The self," says George Herbert Mead, "is essentially a social structure, and it arises in social experience" (1944, p. 199).

Building on this insight, developmentalist Alan Fogel (1994) has persuasively shown how our sense of self is not a given entity but grows through a lifelong series of relationships with others, first with our primary caretaker, then with family, friends, mentors, and colleagues. From the ongoing intercourse with these others, we internalize voices, a *dialogue* that becomes who we are. "The self," he tells us, "is the developmental history of these participatory and imaginative cognitive relationships" (p. 139). In fact, at least since Mead (1944) and Dewey pointed to the importance of social experience in the formation of the self, it has been recognized that what we think of as our "self" can usefully be construed as being made up of a number of different voices, packaged as a kind of internal committee. Each voice plays a vital part, is recognized to a greater or lesser extent by the other members, and exercises a correspondingly variable influence.[6] We are quite literally, a self-organizing system.

In a charming little essay called "The Selves," biologist Lewis Thomas (1979) plays with the idea that he may not be a single, clearly delineated "self," but rather is made up of a whole conversation of selves picked up from various experiences at various times throughout his life. He goes on to describe the company of "selves," suggesting that to have a number of different selves ought to be considered a normal phenomenon rather than a clinical condition. The trick, he says, is to get them talking together rather than at cross-purposes. "We never get anything settled," he grumbles, and "In recent years I've sensed that...what they are beginning to want more than anything else is a chairman" (p. 44). But our dialogues do not take place only with other human beings. In a widely influential book, philosopher/ecologist David Abram (1996) shows how deeply our species has been formed out of its relationship with the natural world—what he prefers to call "the more-than-human-world." Demonstrating how seamlessly the self in oral cultures is formed in dialogue with that more-than-human-world, and showing how firmly language is rooted in direct experience, he goes on to argue that by removing us from that experience, the technology of the written language has dangerously cast us adrift from that vital connection with our surroundings on which, ultimately, our lives rest.

Why does all this matter? As our awareness of the importance of both social and ecological diversity grows, it is important that we understand ourselves not as monolithic entities standing over and against this diversity, but rather as beings constructed of the very stuff of that surrounding diversity—not coterminous with it, yet not as distinct from it as some members of our inner committee might wish. As Bateson (1994) put it, "flexible boundaries of the self open up attention to the environment that may ultimately be essential to survival, for it is not the individual organism that survives but the organism in the environment that gives it life" (p. 74). Thus, by recognizing how we are walking versions of the world that has shaped us, we will find a new capacity to work effectively in a diverse and complex world.

But something else may be happening as well—a kind of meta-learning— the process by which we learn how to learn. A Peace Corps volunteer, who lived, say, in Thailand for two years, is more likely to feel comfortable in Guinea-Bissau than someone who has never left Iowa City. It's as though when we deeply hear the voice of one who was formerly "other," we develop a channel through which we can begin to hear voices of the other *in general.*[7] Thus, it may be that in addition to growing a richer inner conversation, we are also developing a greater capacity to welcome such outer conversations. It may be that the boundary between what we have thought of as our "self" and our "not-self" is growing more porous, more flexible, even while becoming more distinct.

Thomas Berry (1999) moves us yet further when he observes, "The universe is not a collection of objects; it is a communion of subjects." To realize the radical truth of this observation fully may take most of us our lifetimes. The gradual apprehension of reality as deeply participatory rather than purely objective and "other" is a profound epistemological and spiritual task—one fraught with the risk of delusional solipsism on one side and alienation on the other. The challenge is to learn to see ourselves as nodes in a dance with the universe—what Hindu tradition describes as "Indra's net" and Thich Nhat Hanh (1988) refers to as a state of "inter-being."

Practicing Dialectical-Paradoxical Thought

Toward the end of a recent article on transformative learning, Robert Kegan (2000) calls for a way of making meaning (which he calls the "self-transforming mind") in which "we can even embrace contradictory systems simultaneously" and ultimately become conscious participants in our own evolution. To do this will require that we be able to recognize our own systems of thought as partial and hold them up along with other, equally partial systems. It will also require a rich capacity to think dialectically—to recognize knowledge as emergent rather than static, reality as constructed rather than given, and reason as the result of the ongoing resolution of contradictions rather than simply the application of fixed rules of logic. Dialectical thought of this sort has become widely recognized as a further evolution of cognitive development beyond formal operations. While occasionally encountered among traditional undergraduates, it tends to appear more frequently in graduate education and adult work settings where competing frames of reference are common. An educator with a lifetime of experience in cross-cultural settings put it this way:

> My speaking brings me in front of other people who may be thinking about things in a totally opposite way...which raises new questions. Or some people have thought about different facets of it and come from a different line of questioning. Or some may be sympathetic but suggest a different viewpoint. These are moments of growth for me. (Daloz et al., 1997, p. 120)

To work effectively in this stance requires a high level of self-confidence and maturity. One must be willing to listen attentively, take the perspective of the other imaginatively, and let go of one's own certainties—at least for the moment—without fearing that one will be swept up in the convictions of the other. It requires a kind of openness that is finally, like most transformative learning, more a matter of courage and love than intelligence.

In his poem, "Two Tramps in Mudtime," Robert Frost (1957), a master of the dialectic, dances on the tension between the work one must do to make a living and the work one loves. Here are the final lines:

> ...But yield who will to their separation
> My object in living is to unite
> My avocation and my vocation
> As my two eyes make one in sight.
> Only where love and need are one,
> And the work is play for mortal stakes,
> Is the deed ever really done
> For Heaven and the future's sakes. (p. 359)

Finally, neither one nor the other alone is adequate; what is needed is a third alternative that contains the truth of both: "as the two eyes make one in sight." This capacity to generate a novel possibility from the creative intersection of more limited perspectives lies at the heart of transformation, for in this kind of both-and thinking lies the power to move through the impasse that often marks the last stand of a crumbling worldview. What is needed is not new ideas but a whole new way of thinking.

But the contradictions are not always resolved at once—or even at all. In the *Common Fire* (Daloz et al., 1997) study we frequently heard people balancing themselves on both ends of the dichotomy, living the contradiction. "Even though I feel a tremendous urgency to stop the suffering," said one, "I also know this work will take many lifetimes." And another observed, "I try to see the contradiction in a larger context, and to sort of let it be and let it flow. Usually it settles down and there is a greater integration—in the future if not now" (p. 122). While there is still ample room for logical analysis, this strategy of resisting premature closure seems to be a more effective way of dealing with complex, ambiguous, and shifting issues than simply locking in on a single position. Sometimes simply holding the contradiction will enable it to resolve itself in its own way and time.

Standing on the Cusp of Mystery

I confess that I am not reading much these days about adult education. But what I *am* reading has been an extraordinary education for this adult. When I was a college student, we learned in our biology course that there were two kingdoms: plants and animals. That had been the conventional wisdom for the preceding several thousand years and there was little reason it should change. And yet over the past three decades, a revolution of extraordinary magnitude (made possible by the decoding of the structure of DNA) has revealed literally dozens of other kingdoms, a galaxy of microbial life making up more than two-thirds of the genetic diversity of all known life. Indeed, there are greater genetic similarities between slime molds and human beings than among many of those other forms of life that we once lumped under the term, "bacteria." Plants and animals are mere adjacent twigs on the new tree of life.[8]

Similar revolutions have taken place, as we know, with the introduction of plate tectonics to geology and quantum theory to physics. Science, Thomas Kuhn (1970) has suggested, is not so much the story of a "slow, steady advance of knowledge" as it is a series of dramatic paradigm changes. The same is true, as well, of human development. We "grow up" not in a simple accretion of years and knowledge, but through a sequence of qualitatively significant revolutions in how we make meaning.

What's interesting in all this, however, is that at each stage—whether in the history of an individual or a culture—we tend to be convinced that our present reality is the one that is "really" real. *Now* we've got it figured out! *Now* we stand at the end of history! As educators, we are particularly vulnerable to this conviction because our power rests in the knowledge we have acquired and in our capacity to pass it on to others. With a few Socratic exceptions, we go about our business layering answer upon answer and in the process all too often neglect to notice that the whole edifice may rest on a construal of reality that is limited by the length of our own bootstraps.

In a recent book, Wendell Berry (2000) takes to task the great naturalist E. O. Wilson for his embedded assumption that although science may not have provided a comprehensive, empirical explanation of life to date, it will eventually. Not so, says Berry. That is not the nature of the universe and to assume so does fundamental damage to our humanity by framing our existence as ultimately knowable rather than intrinsically enigmatic. "As soon as a mystery is scheduled for solution," he observes, "it is no longer a mystery; it is a problem." He goes on to argue that "to know everything" would be not only impossible but its pursuit a chimera. "The real question that is always to be addressed is the one that arises from our state of ignorance: How does one act well—sensitively, compassionately, without irreparable damage—on the basis of *partial* knowledge?" (p. 149). Reality is ultimately a subset of mystery, not the other way around.

I think Berry (2000) has got it right. Life is infinitely more wondrous, complex, and incomprehensible than we can imagine for the simple reason that we are limited by our own capacities to make meaning, and hence, ever to construe a mental model fully adequate to the possibilities inherent in the universe. The world, as we know it will never be complete because *we* will never be complete. If we are willing to accept this, then we may be able to add to the power of our knowing the complementary power of *not knowing*. The task, it seems to me, is to honor our givens while holding them up for scrutiny, to grasp our truths with what Goethe called "a delicate empiricism," reliable enough to hang from, but always subject to revision. To hold thus, smack in the center of our knowing and our not knowing, is ultimately a spiritual challenge; it requires something like faith. And finally, what choice have we? For in the end, transformative learning—learning that upends the very basis of our knowing—demands that we step out beyond our present certitude and welcome the wonder and amazement of life lived on the creative cusp of existence.

A Context for Learning Interdependence

Over the past several years at the Whidbey Institute we have designed and led a series of weekend leadership retreats (Parks et al., 2002)[9] informed by these elements and designed to inculcate a commitment to bioregional citizenship infused with a sense of the commons. We have learned that if people have not had an experience of the commons in some micro form, it is difficult for them to grasp the commons on a larger scale. We seek to serve the formation of leadership that can take into account the interconnection between the ecology of the human and of the more-than-human in the service of a world that works for all.[10] Such leadership will necessarily address what Ronald Heifetz (1994) refers to as "adaptive learning" as it works to bring about cultural transformation in the bioregion.

We have identified seven key factors that contribute to the development of an interdependent consciousness. Here are brief descriptions.

1. *Multiple frames in a context of the whole.* The metaphor of the commons—a bounded, public space where all the elements of the community are represented and have a voice—is a vital image for the formation of practices of interdependence.

2. *A safe mentoring community of recognition, support, challenge, and inspiration.* An environment that cultivates growth, provides a safe place for change, free of judgment and rich in difference. Within the context of an overarching sense of purpose, participants are encouraged to identify and explore their vital differences and learn from each other.

3. *Conscious focus on vocation.* Essential to the formation of purpose is a sense of calling that integrates one's own inner longings with the very real needs of the outer world. This may well surface as an evolving life-dream at several times during the life span.

4. *Judicious use of ritual.* Conscious use of ritual practices at the opening and closing of gatherings—as with the reading of a poem or lighting of a candle—serves to break continuity with "ordinary time and space" and to create a special opportunity for transformational processes to work.

5. *Contemplative time.* The sense of being rushed is anathema to the work of the soul. It is vital to schedule time in a leisurely fashion—to allow extended periods for silent meditation, journal writing, or deep conversation.

6. *Reliable information on critical issues.* Unlike programs that focus exclusively on inner transformation, we place importance on keeping the outside world present at times as well. Thus, we provide relevant readings on such key issues as water use, bioregionalism, or climate change and encourage thoughtful discussion to integrate inner change with outer action.

7. *Beautiful natural surroundings.* We have found that the beauty of unspoiled natural surroundings with time for long walks along with comfortable, home-like lodging with space for deep conversation creates an undefinable but powerful ethos for transformative work.

Woven together, these elements offer a milieu in which the transformations of consciousness that are now needed can be encouraged. The practice of this kind of education with the flow of the adult years is part of the great work of our time. Educators across sectors can be a part of reawakening us to our participation in the great dance of life.

Notes

1. See www.well.com/user/davidu/extinction.html.
2. See www.earthcharterusa.org.
3. The Thomas Berry Seminars, convened by Mary Evelyn Tucker and Brian Swimme, are held annually at the Whidbey Institute.
4. For a particularly clear and compelling example of systems thinking applied on a global scale, see Meadows et al. (1992).
5. The reference is to #15. Gratitude to Sam Magill for bringing the power of this metaphor to my attention.
6. One of the most persuasive compilations of this work appears in a now-classic article called "The Dialogical Self" by Hermans et al. (1992).
7. In *Common Fire*, we found that "a constructive engagement with otherness" during the formative years was the single strongest correlate with subsequent commitment to the common good of any factors we surfaced (Daloz et al., 1997).
8. For a wonderful discussion of this, see Wolfe (2001). See esp. chapter 3.
9. For more information, see www.whidbeyinstitute.org.
10. See the work of Sharif Abdullah, especially *Creating a World that Works for All* (1999).

References

Abdullah, S. (1999). *Creating a World that Works for All*. San Francisco: Berrett-Koehler.

Abram, D. (1996). *The Spell of the Sensuous: Perception and Language in a More-Than-Human World*. New York: Pantheon.

Bateson, M. (1994). *Peripheral Visions: Learning Along the Way*. New York: HarperCollins.

Belenky, M., Clinchy, B., Goldberger, N., and Tarule, J. (1986). *Women's Ways of Knowing: The Development of Self, Voice, and Mind*. New York: Basic.

Berry, T. (1999). *The Great Work: Our Way into the Future*. New York: Random House.

Berry, W. (2000). *Life is a Miracle: An Essay Against Modern Superstition*. Cambridge, MA: Perseus Books.

Brookfield, S. (1987). *Developing Critical Thinkers*. San Francisco: Jossey-Bass.

Daloz, L. (2000). "Transformative Learning for the Common Good." In J. Mezirow (Ed.), *Learning as Transformation: Critical Perspectives on a Theory in Progress* (pp. 103–123). San Francisco: Jossey-Bass.

Daloz, L., Keen, C., Keen, J., and Parks, S. (1997). *Common Fire: Leading Lives of Commitment in a Complex World*. Boston: Beacon.

Eliot, T. S. (1958). "Little Gidding." In *The Complete Poems and Plays: 1909–1950.* New York: Harcourt Brace.

Fogel, A. (1994). *Developing Through Relationships: Origins of Communication, Self, and Culture.* Chicago: University of Chicago Press.

Frost, R. (1957). "Two tramps in mudtime." In *Complete Poems of Robert Frost.* New York: Holt.

Harvell, D. et al. (2002, June 21). "Climate Warming and Disease Risks for Terrestrial and Marine Biota." *Science* 2158, 314–328.

Heifetz, R. (1994). *Leadership Without Easy Answers.* Cambridge, MA: Harvard.

Hermans, H. J. M., Kempen, H. J. G., and van Loon, R. J. P. (1992, January). "The Dialogical Self." *American Psychologist* 47, 23–33.

Kegan, R. (1994). *In Over Our Heads: The Mental Demands of Modern Life.* Cambridge, MA: Harvard.

Kegan, R. (2000). What "form" transforms? In J. Mezirow and Associates (Eds.), *Learning as Transformation: Critical Perspectives on a Theory in Progress* (pp. 35–70). San Francisco: Jossey-Bass.

Kingsolver, B. (2002). *Small Wonder.* New York: HarperCollins.

Kuhn, T. (1970). *The Structure of Scientific Revolutions.* Chicago: University of Chicago.

Mead, G. (1944). *Mind, Self, and Society.* Chicago: University of Chicago.

Meadows, D. H., Meadows, D. L., and Randers, J. (1992). *Beyond the Limits.* Post Mills, VT: Chelsea Green.

Mitchell, S. (1988). *Tao te ching: A New English Translation.* New York: Harper & Row.

Nhat Hanh, Thich. (1988). *The Heart of Understanding.* Berkeley, CA: Parallax Press.

Oliver, M. (1992). "The Summer Day." In *New and Selected Poems: Mary Oliver.* Boston: Beacon.

O'Sullivan, E. (2002). "The Project and Vision of Transformative Education." In E. O'Sullivan, A. Morrell, and M. A. O'Conner (Eds.), *Expanding the Boundaries of Transformative Learning.* New York: Palgrave.

Parks, S. (2000). Big Questions, Worthy Dreams: Mentoring Young Adults in Their Search for Meaning, Purpose, and Faith. San Francisco: Jossey-Bass.

Parks, S. (1989). "Home and Pilgrimage: Companion Metaphors for Personal and Social Transformation." *Soundings* 72 (2–3), 297–315.

Parks, S., Magill, S., Hanson, K., and Daloz, L. (2002). *The Powers of Leadership: Re-Inhabiting the Seasons on the Commons.* On-line: www.whidbeyinstitute.org.

Perry, W. (1999). *Forms of Ethical and Intellectual Development in the College Years: A Scheme.* San Francisco: Jossey-Bass.

Piper, T., Gentile, M., and Parks, S. (1993). *Can Ethics be Taught?* Cambridge, MA: Harvard Business School.

Selby, D. (2002). "The Signature of the Whole: Radical Interconnectedness and Its Implications for Global and Environmental Education." In E. O'Sullivan, A. Morrell, and M. A. O'Conner (Eds.), *Expanding the Boundaries of Transformative Learning* (pp. 77–94). New York: Palgrave.

Swimme, Brian. (1996). *The Hidden Heart of the Cosmos: Humanity and the New Story*. Maryknoll, NY: Orbis Press.

Thomas, L. (1979). *Medusa and the Snail*. New York: Viking Press.

Tucker, M. E. (2002, July 14). Address delivered at the Whidbey Institute.

Wolfe, D. (2001). *Tales from the Underground: A Natural History of Subterranean Life*. Cambridge, MA: Perseus Books.

CHAPTER 3

Learning Ecology. A New Approach to Learning and Transforming Ecological Consciousness

Stuart B. Hill, Steve Wilson, and Kevin Watson

Introduction

In this chapter we describe our emerging approach to learning (*learning ecology*), provide examples of teaching/learning in tertiary and community settings that illustrate this approach, and discuss its implications for transformative learning relevant to raising the level of ecological consciousness.

We believe that although transformative learning that expands consciousness in general will also be likely to raise ecological consciousness, this will be much more effectively achieved if our particular approaches to teaching/learning are informed by ecology and our deepest and most profound understandings of nature. Such understanding has radical (root-level) implications for both the frameworks that are used to design educational programs, and also the content of the learning materials and experiences.

Further, we believe that raising ecological consciousness will result in an increasing proportion of the population identifying as environmentalists. Most who presently identify themselves in this way are painfully aware that links exist between our environmental crises, low ecological consciousness, and cultures of detachment from nature. In endeavouring to address these challenges, most environmental activists are involved in educational activities designed to facilitate transformational learning that can raise ecological consciousness, and also in more direct political activities designed to critique, challenge, and transform the oppressive aspects of our cultures. As such, they are involved in the facilitation of personal development, deepening and broadening relational ways of being in the world, the creation of collaborative capacities, community building, and the psychosocial evolution of our species (Huxley, 1952; DeMause, 1982; Lauer, 1983, 1999; see also Beck and Cowan, 1996; Wilber, 2000). Few, however, would be likely to describe their work in this way, or to refer to the underlying process as *learning our way into the future*, as we do (Hill, 1999; 2003). Sadly, most would have to acknowledge that few, if any, of their efforts have resulted in the changes that they had hoped to help bring about. Clearly, this indicates a need for improvements in our educational approaches.

Based on the forementioned beliefs and our observations—particularly our observation that most learning continues to be fragmented, decontextual, disembodied, and lacking in content relevant to the development of ecological consciousness—and on our long experience with effective nonconventional approaches to learning within tertiary and community education, with our colleagues, we have recently become engaged in further developing and naming our particular approach to learning. We call it learning ecology, first because it uses ecological thinking and ecological frameworks to better understand and work effectively with learning as a process, and second because of the need to much more extensively integrate ecological understandings into the processes and content of most of our learning activities. Prior use of the term learning ecology, which has been very limited, hardly overlaps with our usage (that by Jan Visser [2001] is the closest and most developed).

Ecology as a Conceptual Framework for Learning Ecology

Ecology is concerned with understanding the complexities involved in the relationships between organisms, from individuals through populations and communities to species and the biosphere, with their total environment. The value of such understanding lies in its ability to not only better enable humans to learn more effectively, but also to choose to relate to nature (including ourselves) in ways that support rather than undermine its web of life-sustaining structures and processes. As we realize that humans are no more or less expressions of life than any other species, the connection between our supportive responsibility noted earlier, the maintenance of high functional biodiversity, and the well-being and persistence of all species, including our own, will become increasingly apparent (Dale and Hill, 1996). Such understanding has important implications for what and how each of us must learn if we are to function as responsible ecological citizens (Mulligan and Hill, 2001, p. 305).

Processes in nature are complex, and our understanding of them is fragmentary. Because of this, and because most ecologists are more interested in the functioning of whole systems than their fragments, ecology tends to be more open to holistic and intuitive understandings than most other branches of science. It is also accustomed to considering diverse time and space frames, from nanoseconds to geological eras, and from microhabitats to the planet as a whole. It emphasizes nonlinear, cyclical, and successional processes, limiting factors and unique opportunities, and recognizes the importance of diversity, mutualistic relationships, and margins and edges as the sites where creativity and productivity are highest. Other core concepts in ecology, and expressions of thinking ecologically, are listed in Hill (2001a, in press a). All of these understandings have radical implications for the redesign of our approaches to education, particularly for designs aimed at increasing ecological consciousness. Projects with cultural transformation as their goal that have already emerged, partly from this expanded awareness, include social ecology, deep ecology, green politics, ecological economics, ecofeminism, ecopsychology, ecospirituality, ecological agriculture, and industrial ecology (Hill, in press b), to name just a few such ecological initiatives. We believe that learning ecology can provide a parallel opportunity to apply the wisdom of ecology to learning in general, and to transformational learning (Mezirow, 1991; Heron, 1992; Elias, 1997; Kasl and Yorks, 2000) and the development of ecological consciousness in particular (O'Sullivan, 1999; O'Sullivan et al., 2002). An ecological approach to learning might start by endeavoring to understand the complex relationships between the diverse qualities of learners, supportive environments, and effective teachers and the things they do and do not do, the teaching aids they use, and the experiential opportunities they provide.

Learning Ecology and Its Relevance to Raising Ecological Consciousness

Learning ecology is first *a new paradigm that places learning within a holistic meta-framework that is both ecological and cosmological* (O'Sullivan, 1999). It can enable us to better reflect on the strategic, moral, and philosophical outcomes of the various approaches to learning, and so make wiser choices about both its content and methods of learning. Second, learning ecology provides *a means for understanding and working with the complex and diverse ways in which individuals (teachers and students) learn, become more conscious, develop worldviews, change, and act on their values*. It takes a constructivist view (Maturana and Varela, 1988), and acknowledges how our previous life experiences and opportunities, interactions, learning styles, and personalities result in each individual having a unique learning ecology (Cranton, 2000; Keirsey, 1997). For effective learning to take place, both learner and teacher (and, indeed, all who are in relationship) need to have some understanding of one another's learning-ecology profile. Without this, teachers are in danger of acting as inhibitors rather than facilitators of transformative learning and personal development. This understanding has important implications for the notion of appropriate pedagogies, especially in terms of choice, agency, self-directedness, and negotiation in learning, particularly concerning time, place, content, preferred styles of learning, and its measurement. Third, *learning ecology encourages us to consider the complex personal, social, ecological and "spiritual" contexts within which learning and transformation occur, and also the social roles of learning that transcend the needs of the individual.* Such socially responsible learning involves the construction of mutualistic relationships between the various stakeholders (individuals, families, groups, communities, teachers, etc.). Meaningful social understanding, critique, action, and transformation are recognized as occurring across all such social boundaries. Inevitably, this involves clarifying and deepening the relationships human beings have with themselves, one another, other species, the planet, and the cosmos (all of which we recognize to be still largely mysterious and unknown; cf. Voisin, 1959, figure 1). Valuable insights for working effectively with this, and for improving relational competencies, are provided by Ruthellen Josselson (1996), Samuel Shem and Janet Surrey (1998), Alison Stallibrass (1989), and Scott Williamson and Innes Pearse (1980). Thus, learning ecology is about finding better ways, using ecological and transformative frameworks, to understand what enables us to develop meaningful and ecologically responsible abilities, and how this can be effectively supported and facilitated.

The following six provisional position statements provide a background to our enthusiastic promotion of learning ecology.

1. Although consciousness involves being aware of both parts and wholes, because the former lends itself to description, measurement, and tidy experimentation, and the latter does not, analytical or instrumental consciousness has been emphasized over holistic consciousness, which is also often ridiculed and labeled as irrational and the province of belief and religion (see also chapter 1 in this volume; Hubbard, 1998; Russell, 2001). The associated domination of our lives by materials, economics, science, technology, and political systems that service these preoccupations, have led to the neglect of life, the complex relationships upon which life depends, and of the sustainability/system maintenance responsibilities that such an awareness places upon our

species. Linked to this, we have created cultures of fear (Tuan, 1979) in which decisions based on love are marginalized. Whereas the development of rational thinking and analysis is overemphasized within most of our educational systems, the development of imaginative and holistic thinking continues to be largely neglected (O'Sullivan, 1999; Kaplan, 2002). Learning ecology, through its inclusiveness and depth of understanding, seeks to address this imbalance, and to reawaken and provide effective support for our passion for life and learning.

2. Humans, more than any of the other possibly 30 million species with which we share planet Earth, have evolved lifestyles and cultures that are now damaging the life support systems of all species. We are doing this in ways and on such a scale that we are now living in a major period of extinction, with perhaps 200 species being lost every day. One outcome is that the well-being and survival of future generations of most species, including our own, are being seriously compromised. Clearly the ways in which most humans live, particularly those in the so-called developed world, are unsustainable. The challenge facing us is to acknowledge this and collaborate in learning our way toward holistically conscious and sustainable futures (Dale, 2001; Dale and Hill, 1996).

3. Those most responsible for this damage are also those within our society who have the most power (in the conventional sense of political influence, ownership, and control). They are also the ones who exhibit the greatest denial about the significance of this damage, and they tend to focus on responses that are either unlikely to threaten their access to power and control, or to increase it (Jackins, 1997). These responses typically include pollution control, waste management, improved resource use efficiency, resource and product substitution, and creative and distractive public relations and advertising campaigns. Such initiatives are compatible with their underlying goals of increasing resource and market-capture, overall consumption, economic growth, and in some areas also population growth (more cheap labor and consumers of their goods and services). Those not in such denial are marginalized and often labeled as luddites, greenies, and even enemies of the state. Partly as a consequence of this, a diverse range of expressions of acting-out against those in positions of power continue to capture much of the energy of the latter group. Clearly, considerable learning opportunities, and a need to deepen consciousness, exist within both of these groups.

4. Although our education systems have provided some support for understanding and addressing this situation, radical reform and

redesign will be required if they are to realize their potential in enabling the cultural transformation needed for our societies to become socially just, ecologically conscious, and sustainable (Hill, in press b). This will include extending the conventional boundaries put around learning in time (primarily during one's youth), place (schools, colleges, and universities), and curriculum (imposed, fragmented, selected disciplines) to include more integrated programs of lifelong learning, learning within our homes, communities, and places of work and recreation, and facilitation of the development of holistic and ecological consciousness.

5. Most of the elements required for such a cultural transformation are already present within our societies; and enormous potential exists in every area, including education, for their activation and further development. It will be as a result of such developments and their integration with existing elements into people's movements that the critical thresholds for change will be reached and that ecologically conscious and sustainable cultures will emerge. We find it helpful to consider this as a process of re-storying our ways of being and doing (Freedman and Combs, 1996; White, 1997). The learning implications of this, and the need to work more effectively with socially just and sustainable processes of change, are enormous. This is a core focus of learning ecology.

6. Ecology, as the most integrative area of understanding, and the area most relevant to issues of sustainability, can (together with our other understandings, particularly of biology and our psychosocial evolution) provide us with both comprehensive frameworks for engaging with this project of cultural transformation, and also with key directions for achieving ecological consciousness and sustainability (Bateson, 1972; Harries-Jones, 1995). Although some progress in this direction has been made in areas such as resource management (e.g., ecological agriculture and forestry [Hill, 1998, 2001b, in press c]), enormous opportunities exist for parallel developments to be made in education and learning. Our promotion of learning ecology is presented here as a contribution toward addressing this need.

The imperative to become more effective in learning our way into the future has never been so great. This is because the overall relationship between our species and the Earth has now become so unsustainable that extinction is clearly a possible outcome, unless we soon learn how to live mutualistically. In particular, this will require that all of us develop a much higher level of ecological consciousness, this in turn being linked to developments within individuals, including our "spiritual" awareness, and in our relationships with our partners, within families, groups, organizations, communities, societies, and as a species within the cosmos, particularly as members of the total biological community of our amazing and precious planet Earth.

Applications of Learning Ecology in Tertiary and Community Education

Our current learning-ecology work is grounded in the mission statement of our School of Social Ecology and Lifelong Learning at the University of Western Sydney (UWS). It stresses our commitment to developing ecological consciousness through praxis. We strive to understand, develop, and apply forms of learning that will contribute to sustainable futures for our planet, its environments, and its people (learning for sustainable futures). For us, sustainability relates to ways of thinking about the world, and forms of social and personal practice that lead to:

- ethical, empowered, and personally fulfilled individuals;
- communities built on collaborative engagement, tolerance, and equity;
- social systems and institutions that are participatory, transparent, and just; and
- environmental practices that value and sustain biodiversity and life-supporting ecological processes.

Grounded in this mission, learning-ecology principles and practices have been most successfully implemented in our undergraduate and postgraduate programs in social ecology. Stuart Hill (1999) defines social ecology as "the study and practice of personal, social [including all of its cultural, political, economic and technological expressions] and ecological sustainability and progressive change based on the critical application and integration of ecological, humanistic, community and 'spiritual' values" (p. 199).

All programs in social ecology comprise groups of complementary courses (these are currently referred to as units within our university). At the undergraduate level, an individually designed program might include such courses as: introduction to social ecology, cultural ecology, sense of place, imagination in action, ecological feminism, ecopsychology, human ecology, learning and creativity, writing, creativity and change, chaos and complexity, identity and culture, communities and change, group processes, ecospirituality, wilderness values, qualitative research design, and independent study. Our aim is to support integrated, holistic, whole person (embodied) learning within learning communities.

In all courses we aim to extend the boundaries of thinking of participants so that they are more able to develop their ecological consciousness, appreciate and understand the complex, relational and emergent/coevolving nature of our world, and reflect and act upon such understandings in meaningful, collaborative, and responsible ways.

Undergraduate Experiences

A foundational course in the undergraduate program, Introduction to Social Ecology, represents an appropriate case study in the application of learning ecology as a vehicle for developing ecological consciousness. It aims to introduce many of the themes explored in more depth in other courses in both the undergraduate and postgraduate programs.

The class meets once a week for a three-hour period, which is used for focussed staff and student presentations, experiential workshops, fieldtrips, and discussions. During a week-long camp in the third week of the course, deep in the bush in the Blue Mountains, students are provided with numerous opportunities to get in touch with their deeper "self/selves" (particularly through a solo reflective experience at the end of the week), place (partly by conducting ecological surveys, creative writing, and art work), and community (especially around the camp fire).

The following four core themes are central to our particular approach to social ecology (and to the development of holistic and ecological consciousness). They also represent one expression of our learning-ecology approach to education. Edited descriptions of these themes, taken from the course booklet for Introduction to Social Ecology, are provided here. They include interactive questions for the students in the course.

1. *Understanding and working with complexity, power, gender, and otherness/difference.* As part of our "natural" tendency to simplify, we often forget that everything is, in fact, extremely complex, that is, there are always lots of interacting factors and our current understanding of them and their interrelationships is always partial. For example, how we feel and act is never simple. It is always influenced by our physiological make-up, our subconscious and conscious memories of the past, our understandings and competencies, and the nature of the present environment and our responses to it. Similarly, the use of pesticides against pests is complex. It results in the poisoning of other species including

ourselves, the inevitability of the pest becoming resistant, and often the development of new pests that were previously effectively controlled by predators and parasites killed by the pesticide. More appropriate "solutions" would involve creative approaches to the design and management of ecosystems, and changes in values, such as valuing nourishment over cosmetic perfection of foods. What similar examples can you think of? Equally unacknowledged are the underlying power structures that determine who in society has a voice, the questions that get asked, the priorities that are chosen for attention, the apportioning of resources and rewards, and who actually makes the decisions (or controls who makes them). What are your thoughts on this, including your related experiences?

2. *Exploring diverse ways of knowing.* Our society tends to emphasize certain ways of knowing and particular types of knowledge ("objective" and scientifically derived knowledge), and to neglect others (women's, intuitive and indigenous knowledge [Belenky et al., 1986; Cajete, 1994]). Becoming more aware of biases affecting our consciousness can help us to expand and deepen it. Doing this and investigating "other" ways of knowing is a prerequisite to "seeing more of the picture," recognizing the great diversity of options and interacting factors (many of which are commonly ignored), and to acting more collaboratively, imaginatively, effectively, and justly. What are your experiences relating to diverse ways of knowing?

3. *Imaginative visioning and designing.* Most people in our society spend much of their lives being unaware or reluctantly following the agendas of others whose values they do not completely share. How many of us, for example, really agree that the "economic bottom line" should dictate our activities to the extent that it does? Tools that can help us to uncover and address such biases include insights from general systems, chaos, and complexity theories, systemic, paradoxical, and lateral thinking, deep ecology, programs of personal development, coevolution, and psychosocial transformation, and creative imagining and designing/redesigning. What are some of your visions and design ideas for a "better" world?

4. *Effective communication and other "professional" skills.* Such skills as goal setting, project planning, and implementation; collaboration, facilitation, leadership, efficient time and resource management, organization, competence using appropriate technologies, information retrieval, record keeping, and budgeting are all needed sooner or later in most fields of work. The sooner you develop them, the easier your life will be as a student, and the more successful you are likely to be in eventually finding

meaningful and remunerative work. Reflect on how you will use this experience to develop these abilities. Although our emphasis is still on written and oral communication, we encourage the inclusion and integration of diverse art forms in your assignments and projects.

As with most courses in our social ecology programs at UWS, learning experiences in Introduction to Social Ecology utilize interactive workshops that value constructivist principles of learning. As such they build on the diverse understandings and worldviews that participants bring to their learning. In relation to these, students and academics explore the themes outlined earlier, largely through discursive practices supported by selected readings and presentations, exploratory activities, and the life experiences of the participants. In the process of reflecting on and further developing their views and practices, participants are encouraged to use a variety of resources, including critical reflection, their own emotional and "spiritual" awareness, and a variety of modern and postmodern concepts. Many of these are quite contradictory, but working with such difference is regarded as an essential part of the learning journey undertaken by participants as they consider the basis of their thinking about the world as a living, coevolving, relational entity.

A key feature of all programs and courses offered by our school, and of the social ecology programs in particular, is the use of assignments as a means of challenging participants to confront and to express changes in their thinking and action, and to document their personal learning journeys. In Introduction to Social Ecology, as in all of our social ecology courses, there are no exams; all evaluation is based on projects, group work, and class participation.

In the first "mapping" assignment, participants are asked to: "visually document the ways in which you are a member of an 'ecological web' (noting your relationships with the physical environment—air, water, food, and other 'consumer' products and services, energy sources, material flows, landscapes, other species, etc.—and your relationships within society)." These are usually done on a large sheet of cardboard, although some students produce more ambitious three-dimensional webs. In addition, participants are asked to construct a second web, mapping "a selected institution, business or commodity (noting its inputs, outputs and effects)."

In the "group presentations" students research key personal, social, ecological, and "spiritual" issues (such as love, child rearing, consumerism, globalisation, peace, shamanism, etc.) and design and present skits to highlight key concepts and issues.

The final assignment, which is submitted at the end of the course, is introduced by the following paragraph. "This is your story of your learning during this course. While preparing it, it may help to think of this as two parallel columns—on the left the highlights of your personal learning journey (including especially any new understandings and initiatives that you have taken) and on the right all the things that informed it (references, experiences, assignments; with dates and critical reflections). It should also include a self-assessment and at least one peer assessment, as well as the ISHMAEL letters [explained below], and reflections on all other readings (prescribed and self-selected). You must refer to at least six articles in the Course Reader." The 2003 Reader contained 46 selected readings arranged under the headings: Reconnecting and Finding New Stories; Australia: Politics, Place and Cultures; Ideas and Frameworks for New Stories; Revisioning the "Self"; Relating with Nature; Ecological Stories; Visions of Sustainability: Social, Political and Economic Implications; Environment and Health; Processes of Change; Background Foundational Stories.

It is common for participants to put a huge amount of effort into constructing their final documents as they wrestle with the meaning of ecological thinking in relation to their own development and practices, social norms, visions of the future, and the tools they have encountered as a means of constructing the world differently. These documents commonly include poetry, photographs, and other visual and creative media. Most students spontaneously record their transformative learning and other meaningful experiences. Some of these relate to an assignment that students do after reading Daniel Quinn's (1992) book *Ishmael* (in which the wise mentor character is a gorilla named Ishmael!). The students choose to respond to one of a dozen questions (or construct their own question) in the form of a letter to Ishmael. I (Hill, as Ishmael) reply to each of these in the form of a hand-written confidential letter. A small part of the book is about Ishmael claiming his identity, so one of the questions is, "If you are not (whoever you have been constructed as by others) who are you really? Tell me about your essence. What in you is waiting to be recognized and further expressed?" For most students who choose to answer this question it is a cathartic, liberating, and transformational experience. For some, what is most important is sadly the rare experience of being listened to and responded to with respect and depth. Some students still correspond with me (Hill) several years later and share how they have followed the dreams that they articulated and that were acknowledged and nurtured in that class, and particularly through this letter-writing experience. There are many aspects of this experience that illustrate our learning-ecology approach. Perhaps the most important is the realization that a very small act, in this case writing a single heartfelt letter, can be profoundly transformational, for both students and staff. We have found that all of the activities described here are effective in developing ecological consciousness.

Postgraduate "Residential" Experiences

Each semester all coursework and research postgraduate students in our social ecology programs attend a week-long "residential" during which invited scholars address topical themes, and opportunities for experiential learning are provided by our staff and students. These are commonly transformative experiences for both staff and students. At the Autumn 2003 "residential" the focal theme was the celebration of 25 years of offering experiential "residentials" (note, our praxis of "experiential" learning is much broader than that described by Kolb [1984], and integrates the insights of Heron [1992]). This provided a unique opportunity to conduct in-depth interviews with past and present students to deepen our understanding of the manifestation of learning ecology in our social ecology programs. The transcripts were then analyzed in terms of how participants exhibited the features, characteristics, and indicators of learning ecology, as described earlier. The transcripts illustrating learning ecology and transformative learning were further examined to identify common features that may have contributed to their transformative learning experiences. The following represents our preliminary analysis of these transcripts. The names have been changed to protect anonymity. Almost all participants recognized the experiential nature of their social ecology learning:

> *Social ecology really feeds the way I learn. It uses a lot of experiential learning strategies. You have to get to your feet and do it. You have to think there and then—you learn fast.* (Matthew)

One feature of learning ecology described here is its holistic nature, its interconnections and interrelationships. Examples of how this feature came through in the interviews were:

> *It is inherently multidisciplinary—there is no track of narrow specialization.* (Matthew)

> *Social ecology is multidisciplinary. You don't put knowledge into silos. There is this capacity to actually cross borders and boundaries.* (Ruth)

There was also evidence that students were encouraged to think differently and view their environment from a perspective not encountered before. This is also described as a feature of a learning ecology, where synergies and synchronicities lead to a diverse range of thinking pathways (note also the ecological symbolism in this comment):

There are layers of learning and understanding as well as layers of knowledge. Its like a rainforest where everything is different, but they weave together and there's always a pathway through and always different. You follow the light. (Ruth)

Valuing complexity as a richness of understanding is an ecological learning feature that came through in many of the conversations:

The concept of a social ecology itself is complex. It has the notion of complexity and the sense that the human world is an enormously complex process . . . making me a lot more sensitive to the complexities of the environment, and to the degree of diversity of views and motivation that went into creating that complexity. (Matthew)

The idea expressed by many participants that diversity of views is not only healthy for an individual and a community, but also necessary for survival, is an important feature of learning ecology:

Hearing different points of view and actually listening to what people are saying, and what they are meaning to say, allows me to have a broader sense and expand my own awareness. (Sam)

This was paralleled by the idea that learning ecology can help to open up our minds and promote diverse ways of thinking:

Social ecology was a collection of challenges that opened up my mind to thinking—really thinking about the world as a construct . . . everybody is different in the way they see the world. Even if you don't understand the way other people think, you learn not to judge them. (Stan)

It also opens up the mind to creativity:

I have now found my creativity . . . I know more about myself and the world I am in. I'm aware of my different persons and can combine them with the community and be creative. (Val)

Learning ecology enables individuals to rediscover, further develop, and express their "otherness"—to embrace not just their cerebrally definable knowledge and skills, but also to feel and experience their knowing at multiple levels:

> ...*being in the environment and feeling it through my skin empowers me. Information is coming into me at all levels and... developing a consciousness at all levels.* (Naomi)

> *There is more to knowledge than just the objective scientific description of things. An emotional change is part of knowing this world and the changes in me were probably more emotional and psychological than technical. It's been an emotional maturing or kind of learning that occurs in your feelings and in your body, not just in your mind. It's the creativity and imaginative and artistic parts—the song and dance, and being able to express it. It encourages me to think differently.* (Tom)

This moves into developing and deepening consciousness. In addition to Tom, other participants acknowledged their learning at this level:

> *You begin to think differently about the contact you've had with theories and practices. You become aware of your growing subconscious communications.* (Stan)

Some participants were able to talk about how they had applied their insights to learning, and what they had learnt in their everyday lives. Some recognized that the concrete transformations in their lives were a result of their experiential learning. Some used the term "transformative" to emphasize the importance of the changes that had taken place:

> *It's been a wonderful experience in transformation. Not just learning for the sake of learning, but actual deep-seated change in one's being and ability to function. This transformation in me is a kind of change that cannot be entirely put into words because you have to experience it. It's another way of knowing and getting beyond the rational description in words of what you've learnt. You actually learn to access those deep and different parts of your brain and use them.* (Tom)

Others referred to more specific changes in their lives:

> *I have a different relationship to the bush. I took this to another level and now I feel empowered in all my relationships.* (Val)

> *In my job I decided to take a social ecology approach to learning. The students*

are surprised at how well they can think. I took this as affirming this approach to changing things. (Mark)

Overall, it seems that our learning-ecology perspective is able to effectively facilitate transformative learning, and that this leads to significant changes in participants' ways of being, relating, and acting in the world. It also seems that a common denominator to such transformation is developing a learning ecology that incorporates experiential learning. A learning-ecology perspective that promotes transformative learning is characterized by interdisciplinary, multidisciplinary, and transdisciplinary processes that cross borders and boundaries, that promote thinking at the edges, that value and incorporate complexity, diversity of views, open and expand the mind, promote creativity, and embrace diverse ways of knowing that include direct knowing through intuition and feelings. Most importantly, learning ecology can help to expand consciousness, including ecological consciousness, and this allows people to work more effectively with complexity, embrace challenges, critically reflect, think creatively, clarify their worldviews, and be more effective in facilitating "progressive" change. In relation to whole person transformative learning, one participant recognized that they were able to practice conscious communication with the subconscious. Put another way, they were able to expand their consciousness, becoming more aware of, and able to access and integrate their subconscious knowing. We believe that this is a particularly fertile area for further research.

Community Experiences

Learning-ecology approaches have been used extensively in our community work. The following example illustrates one way in which we have connected learning in the classroom to social change within the wider community in an effort to facilitate transformative change and raise consciousness. In this initiative, Hill required all students in a course on social change to "adopt" a person with positional power within their local environment (CEOs, political or religious leaders, university presidents, school principals, union bosses, etc.) and assume responsibility for supporting their "whole person development." Students closely observed their behaviors and activities and, while engaging with and validating their whole beings, provided heartfelt, specific positive feedback for "core" behavior, and de-personalized, nonjudgmental understanding, and constructive critique of "non-core," compensatory, maladaptive, fragmented behavior. Discoveries included the incredible potential of such small initiatives to contribute to significant personal and social change, the rarity of access to such honest feedback by most individuals with positional power, and the capacity of such a daring, yet do-able, initiative to lead to transformative change in all involved.

Learning-Ecology Implications for Transformative Learning Relevant to Raising the Level of Ecological Consciousness

Learning ecology has enabled us to both broaden and deepen our approaches to transformative learning. By integrating ecological understandings into all learning processes and curricula, learning ecology has provided an effective framework for designing and delivering educational programs that are capable of raising ecological consciousness. Although we are still at an early stage in the development of learning ecology, we are encouraged by our experiences in teaching social ecology at the undergraduate and postgraduate levels, and in our outreach programs in the wider community. What we have presented here is indicative of these applications, and in no way aims to be comprehensive. As we learn our way forward we are constantly being reaffirmed by the value and relevance of the ecological framework that we have chosen to inform our work. Indeed, even in these most challenging times, it has enabled us to remain optimistic about the potential for our species to continue to evolve psychosocially, and to significantly raise our level of ecological consciousness, and so be more able to live ecologically sustainable, socially just, and meaningful and peaceful lives.

References

Belenky, M. F., Clinchy, M. McV., Goldberger, N. R., and Tarule, J. M. (1986). *Women's Ways of Knowing: the Development of Self, Voice, and Mind.* New York: Basic Books.

Bateson, G. (1972). *Steps to an Ecology of Mind: Collected Essays in Anthropology, Psychiatry, Evolution and Epistemology.* London: Intertext.

Beck, D. E. and Cowan, C. C. (1996). *Spiral Dynamics: Mastering Values, Leadership, and Change: Exploring the New Science of Memetics.* Cambridge, MA: Blackwell.

Cajete, G. (1994). *Look to the Mountain: An Ecology of Indigenous Education.* Durango, CO: Kivaki.

Cranton, P. (2000). "Individual differences and transformative learning." In J. Mezirow and Associates (Eds.), *Learning as Transformation: Critical Perspectives on a Theory of Progress* (pp. 181–204). San Francisco, CA: Josses-Bass.

Dale, A. (2001). *At the Edge: Sustainable Development in the 21st Century.* Vancouver, BC: University of British Columbia.

Dale, A. and Hill, S. B. (1996). "Biodiversity Conservation: A Decision-Making Context." In A. Dale and J. Robinson (Eds.), *Achieving Sustainable Development* (pp. 97–118). Vancouver, BC: University of British Columbia.

DeMause, L. (1982). *Foundations of Psychohistory*. New York: Creative Roots.

Elias, D. (1997). "It's Time to Change Our Minds: An Introduction to Transformative Learning." *Revision* 20 (1), 2–6.

Freedman, J. and Combs, G. (1996). *Narrative Therapy: The Social Construction of Preferred Realities*. New York: Norton.

Heron, J. (1992). *Feeling and Personhood: Psychology in Another Key*. London: Sage.

Harries-Jones, P. (1995). *A Recursive Vision: Ecological Understanding and Gregory Bateson*. Toronto, ON: University of Toronto.

Hill, S. B. (1998). "Redesigning agroecosystems for environmental sustainability: A deep systems approach." *Systems Research and Behavioural Science* 15, 391–402.

Hill, S. B. (1999). "Social Ecology as Future Stories." *A Social Ecology Journal* 1, 197–208.

Hill, S. B. (2001a). "Transformative Outdoor Education for Healthy Communities Within Sustainable Environments." In *Education Outdoors—Our Sense of Place* (pp. 7–19). Bendigo, VIC, Australia: 12th National Outdoor Education Conference.

Hill, S. B. (2001b). "Working with Processes of Change, Particularly Psychological Processes, When Implementing Sustainable Agriculture. In H. Haidn (Ed.), *The Best of ... Exploring Sustainable Alternatives: An Introduction to Sustainable Agriculture* (pp. 125–134). Saskatoon, SK: Canadian Centre for Sustainable Agriculture.

Hill, S. B. (2003). "Autonomy, Mutualistic Relationships, Sense of Place, and Conscious Caring: A Hopeful View of the Present and Future." In J. I. Cameron (Ed.), *Changing Places: Reimagining Sense of Place in Australia*. Double Bay, NSW: Longueville.

Hill, S. B. (in press a). "Social Ecology as a Framework for Understanding and Working with Social Capital and Sustainability within Rural Communities." In R. Coté, J. Tansey and A. Dale (Eds.), *Social Capital and Sustainable Community Development: The Missing Link* . Vancouver, BC: University of British Columbia.

Hill, S. B. (in press b). "Redesign as Deep Industrial Ecology: Lessons from Ecological Agriculture and Social Ecology." In A. Dale and R. Cote (Eds.), *Industrial Ecology: A Question of Design?* Vancouver, BC: University of British Columbia.

Hill, S. B. (in press c). "Redesigning Pest Management: A Social Ecology Approach." *Journal of Crop Production.*

Hubbard, B. M. (1998). *Conscious Evolution: Awakening the Power of Our Social Potential*. Novato, CA: New World Library.

Huxley, J. (1952). *Evolution in Action*. London: Scientific Book Club.

Jackins, H. (1997). *The List*. Seattle, WA: Rational Island.

Josselson, R. (1996). *The Space Between Us: Exploring the Dimensions of Human Relationships*. Thousand Oaks, CA: Sage.

Kaplan, A. (2002). *Development Practitioners and Social Process: Artists of the Invisible*. London: Pluto.

Kasl, E. and Yorks, L. (2000). "An Extended Epistemology for Transformative Learning Theory and Its Application Through Collaborative Inquiry." In

64 • Hill et al.

Challenges of Practice: Transformative Learning in Action (pp. 175–180). Columbia
University, New York: 3rd International Transformational Learning Conference.

Keirsey, D. (1997). *Please understand me II: Temperament, character and intelligence*
(S. Montgomery, Ed.). Amherst, NY: Prometheus.

Kolb, D. (1984). *Experiential Learning: Experience as a Source of Learning and
Development*. Englewood Cliffs, NJ: Prentice Hall.

Lauer, R. M. (1983). "An Introduction to the Theory of Adult or after Piaget what?"
In M. Levy (Ed.), *Research and Theory in Developmental Psychology* (pp. 195–219).
Lovington, NY: N.Y. State Psychological Association.

Lauer, R. M. (1999). *Learners of the World Unite!* Unpublished manuscript.
Columbia University, New York.

Maturana, H. R. and Varela, F. J. (1988). *The Tree of Knowledge: The Biological Roots
of Human Understanding*. Boston: Shambala.

Mezirow, J. (1991). *Transformative Dimensions of Adult Learning*. San Francisco, CA:
Jossey-Bass.

Mulligan, M. and Hill, S. B. (2001). *Ecological Pioneers: A Social History of Australian
Ecological Thought and Action*. Melbourne, VIC: Cambridge University.

O'Sullivan, E. (1999). *Transformative Learning: Educational vision for the 21st century*.
London: Zed Books.

O'Sullivan E., Morrell, A., and O'Connor, M. A. (Eds.) (2002). *Expanding the
boundaries of Transformative Learning*. New York: Pelgrave.

Quinn, D. (1992). *Ishmael*. New York: Bantam.

Russell, P. (2001). "The light of consciousness." *Network* 76, 2–3.

Shem, S. and Surrey, J. (1998). *We Have to Talk: Healing Dialogues Between Women
and Men*. New York: Basic Books.

Stallibrass, A. (1989). *Being Me and Also Us: Lessons from the Peckham Experiment*.
Edinburgh: Scottish Academic.

Tuan, Yi-Fu (1979). *Landscapes of Fear*. Minneapolis, MN: University of Minnesota.

Visser, J. (2001). Integrity, completeness and comprehensiveness of the learning envi-
ronment: Meeting the basic learning needs of all throughout life. In D. N. Aspin,
J. D. Chapman, M. J. Hatton and Y. Sawano (Eds.), *International Handbook of
Lifelong Learning* (pp. 447–472). Dordrecht, The Netherlands: Kluwer Academic.

Voisin, A. (1959). *Soil, Grass and Cancer*. London: Crosby Lockwood.

White, M. (1997). *Narratives of therapists' lives*. Adelaide, SA: Dulwich Centre.

Wilber, K. (2000). *Integral psychology: Consciousness, spirit, psychology, therapy*. Boston,
MA: Shambala.

Williamson, G. S. and Pearse, I. H. (1980). *Science, Synthesis and Sanity*. Edinburgh:
Scottish Academic.

CHAPTER 4

Graduate Leadership Education in a Socio-Ecological Perspective: Working at the Paradigmatic Interface

Don W. de Guerre and Marilyn M. Taylor

> Years after systems thinking and ecological thinking and cybernetic thinking have penetrated into our culture in general and organizational rhetoric in particular, they are only occasionally reflected in practice.
>
> Jeremy Shapiro

G lobal turbulence impacts all aspects of our lives including our workplaces where we derive our livelihoods and most of us spend half of our waking hours. As economic conditions fluctuate radically, as instant worldwide communication and rapid travel bring diverse cultural impacts and accelerating innovation, reliable planning horizons are shortened abruptly. Command and control structures are increasingly under pressure. In search of the change that will reduce organizational vulnerability, we see unending cycles of mergers and acquisitions, downsizing, right-sizing, and other forms of restructuring while both material and human costs mount.

Unpredictable environments require maximum flexibility and a highly tuned adaptive capacity for people and organizations to their environments. There is an emerging recognition that this implies a fundamental shift from hierarchical leadership and organizational structures to increasing decentralization of decision-making responsibility and self-organization. We believe that this trend has an exponential significance reaching far beyond the workplace. Poised at a point of both enormous potential for human betterment and also for human exploitation and ecological devastation, these fundamental new forms of leadership and organizational are also likely to be *schools for a socio-ecological or systemic consciousness*[1] (Kegan, 1994).

Over the past 50 years, theory and practice of designing and implementing self-managing human systems have become highly evolved in diverse organizational and community settings internationally (cf.: Emery and Trist, 1972; Emery and Emery, 1979; Van Beinum, 1986, 1990; Bunker and Alban, 1997; Devane and Holman, 1999; Axelrod, 2000). These innovations have been driven by strongly held values for enhancing life and work contexts in the face of the dehumanizing effects of the industrial, mechanistic imagination.

In this chapter, we focus on the profoundly different meaning and practice of leadership required in these emerging organizational forms and we offer an approach to leadership education consonant with these. It embodies a socio-ecological or systems perspective in leadership that is emerging in the literature, in the minds of visionaries, and a small minority of scholar practitioners. If designing educational programs from an ecological perspective is one level of innovation, the second is how to respect the fragility of such ecological practices and sustain them in a culture of modernism with its dominant organizational form, bureaucracy. The few that have survived do so only with enormous strain. We explore briefly this paradigmatic interface for alternative ways to situate sustainable systemic leadership education.

The Leadership Education Challenge

Current educational contexts and pedagogical practices for leadership education are, for the most part, inspired by instrumental individualism consonant with the modern industrial context. As observed in the introductory chapter, education is "understood primarily as the formal dissemination of knowledge that has been generated through formal research and scholarship" delivered in a "highly compartmentalized structuring of knowledge" in highly bureaucratized educational institutions (p. 9). Knowledge is assumed to be stable, enduring, and applicable regardless of context. Several additional modernist assumptions specifically relevant to leadership education are: the whole is equal to the sum of its parts; and everything can be fixed by a smart person with the right tools and methodologies. This stance of instrumental individualism makes it the responsibility of the leader to maintain expert control through applying his/her received knowledge. In this perspective, the essential interdependencies are rendered invisible and the indeterminacies are ignored.

The leadership education literature highlights five thematic types of change needed in conventional leadership education (Taylor et al., 2002). First and most frequently, there is a need to close the gap between received knowledge (theory) and the realities of the workplace (practice) and the capability to apply knowledge in practice (Linder and Smith, 1992). Second, leaders need to learn more effectively how to relate to others than they typically do now in conventional leadership education. "Effective working alliance relationships become more and more important as organizations move away from bureaucratic control towards matrix structures, project teams and organic networks" (Clarkson and Shaw, 1992, p. 23). The third theme is the need for fostering the development of a systems perspective, that is, an awareness of the interrelationships among elements of social relationships and organizations. Fourth, in navigating the changing workplace, the development of personal strength is an important need in leadership education. Self-awareness in social processes and relationships and opportunities to provide constructive influence (Boyzantis and Kram, 1999) and clarity about values and ethics (Nodoushani and Nodoushani, 1996) are important anchors for leaders. Finally, leadership education needs to do more about enabling aspiring leaders to learn continuously (Finegold, 1994; Boyzantis et al., 1995).

An Alternative Practice of Leadership Education

We offer a systemic leadership approach that, designed for a dynamic changing world, obviates the gaps of conventional leadership education. It is designed on the basis of the six principles depicted in figure 4.1.[2]

A systemic educational approach, a fundamentally different cultural and epistemological perspective from conventional professional education, can be characterized as reversing six priorities:

- Practice is primary; theory illuminates practice; learning and knowledge are embodied.
- Systems-in-environments are the primary focus; the significance of parts derives from their relation within the system. The nature of a system cannot be discerned from an examination of each of its parts.
- Process (what things are becoming) is central; states (what things are) are rapidly changing.

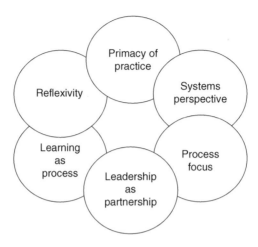

Figure 4.1 Six Interrelated Educational Design Principles.

- Learning to learn is figural; knowledge acquisition is ground.
- Collaboration is primary; individual action is a constituent element contributing to and supported by collaborative interaction.
- Reflexive understanding incorporates but goes beyond detached analysis. The knower is part of the world that s/he seeks to know.

The entire intellectual "platform" on which we build action and knowledge is shifted here. We see this shift as congruent with the movement from our culture's predominantly modernist worldview to one consistent with what Kegan (1994) has called a reconstructive postmodern perspective, as discussed further in the following.

An important educational implication is that the form and practice of the educational program is as critical to the learning as are the ideas that inform it. The new leadership requires practical wisdom, or what the Greeks called, *phrónêsis*, being grounded good judgment in matters concerning human conduct. Leadership education that fosters understanding of ourselves as integral to our context and recognizes our fate as co-terminus with our environment reflects an ecological consciousness in the way we, as leadership educators. It requires us to reexamine our most basic assumptions about what it means to educate, what it means to be an educator, and it requires that we redesign the way we teach, the way we organize curriculum, the way we relate to our colleagues and to students, and, certainly, how we structure educational institutions.

Socio-Ecological Leadership Education

An example of a systemic approach to graduate leadership education was developed by the authors and their colleagues (Taylor et al., 2002). Enacting the principles cited earlier, the program was intended to enable participants to *experience* systemic leadership. About 20 persons, comprising a cohort, become both participants and observers in a number of nested human systems within and around the cohort. Three levels of organization evolved distinctively in each successive cohort provide contexts for in-vivo learning with the faculty serving as "boundary managers"—leaders at the interface between the system and wider educational context. The cohort learning system identifies its own specific common values, generates norms, and learning priorities within the broad objectives of the program. It also serves as a process consulting or action research organization for client systems (community, public service, and private enterprise) in its immediate task environment or social eco-system. Self-managed learning and work groups are developed within the cohort that produce work and support participative learning. All cohort-wide decisions illustrate large group processes, such as dialogical town hall meetings. Learning and coaching triads provide a venue for ongoing learning support among participants as colleagues (see figure 4.2).

In the latter phase of the program, the learning system as a whole develops an interorganizational or trans-organizational intervention for a group of community agencies, and each participant, supported by their colleagues as well as their faculty coaches, demonstrates his/her practical capability and understanding in conducting a process consultation with a client system as a thesis-equivalent M.A. Project.

Table 4.1 summarizes some of the practices of systemic education that instantiate the new priorities.

Intensive format learning sessions are critical to systemic leadership education that emphasizes relationship and learning, practice and reflection. In this model intensive format learning sessions were two one-week sessions at the beginning of each of the two years and monthly three-day weekends.

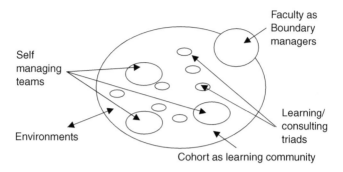

Figure 4.2 Participant Cohort as learning Community.

Extended periods of time permit full engagement with practice, the development of collaborative learning relationships with others, the generation of effective participative decision processes, fostering practical expertise, and the conscious formation of constructive norms and values.

Dealing with the Paradigmatic Interface with the Conventional University

The paradigmatic interface is a place of high potential for learning and high tension. It is about friction, perhaps best represented by the image of "fire," a symbol of transformation. As a paradigmatic change intervention, systemic leadership education is a disturbance on many levels—logistical, administrative, intellectual, and political—in a conventional university. Difference can be met by curiosity and a welcome sense of challenge. More often, when conventional assumptions are contradicted the response is unwelcome confusion, aggravation, anxiety, and sometimes anger. For some and perhaps at first, the differences are subtle and may go unnoticed. Indeed, one of the dangers is that the critical features of this educational approach can be conflated with conventional practices. What difference does it make to have courses given in modules within the program by individual professors instead of interwoven, team-taught courses? With attention exclusively on course content, the process learning is imperceptible. For others, the differences are surprising. What kind of a university permits participation by students in courses that generate high emotion and interpersonal conflict? The exclusive

Table 4.1 Contrasting Educational Paradigms

	Illustrative practices of divergent priorities	
Systemic education		Instrumental education
Practice is primary; theory serves practical ends.		*Theory is primary and a template to design and assess practice.*
As *practitioner scholars*, faculty members are able to practice what they teach and fully conceptualize and contextualize it in value perspectives.		Faculty members are exemplary in the world of ideas, experts in their subject matter.
Student admissions requirements include practical experience, relevant professional goals, and social psychological capabilities as well as academic achievement.		Admissions typically based entirely on prior academic achievement and admissions tests; other requirements if any are secondary.
Successful completion of the program requires practical expertise with an intellectual understanding of the practice.		Successful completion of the program typically requires a high level of conceptual fluency.
Knowledge is generated in action–reflection arcs, the formal model of which is action research.		Knowledge is generated in statistical distributional and sometimes qualitative studies.
Systems are the primary focus for attention, sources of knowledge and intervention.		*Parts are the objects of attention and study, and focus for intervention.*
This cohort program is designed to enact systemic organizational and leadership principles, itself evolving as a dynamic human system. This requires an intensive format, that is, extended periods of time together.		People are admitted and educated as individuals. Attention is on learning as an individual cognitive activity best delivered in weekly course formats.
Courses are interwoven and collaboratively designed and delivered by a faculty team and adapted to participants' learning processes.		Courses are designed by individual professors and divided up according to subject matter distinctions.

Table 4.1 (Continued)

Illustrative practices of divergent priorities

Systemic education	Instrumental education
The intellectual framework for intervention focuses on changing the way in which people and systems relate in conducting their work and in how they relate to their contexts.	*The intellectual framework for intervention focuses on changing individuals, individual organizational entities, their communications and task processes.*
The primary attention is on apprehending processes and patterns of change over time. Conceptual frames incorporate the dimension of time and patterns of change. Participants learn to observe and intervene in processes recurrently.	*The primary attention is on learning how the nature of things how they work.* Key concepts and theories describe states, relationships among variables. Students learn to gather data, analyze variables, and derive logical conclusions.
Intellectual competence is demonstrated in ability to learn in action and to critically examine and revise one's interventions and understanding. Course work is designed to generate double loop learning (improving *how* we do things together) and triple loop learning (reworking a fundamental perspective that enables us to understand why we can do things more effectively).[3]	*Intellectual competence is demonstrated in the abilities to acquire existing information and theories, and critically examine research and theory.* Coursework is subject matter focused and possibly revisions of one's thinking.
Collaborative leadership and intervention is the primary focus. Faculty members model collaborative leadership with each other promoting each others' learning and working to produce optimal design and conduct of the program	*Individual leadership and achievement is the primary objective.* Faculty members model the achievement of individual expertise in a subject area and in teaching.

Faculty members work as coaches building partnerships in learning with participants, fostering interdependence and independence among learners who retain responsibility for their own learning.
Collaborative leadership in the form of process consultation is an essential competency for graduation.

The most advanced form of knowing is reflexive understanding in which places oneself within the inquiry.
Faculty members consider that optimal performance is a willingness to examine and revise their choices, behavior, and decisions with colleagues and participants.
Participants learn to open themselves to inquiry with others. Learning and performance are balanced.

Faculty members transfer their knowledge to learners and evaluate the results. Dependence and relationship dynamics between professor and student is not a primary focus of attention.
Individual achievement in knowledge and theory about leadership and organizations is required.

The most advanced form of knowing is a detached and rigorous analysis.
Faculty members consider that optimal performance is a seamless demonstration of individual academic expertise.

Students learn to present near-perfect work for examination by the professor.

focus on logic, abstraction, and detached inquiry precludes the development of practical wisdom in human conduct. *Phrónêsis*, practical wisdom, requires full engagement in practical challenges, embracing mistakes and messes, insight through reflection, and revision of personal practices.

In leading this kind of educational change, our own learning through engagement has been intense, our mistakes and messes sources of great insight, and our learning has been extremely valuable. We offer the following four themes in practical wisdom for managing our own behavior, for selecting our initiatives, and for working with others at the paradigmatic interface. First, we found it very helpful to be mindful of our place in our wider environment and moment in history and its implications for our opportunities and limitations for practice. Second and related to the first, we found it is critical to understand paradigms at play—our own and those of others. We identify our educational perspectives as exemplifying reconstructive postmodernism, while the more prevalent and influential perspectives in the university represent the modernist synthesis and deconstructive postmodernism or antimodernism. Third, we learned it is critical to promote and excel at dialogue across paradigmatic difference as an alternative to defending the innovation in the conventional political institutional ways. Finally and consequent to the prior three themes, we learned about the nature of the "econiche"[4] or institutional conditions necessary for sustainability of systemic leadership education.

Our Wider Environment and Our Moment in History

We understand ourselves to be on the front edge of the enormous transformative wave of our times. While many organizations and leaders have been inventively adapting to their unpredictable environments, many have not. Further, while leadership educators are beginning to identify gaps between what is offered and what is needed, as cited earlier, institutional higher education has not yet experienced the full force of current, paradigmatically challenging global change. Innovations are at the level of content (e.g., more emphasis on the international environment) or technology (e.g., Web CT for coursework, access to electronic databases). Rising enrolments encourage schools to be doing what they have always been doing. Without direct challenge to universities from the wider environment, faculty members who are attending to the environmental messages and are educational program innovators become the only force for fundamental innovation. We must expect, therefore, to expend enormous energy creating space for the innovation, for dialogue to promote understanding of the innovation among colleagues and within the institution, as discussed here. A further environmental element, at least in our current Canadian context, is serious underfunding of education. Universities, virtually all being under public funding guidelines, are stretched between restrained student fees and reductions in government funding. In this economic environment, innovations that are supported are those that increase the number of students per class and other efficiencies. Innovation, in general, is seen costly (e.g., time for faculty learning and development of new pedagogical initiatives) and typically not supported in the climate of economic constraint.

Understanding Paradigmatic Differences

The systemic leadership program described earlier is evolved from a socio-ecological perspective, a constellation of assumptions that is profoundly divergent from the two academic perspectives currently prevalent in the academy—modernism and deconstructive postmodernism. We have found that "seeing paradigms" is critical, especially for the minority perspective. Otherwise, disagreements about pedagogical practices and organization can be interpreted as educators being unreasonable and uncooperative rather than understood as representations of fundamentally distinctive practices generated by different underlying educational assumptions, beliefs, purposes and values. Here we exemplify how these challenges at paradigmatic inter-faces arise in practice in order to illustrate the differences among the three perspectives.

As we have seen in the Introduction, organizations and institutions in Western society are expressions of the modernist imagination. The university is no exception. It is a bureaucracy, in this case, designed to transmit largely theoretical knowledge that is derived from empirical rational research and intellectual debate. Knowledge, like the organization itself, is compartmentalized into logically delimited disciplines and packaged into manageable portions in courses to be delivered, largely through lectures and seminars, by professors. Union agreements about "teaching loads" are based on this structure.

In a socio-ecological approach to education, courses as distinguished in a university calendar are interwoven into an entire program designed on the basis of participants' *process of learning* that emerges from practical experience generated within the program and relevant conceptual material. Since the learning from one course is interrelated with that of other courses, and since the design of courses is learning-oriented, it is essential that faculty members collaborate in their teaching to foster that integrity in the learning experience.

Yet, for the conventional university educator who regards knowledge as a primary theoretical, encoded in text, it is not at all clear why the courses in this program cannot be offered as distinct entities, as usual, that can be taught by individual faculty members in the usual teaching schedule. Isn't it the same content? Even the more innovative educator who includes experiential exercises, cases, and student discussions of these and other experiences within the regular class format, cannot achieve the possibility of *knowing from within* the dynamic life of a temporary *learning system*. The significance of the mode of the program delivery as integral to the "curriculum" as well as the organizational implications challenge multiple layers of the modernist educator's assumptions.

The second prevalent paradigm in the academy is deconstructive postmodernism (Kegan, 1994), a powerful critique of modernist assumptions from yet another perspective. Three defining features of this viewpoint are: (1) rejection of absolutes—"no key ruling theoretical framework," no metanarrative; (2) power and dominance as a thematic focus in all social discourse; and (3) the celebration of difference—plurality as "a constitutive quality of existence" (Burbules and Rice, 1991, pp. 325–326). Deconstructive postmodernism in education is represented in rigorous intellectual analysis aimed at deconstructing institutional practices and propositions. Coherences and syntheses are "unpacked"; where modernism begins with the "parts," deconstructive postmodernism wants to end with the "parts." Systemic or socio-ecological education seen from this standpoint is highly suspect and, perhaps ironically, as another modernist invention. Specifically, the requirement of participation in a learning system, task teams and other groups by either students or faculty is assumed necessarily to constrict individual points of view, to obscure the exercise of power, and to favor hegemony and conformity.

Burbules and Rice (1991) view the deconstructive postmodern position as "unsustainable either intellectually or practically" since it "lacks a clear conception of a 'positive freedom' that identifies social conditions in which freer thought and action are possible; lacking this, antimodernism has not been able to articulate a clear and defensible educational theory" (p. 400). Where modernism can be seen as "stuck" in a synthesis, deconstructive postmodernism can be seen as "stuck" in an antithesis. Reconstructive postmodernism shares the three key features in a different way. Introducing the notion of *processes over time*, it opens up possibility of *temporary social and intellectual syntheses*. These are referenced to practical realities that are emergent. Social and intellectual syntheses are regarded as essential temporary social constructions that, though inevitably succeeded by new forms, constitute in a particular historical moment a step in reaching for a better understanding and conditions for life.

If we are to understand the nature of our differences, it is important for us to understand not only our own fundamental assumptions, but also those of others. We need to *imagine the other* (Saul, 2001) in order to communicate our differences and understand what we are asking of others whom we invite or expect to understand us. Since shifting paradigms involves personal transformation, it is critical in recruiting both participants and faculty to enter into this work that we understand the learning demands and that involvement is value based and voluntary.

Promoting Dialogue Across Paradigmatic Differences

Mindful of our historical moment and our environment, we are aware of ourselves as members of a small minority bringing a socio-ecological perspective to education. Believing in the value of our work, we have come to accept that an important part of that work is relating to colleagues and deans who, not being members of our field of practice and scholarship, are nevertheless impacted by it since we are part of *their* environment.

Universities, when operating at their very best, have been committed to innovation and invention, the generation of new knowledge, the pursuit of excellence, and respect for disciplinary diversity. These common values are a critical "platform" for relating across paradigms. Our experience is that in pursuing this kind of innovation in a conventional university context, academic leaders who are confident and enthusiastically involved in their own disciplines are open to considering educational innovations and other perspectives. There is, in most cases, a respect for different ideas and possibly for different practices if they are understood as having integrity within a different intellectual perspective.

Rendering the distinctive paradigms visible, however, is the considerable challenge. Most often, like fish that cannot identify the water they swim in, we are unaware of them. A form of communication, "dialogue" (Gustavsen, 1992), an inquiry into meanings and assumptions among people, is necessary to surface basic underlying assumptions and beliefs. Without it, practical pedagogical disagreements become intractable and practical initiatives can collide. For example, in leadership education where working with conflict is essential, there are four paradigmatic approaches to conflict. Kegan (1994) describes the traditionalist's primary objective, seeing only one right way, is to win. For modernist, acknowledging diverse interests, the objective is to find a rational solution that satisfies both parties (win–win). A deconstructive postmodern view would emphasize the danger, even the inevitability, of working through conflicts to mutual understanding as domination of one perspective over another. A reconstructive postmodern best possibility is for both or all parties to understand the issue in a new way—conflict being inherent in cross-paradigmatic learning. The way we represent intervention possibilities to students and, indeed, how we work with conflicts in the learning context will derive from our underlying assumptive framework. Interactions based in more than one of these conceptions without recognizing the underlying assumptive differences operate at crossed purposes and communication tends to be distorted and confusing. This generates iterations of angst and aggravation.

There appear to be four conditions for dialogue. First, bringing tacit assumptions and beliefs requires a *safe environment* since we have to be ready to discover things about ourselves that are surprising, things we didn't know we didn't know. We cannot be performing to pressing decision deadlines, or be punished for our assumptions or governed by rules of order. Dialogue is an emergent flow of mutual inquiry. Cross-paradigmatic communication can be vanquished by the refusal of time and confusion of its purposes with university business. Dialogue is, however, consonant with the universities age-old occupation of inquiry. In addition to sessions organized for dialogue concerning specific presenting academic issues, many other dialogical spaces must be continuously created so as to foster a conversation over time (de Guerre, 2000). Some of these include learned lectures, workshops, seminars, research colloquia, and multipartite groupings of participants from different departments within the university and different sectors of the community. Such carefully constructed dialogical spaces can provide the opportunity to engage with each other as persons mindful of the wider world in which we are working (Van Beinum, 1990).

It is important to note that common ground can be created while maintaining difference and disagreements. Through dialogue we need to be open to a range of results: agreement, disagreement with understanding based on common meanings, no common understanding but understanding of differences but partial understanding of the others' position, little understanding but mutual respect of the other for their thoughtful position, and irreconcilable difference (Burbules and Rice, 1991).

There are three more conditions for cross-paradigmatic dialogue. One is that participation is voluntary and in good faith. Caution and tentativeness can be expected and even helpful indications that participants are making their own choice to engage or not. Strict adherence to ideology (e.g., extreme deconstructive postmodernist) or maintenance of political benefits from the state of impasse and confusion precludes genuine participation. Refusal of authentic engagement inevitably suspends the possibility of dialogue.

Another condition is that each participant is equal regardless of institutional roles and status. And the final condition is what Burbules and Rice (1991) call "communicative virtues"—"tolerance, patience, respect for differences, a willingness to listen, the inclination to admit that one may be mistaken..." (p. 411) in the spirit of attending openly to "the other." The presence and development of these virtues we see as interactive with the perceived level of safety in the environment. The more the dialogical space becomes more assuring, the more the communicative virtues will emerge.

Our experience of living on the paradigmatic interface is that it is strenuous and enormously challenging. It is an extremely complex position in the academy, both practically and intellectually. We recognize the vulnerability of systemic educational innovation within a large institution and wider culture whose assumptive frameworks can obscure its fundamental distinctiveness or even unwittingly obliterate it by imposing conventional institutional practices. In this context of fragility, it is easy to become defensive of the project and be drawn into a win–lose stance thus undermining our own position and values. We have missed many critical opportunities to build the conditions for dialogue through the quality of our own participation. The hardest work at the interface is that of sustaining full participation in full simultaneous consciousness of the qualities of the social environment, the relationship dynamics, and ourselves as participants. It is only in this way that we can ensure that our behavior is consistent with our values in the face of threat. This is perhaps the heart of the reconstructive postmodern task.

Qualities of the Econiche for Sustainability of Systemic Leadership Education

The harsh realities of current institutional education—fierce competition for scarce operational and research funding that result in deterioration of collegial relationships and organizational climate—have provoked us to examine carefully the qualities of organizational environments required to sustain a paradigmatically innovative educational practice. The demand for efficiency has led to trying to produce more with fewer resources, eliminating "unproductive" experimentation and reflection, and reinforcing hierarchical bureaucracy. In such an institutional context dealing with the paradigmatic interface through the establishment of some common ground across paradigms becomes impossible. Creativity cannot flourish nor does the human spirit from which it springs.

We see three alternative foundational elements in an organizational "platform" for socio-ecological or systems leadership education. Such a "platform" could be in association with a conventional university through a contractual partnership or it could be constituted separately. Whatever its venue, its nature would need to be reflected in its formal and legal constitution.

The first foundational element is intellectual, that is, the educational mission is the cultivation of practical wisdom, *phrónêsis, the intellect of practice.* The educational and research programs would be based on the hermeneutic between practice and theory as iterative and ongoing processes. There is an emerging interest in what has been called the "third educational alternative," that is, an alternative to the traditional research university and conventional professional schools. It characteristics are: highly interactive education; participants who are mature adults; a focus on enhanced life appreciation; driven by complex life changes; multidisciplinary; and organized for accessibility (price and time).

The second foundational element is the design and operation of the educational organization itself, namely, an econiche that is governed by the same values and principles informing the program itself. Members of the organization need to be recruited on the basis of their commitment to these values and principles as much as their professional expertise. Designed and redesigned by its members as new realities emerge, the organization would attend to the quality of relationships among its members and with clients and program participants as integral to the organization's task objectives. Members would be meaningfully involved in making decisions that affect their participation in the organization fully explored in dialogical spaces preferably by consensus. Attention to its wider environment would be extensive and continuous. Such an organization would have the flexibility to be actively adaptive to student and organizational needs in the larger society and move nimbly in the turbulent environment. Importantly, there would be congruence between the systemic educational paradigm and the organization of its educators who would be practicing what they teach.

The third foundational element is that financial support for the organization would come from those who understand or genuinely want to learn its purpose and principles, that is, those who are committed to it and who benefit from it. Contract research between the organization's scholar-practitioners (faculty and student interns) and practitioner-clients is one source of funding that is simultaneously a vital way to ensure the integration of research and practice. Program tuition fees would be commensurate with program operating expenses so that participants are responsibly supporting the educational services from which they benefit. Endowments and other contributions would need to be from multiple sources precluding reliance on any single source of income to preserve intellectual freedom in education and research. At this moment in our history, we believe it especially important to overcome the constraints on research and pedagogy that derive from modernist assumptions in funding criteria.

Conclusion

Pursuit of practical wisdom is an ongoing process for us all. Our purpose has been to develop an educational practice that enables leaders of the future to value and influence social processes and structures in a socio-ecological perspective. We have called this systemic leadership, a form of leadership critical to survival and nourishment of human creativity and spirit in a complex and turbulent environment. Through providing innovative education in a conventional university, we were provoked in our own learning at the paradigmatic interface. We have offered our best current understanding about organizational conditions to sustain and advance an educational innovation that holds great promise for learning toward an ecological consciousness.

Notes

1. Systemic consciousness includes at least, awareness of self, awareness of the awareness, and awareness of social and ecological aspects of the global environment.
2. This program design is more fully elaborated in Taylor et al. (2002).
3. William Torbert along with theorists like Bruner (1986) and Bateson (1979), make distinctions among levels of learning. Torbert and Fisher (1992) speak of "single loop" learning is "empirical, technical, and ahistorical: it permits us to achieve a goal over time . . . a person or organization learns to change specific behaviour or operation, in order to more effectively achieve a pre-determined and constant goal or project." "Double loop learning" is "theoretical and structural: it gives us a distinct, systematic perspective on events . . . a person or organization learns in a way that changes the very structures, strategies, and goals within which single-loop learning occurs, in order to more effectively approach a relatively intangible mission, purpose, or principle . . . . A person acts in a qualitatively new way." "Triple loop" learning derives from feedback from which "the very taken for granted purposes, principles, or paradigm . . . may be reintuited . . . . Inconsistencies among mission, strategy, operations, and outcomes are observed as they occur . . . [consistent with] the action inquiry paradigm of social science" (p. 195).
4. Merrelyn Emery (1999) defines "econiche" as "a consistent and intermediate level of environment which . . . is analogous to concepts such as 'task or learning environment' . . . which is afforded by an organization" (p. 27).

82   •   Don W. de Guerre and Marilyn M. Taylor

References

Axelrod, R. H. (2000). *Terms of Engagement: Changing the Way we Change Our Organizations.* Toronto: Berrett-Koehler.

Bateson, G. (1979). *Mind and Nature: A Necessary Unit.* New York: Dutton.

Boyatzis, R., Cowen, S., and Kolb, D. (1995). "A Learning Perspective on Executive Education." *Selections* 11 (3), 47–56.

Boyzantis, R. and Kram, K. (1999). "Reconstructing Management Education as Lifelong Learning." *Selections* 16 (1), 17–27.

Bruner, J. (1986). *Actual Minds, Possible Worlds.* Cambridge, MA: Harvard University Press.

Bunker, B. and Alban, B. (1997). *Large Group Interventions: Engaging the Whole System for Rapid Change.* San Francisco: Jossey Bass.

Burbules, N. and Rice, S. (1991). "Dialogue Across Differences: Continuing the Conversation." *Harvard Educational Review* 61, 393–416.

Clarkson, P. and Shaw, P. (1992). "Human Relationships at Work in Organizations." *Management Education and Development* 23 (1), 18–29.

de Guerre, D. W. (2000). "The Co-Determination of Cultural Change Over Time." *Systemic Practice and Action Research* 13 (5), 645–663.

Devane, T. and Holman, P. (1999). *The Change Handbook: Group Methods for Shaping the Future.* San Francisco: Berrett-Koehler.

Emery, F. and Emery, M. (1979). *Project Australia: Its Chances.* Melbourne: P.A. Consulting Services ANU/CCE.

Emery, F. and Trist, E. (1965). "The Causal Texture of Organizational Environments." *Human Relations* 18, 21–32.

Emery, F. and Trist, E. (1972). *Towards a Social Ecology: Appreciation of the Future in the Present.* New York: Plenum Press.

Emery, M. (1999). *Searching: The Theory and Practice of Making Cultural Change.* Amsterdam: John Benjamins Publishing.

Finegold, D. (1994). "International Models of Management Development." *Selections* 11 (1), 12–27.

Gustavsen, B. (1992). *Dialogue and Development.* Assen: van Gorcum.

Jeremy Shapiro, http://www.acm.org/ubiquity/interviews/j_shepiro_

Kegan, R. (1994). *In Over Our Heads: The Mental Demands of Modern Life.* Cambridge, MA: Harvard University Press.

Linder, J. and Smith, J. (1992). "The Complex Case of Management Education." *Harvard Business Review* 70 (5), 16–33.

Nodoushani, O. and Nodoushani, P. (1996). "Rethinking the Future of Management Education." *Human Systems Management* 15 (3), 173–181.

Saul, John Ralston (2001). *On Equilibrium.* Toronto: Penguin.

Taylor, M., de Guerre, D., Gavin, J., and Kass, R. (2002). "Graduate Leadership Education for Dynamic Human Systems." *Management Learning* 33 (3), 349–369.

Torbert, W. and Fisher, D. (1992). "Autobiographical Awareness as a Catalyst for Managerial and Organizational Development." *Management Education and Development* 23 (2), 184–198.

Van Beinum, H. (1986). *Arbeid en Arbeidsomstandigheden (Democratization of Work in North America)*. Amsterdam: NAIS.

Van Beinum, H. (1990). "Observations on the Development of a New Organizational Paradigm." Stockholm: Arbetslivscentrum.

Van Beinum, H. (1993). Personal conversation with one of the authors.

CHAPTER 5

The Ecology of Learning and Work: Learning for Transformative Work Practices

Marilyn E. Laiken

Introduction

It has been said that "the unexamined life is not worth living" (Socrates). Yet, in the current work and educational climate of increasing pressure to produce relentlessly, a key to success has been all but eliminated. This is the ability to create a space for collective reflection, learning, and ultimately personal, organizational, and potentially social, transformation.

Our recent research (Laiken, 2001; Laiken et al., in press) has highlighted managing the paradox of task versus process, or action versus reflection, as a critical factor in blocking or facilitating transformative learning. This involves the ability to step back from the task at hand periodically, to reflect on *how* the work is proceeding in order to become progressively more able to manage the task effectively, whether individually, as a work team, or as a whole organization.

At the Ontario Institute for Studies in Education of the University of Toronto, graduate students in our Adult Education specialization, "Workplace Learning and Change," are studying to be change practitioners across work sectors. All of them have an interest in creating authentic, transformative work environments, and are using their graduate education to experience and learn about this for themselves and their constituents.

Authentic learning environments and authentic workplaces have much in common. They tend to be ones in which collaborative partnerships prevail over hierarchical power relationships; leadership is enabling rather than controlling; differences are viewed as rich resources for learning rather than challenges to be "managed"; reflection and critical thinking are encouraged through the development of vibrant communities of practice; conflicting ideas are surfaced through genuine dialogue, often leading to expanded thinking and revised worldviews; and "wholeness" is valued—both in the individual as a whole person (body, mind, emotions) and in the understanding of groups and organizations as living systems.

Probably the most important characteristic of these environments is the prizing of congruence between beliefs and behavior. However this rarely describes the reality. Rather, an authentic learning or working environment is one in which participants may see themselves in a *process* of continuously striving for such congruence. This involves being clear at the outset about one's values and vision of an ideal, and then being willing to acknowledge honestly instances in which the reality may be out of sync with that vision. The task then is to conscientiously work toward closing the gap.

Graduate education programs in traditional universities are challenging places in which to create authentic learning environments that fit this description. Like the traditional workplace, they are generally hierarchically structured and tend to create power-over positions for those in leadership roles, encourage competition as opposed to collaboration through their funding and reward (i.e., grading) systems, use adversarial approaches such as collective bargaining or appeals procedures to resolve conflicts, and often implicitly allow and support critique that is judgmental and silencing as opposed to exploratory and inviting. Most significantly, genuine dialogue, honest expression of feelings, and the opportunity to focus on process as well as content are clearly devalued, making it difficult, if not impossible to close the gap between espoused values and practiced behavior.

And yet, we learn what we live. If our students are to help create transformative environments in their own work organizations, we believe that they must first experience such environments in their graduate education.

Our intention in the Workplace Learning and Change specialization is to engage learners in theory and practice that generates consciousness through interaction and reflection. Although our expectation is that the experience will be personally transformative, we also assume a reciprocal relationship between personal and systemic transformation processes. By creating an environment in which learners can safely experiment with new behavior, reflect on the outcomes, and extrapolate principles that can then be applied in future experiences, our graduate courses foster systemic consciousness through collaborative participation, developmental leadership, and critical reflection regarding current organizational practices.

We believe, as expressed by Fritjof Capra (2002), that:

> To build a sustainable society for our children and future generations, we need to fundamentally redesign many of our technologies and social institutions so as to bridge the wide gap between human design and the ecologically sustainable systems of nature. (p. 99)

We recognize social contexts as potentially transformative, and therefore strive to help our graduate students create work environments in which "the structures, norms and processes embody transformative ecological values— (those of) participation, partnership, mutual respect, and responsibility, reflection, communication and collaborative inquiry, creativity and . . . a sense of the whole" (Taylor, 2002, p. 5). In our program, this is accomplished through courses designed to reflect the values and approaches that we aim to demonstrate and model.

In one of the courses that I teach, entitled: "Developing and Leading High Performing Teams: Theory and Practice" (referred to in this chapter as "course 1107"), we are experimenting with a particular design that surfaces the action/reflection paradox for the purpose of learning how to manage this polarity. This becomes important if we consider that transformational practice is dependent on an opportunity for reflective, critical thinking (Mezirow, 1991; Cranton, 1994).

This chapter examines the design of the course 1107 learning environment in an effort to shed light on how engaging in dialogic conversations helps learners to manage the action/reflection tension, educationally and organizationally. It draws on data from both our recently completed research project, conducted to examine models of organizational learning (Laiken, 2001; Laiken et al., in press), and from the writings of recent 1107 students in their final papers for the course.

The Problem

At the organizational level, across work sectors, our students agree with our research findings that whether the product is defined as services or goods, the general tendency is to view time spent on specific task completion as the only legitimate form of work. Divergent thinking, although touted as an organizational value with phrases such as "thinking out of the box," is in reality only barely tolerated before convergence toward action (or, in Nike's terms, "just do it") overrules.

However, as Capra (2002) notes:

> Being creative means being able to relax into uncertainty and confusion. In most organizations this is becoming increasingly difficult, because things move too fast. People feel that they have hardly any time for quiet reflection, and since reflective consciousness is one of the defining characteristics of human nature, the results are profoundly dehumanizing. (p. 126)

For instance, in one of the organizations from our research (Laiken, 2001, p. 8), a worker comments:

> Oh, they look bored at the meeting, and they don't make notes, and they think, "well, didn't we already discuss this?" So people try to speed up the tempo, you know at the meetings, and it's a good thing, because there's work to do. But on the other hand, it's also a forum where you can think—we need to meet, because there will be issues—you know there are—that we should get a little deeper into.

Decades of experience and research in adult learning (Lewin, 1951; Argyris and Schön, 1978; Kolb, 1984; Cranton, 1994) have convinced educators that an opportunity to reflect on one's lived experience is an absolutely essential component of learning that results in attitudinal and behavioral change. In the workplace, an opportunity for such reflection not only increases productive capacity as well as individual knowledge and skill, but also, in fact, results in personal and sometimes, organizational learning that is transformative.[1] As workers engage in critical, reflective conversations about the results of a mutual project and their interactions within it, they not only devise improved approaches for further work, they also explore their own values, assumptions, and interpersonal processes. Where an unexamined experience may tend to simply be repeated, a conscious examination of learning from direct experience surfaces distorted assumptions and has the potential to revise established worldviews. The paradoxical outcome for an organization is a case of slowing down in order to speed up. Decision-making is improved, effectiveness is increased, and overall productivity and work satisfaction are enhanced through systematically incorporated periods of collective reflection (Argyris, 1990; Senge et al., 2000; Laiken, 2001; Capra, 2002; Laiken et al., forthcoming).

Nevertheless, the workplace persists in devaluing this activity by using derogatory language such as "mushy" or "touchy-feely," and through maintaining systems, processes, and behaviors that relegate critical reflection to an isolated corner, if it is supported at all. As a team member in one of our research sites notes:

> But it does take work, though, I mean, you think about a team—it doesn't just happen on its own. It takes its course—and the problem is, people get so caught up with doing the other work they have to do that they don't take the time to build their team, and so the team work doesn't get improved. (Laiken, 2001, p. 9)

When personality or work-style differences (Kolb, 1984) surface in a team meeting, the pressure to move to task closure reinforces convergent work approaches. The assimilative thinkers who could encourage deeper analysis, or the divergent thinkers who might help expand the possibilities, often play second fiddle to an action orientation that is reinforced by work pressures to make a decision and move on. What is lost in this process is the potential for learning that could both inform future action and expand personal consciousness.

Helen reflects on her own attitude toward process at the start of the 1107 course:

> I personally viewed the frequent "time outs" as being selfish and unproductive to the class goal.... I recognized the time that a team project would take, and feared that if we continued to stop and look at our team process, we would run out of time. As a working parent taking two courses, I valued the task time, and was resistant to seeing value in the process.

Additionally, when one considers the fact that the skills involved in critical reflection are not as valued, and therefore taught or practiced minimally in the action-oriented workplace, it is not surprising that these skills are generally underdeveloped among workers, regardless of personal style differences. Thus, although the need for balance between "task" and "process" is sometimes recognized, the implementation is fraught with difficulties.

One of the key barriers is a disinclination to engage in open dialogue that holds the potential for conflict. Inevitably, as a group of people begins to examine together a shared work experience, the differences that define their uniqueness will surface. In an earlier study (Laiken, 1993) conducted with senior managers, team leaders, and members from two private sector organizations, we found that "an intellectual understanding does not appear to be sufficient. No matter how much it is accepted that surfacing and managing conflict is a normal, healthy productive process in a team's life, most team members and leaders appear to be frightened of the outcomes and disinclined to engage" (p. 33).

Reflecting on the issue of conflict within the 1107 context, Yolande says:

> The team experience, especially the group facilitation with Barbara, helped me discover a part of me that prefers to avoid conflict. If the conflict is of the more factual and neutral nature, I am not afraid to deal with it openly, and I am able to listen to others and build on others' opinions. But if the conflict is more personal, relating to people's feelings, personality, or has a moral or ethical element to it, I tend to avoid it. (Final paper, 1107, 2001)

A Graduate Course Response to the Challenge

How then do we, as adult educators, enable reflective opportunities that have potential learning outcomes to be incorporated into productivity-oriented workplace settings? And how do we personally learn the skills required to engage in such reflection, so that we may teach them to others? These are key questions that have surfaced in course 1107 over the years. Our Adult Education graduate students engage in this inquiry experientially, through a course design that unfolds during seven full-day sessions over a period of 13 weeks.

The first day is devoted to orienting the learners to the course design, beginning to build the group of 12 people as a team, and introducing Paul Hersey and Kenneth Blanchard's Situational Leadership Model (1988) as a skeletal framework from which to build the theoretical components of the course. The theories represent current and classic research on developing effective work teams, and are introduced experientially during the morning sessions of the remainder of the course.

At the end of the first meeting, the students form co-facilitating pairs for each of the remaining six sessions. The course design then proceeds as follows.

In the mornings, theory is introduced covering such areas as the phases of team development; team goal-setting, problem-solving, decision-making, communication and conflict management; managing difference; and dealing with intractable problems as polarities. The purpose of these theoretical frameworks is to provide a "conceptual map" to help students examine their lived experience of team membership and leadership, both in the workplace and during the afternoon peer-led team meetings throughout the course. These pieces are initially introduced and taught by the instructor; however, the content is eventually determined by the interests and learning needs of all class participants, and often involves guest lecturers, films, site visits, and simulated experiences. Examples of such participant-determined content have included an examination of style/personality differences in a team through such instruments as David Kolb's Learning Style Inventory (1984) and the Myers-Briggs Type Indicator (1998), guest lectures to explore Barry Johnson's concept of "Polarity Management" (1992), and an exploration of Peter Senge's "ladder of inference" (Senge et al., 1994) as an approach to managing the leaps of abstraction from observations to assumptions that inevitably occur in a working team.

The afternoon session is divided into two components. The first is an hour and three-quarter meeting of the class group as a working "team," led by the co-facilitating pairs of students chosen during the first class. The task, process, and facilitation of these meetings is entirely decided by the members, who are also asked to determine a method for evaluating their progress as a team in all of these areas. The outcome of this evaluation is worth 50 percent of each student's grade. The instructor acts as a "coach" to the co-facilitators prior to and during the team sessions, if needed. Otherwise she simply observes, collecting data to help with the next segment. The purpose of this component is to generate the team experience that provides grist for the learning mill. It is during this segment of the day that students experience the typical behavior of team members as they complete a task such as setting team objectives, planning for implementation of activities to accomplish these goals, and evaluation of their individual and collective success. The grading task simulates a work team experience of peer evaluation, an activity that is increasingly becoming a norm for progressive teams in organizational settings.

The final hour of the day is devoted to a team "debrief," the ultimate purpose of which is to help students learn the skills of successfully achieving task goals through action, while maintaining an effective team process through reflection. This segment, which is initially facilitated by the instructor, and eventually co-led by all team members, provides a structured reflective opportunity to examine the team's behavior and provide individual feedback to members and co-facilitators. The observations of "team life" are intentionally related back by the instructor and students to theoretical concepts introduced in the morning sessions.

Sarah comments on the impact of this part of the course design:

> The debrief for this session offered many insights into appropriate leadership for this stage. For example, the co-facilitators had prepared an agenda but had realized just before the session that it was too structured, so discarded it. This was a good decision, because it allowed the group

members to have more control over the session, thereby sharing the power.... Because the co-facilitators adjusted their leadership style to be less directive, the group was able to air our differences and work through our issues. (Final paper, 1107, 2001)

The path to this kind of awareness is a dialogic approach intended to encourage critically reflective conversations. Learners practice the skills required to engage successfully in dialogue, including advocating their own views, as well as inquiring into the views of others, with the intention of promoting understanding of differences (Isaacs, 1993; Ellinor and Gerard, 1998; Brenegan, 2000). They are introduced to such concepts as "the ladder of inference" (Argyris and Schön, 1978; Senge et al., 1994), to help them manage the tendency to leap from observed behavior to undiscussed interpretations and assumptions. They practice the skills of self-disclosure and giving and receiving feedback on observable behavior (Luft, 1970), and are encouraged to see conflict and expression of difference as a rich opportunity for learning (Laiken, 1994).

About this experience, Sharon says:

The team enabled a dialogue process to occur by creating a safe, "holding" environment for our discussion. From the early stages of our team development, we had established a supportive, accepting climate for our meetings.... This container had the capacity to hold the diversity within our team. Opposing views were welcomed as an essential contribution, each worthy of consideration. (Final paper, 1107, 2001)

The face-to-face interaction in class is supported by several additional vehicles for reflection, which help reinforce the experiential learning approach. These include a course requirement that each student maintain a personal reflective journal of his or her experience; a learning partnership that is formed early in the course and used in any way the learners choose; and a website (Web Knowledge Forum) that is available for on-line conversations between classes.

Learning to Engage in Dialogue

Though clearly course 1107 has an impact, the question still remains about exactly how this is achieved. In an earlier article (Laiken, 1997), I introduced a variation of Bandura's (1974) behavioral theory model. It helps to examine the various stages of learning through which an individual or group might progress, to enable the kind of collective reflection described in the last section. I have become aware of the fact that this is exactly the process that my 1107 students experience in class and exemplify in their workplaces, as they and their colleagues learn the art and practice of dialogue.

The stages are as follows:

(1) *Lack of awareness (unconscious incompetence).* In this stage, differences in ideas, styles, approaches, commitment, and so on, may cause discomfort, but there is no expectation that it is possible to address this within the work/learning context.

In describing this phase within a client community service team, Evelyn says:

There are conflicts between some professional groups about roles, and some team members have reacted to these and other issues through absenteeism and a general lack of enthusiasm for the task at hand.... Team members tend to talk about the issues outside of the group format, which might help to alleviate some frustration, but does not provide the team with the ability to move forward. (Final paper, 1107, 2001)

(2) *Awareness without action (conscious incompetence).* In this stage, there is an awareness of issues needing to be discussed more openly, but neither the willingness nor the ability to make these discussible in the work/learning context.

A transcript of a conversation from Vanessa's recent nursing team meeting provides an example of this stage in the workplace:

As we simmered down a little, Margaret asked, "So how do we get into this muck? I know we do it, but here we are—nurses, with supposedly great interpersonal skills, grand communication skills and lots of ability for active listening. Where do we go wrong?"

"Well, I think we may be able to listen and empathize, but I think we are not so skilled at giving feedback and talking clearly about our experiences. That's not what they teach you in nursing, at least not when I graduated!" Dorothy interjected, "Yes if someone says something weird or off-base at team, people just shut up or change the subject. We're not really good at clarifying, especially something that is contentious." "Or something that upsets us," added Anne. "We are much more likely to talk about it after the meeting in small groups." "Yes," said Margaret, "and that's where it really can start to get out of hand." (Final paper, 1107, 2001)

The work at these two levels involves helping people to invite feedback on the impact of their behavior on others; helping them explore the assumptions that are driving this behavior; and helping them be open to having these assumptions questioned by others who bring a different perspective to the table. The impact of this type of engagement is to prevent trips up the previously mentioned "ladder of inference" (Senge et al., 1994):

- From observable data gleaned from experiences with each other
- To "data" that we select from what we observe
- To personal and cultural meanings that we add
- To assumptions we make based on those meanings
- To conclusions we draw rooted in our assumptions
- To beliefs we adopt or generalizations that we make
- To actions we take based on those beliefs.

The next stage is:

(3) *The ability to act on awareness, with effort (conscious competence).* In this stage a group is able, possibly with facilitative help, to surface and expose assumptions in order to explore differences more openly.

Here, learners prevent their trip up the "ladder of inference" by becoming more aware of their own thinking and reasoning through critical reflection, and begin to engage genuinely with each other through dialogue. This involves slowing down their thought processes so that they avoid moving quickly from the concrete data of direct observation to a generalization that is not tested. Participants learn to spot these leaps because they often cause confusion and tension in a conversation. At this point, rather than ignoring the tension, they learn to acknowledge the leap, and examine it by testing their understandings against the experience of others.

Reflecting on her engagement with this process in 1107, Tess says:

During our fifth meeting a team member declared: "I don't look forward to coming to this class and I don't know why." That moment held an indescribable intensity in the team…. As the conversation continued, conflicting views and feelings surfaced. I felt the energy begin to shift. The team allowed the space for working through internal and interpersonal conflicts. The collective strength and vulnerabilities of the team began to surface, as individuals shared responsibility for leadership on specific issues. In these moments I began to feel part of a dialogue—with myself and in the group.

Once the differences have surfaced and are understood clearly by all, the last phase of the model becomes relevant. This is:

(4) *The ability to hold the polarities, and maintain the communication (unconscious competence).* This stage involves the ability to interact with others who have qualitatively different views, styles, backgrounds, and so on, in a way that values the other individuals and their ideas, while simultaneously maintaining the integrity of one's own beliefs, and allowing oneself to be influenced by the differences.

As is almost always the case in complex interactions, the issues on the table here are not problems to solve, but polarities to manage. It is likely that a variety of viewpoints will all be potentially credible, while at the same time seeming contradictory. It is in creating a container to hold these differences, and through them to clarify and revise one's own thinking, that the potential for transformation occurs.

In her final paper, Sharon describes how her class team progressed through all four stages within a few weeks:

The first barrier to effective team functioning occurred after our fourth team meeting. Following the session, half of the team met at a restaurant across the street from the school. Emotions ran high. Some of the team members were deeply disturbed by our team's performance. Several individuals who were not present were labeled as "disruptive to our team process" and identified as barriers to achieving our expected team outcomes. (Stage 1)

As a group, we eventually realized that we were responsible for creating the barrier to our team functioning. What could be more damaging to our team development than holding this "gripe" session, labeling team members and raising conflict issues with only half of the team present? We recognized that the only way this barrier could be broken was to address the areas of conflict with the group as a whole at our next team meeting. (Stage 2)

Fortunately, at the next meeting, with support from each other, the team facilitators and the teacher, the team members who were struggling with conflict were able to articulate their issues and successfully resolve them within the team. (Stage 3)

Following this, as a group we reaffirmed our commitment to our team norm of honesty, and the need for each member to call for a "time out" to examine our process when s/he was experiencing a barrier to team functioning. (Stage 4)

Conclusion

In our 1107 course, as in the "learning organizations" of our research (Laiken et al., in press), learners and workers have struggled in their own way with the action/reflection paradox. The class teams and organizations that have been able to actually balance their task and process activities, and include reflective opportunities in the course of a work/learning day, are beginning to demonstrate the ability to manage difference in new ways. In the end, I believe it is this notion of learning in the moment through genuine dialogue, which holds a promise of personal and organizational transformation. Nonaka and Takeuchi (1995) say:

> Although knowledge is always created by individuals, it can be brought to light and expanded by the organization through social interactions in which tacit knowledge is transformed into explicit knowledge.... Tacit knowledge is created by the dynamics of culture resulting from a network of (verbal and non-verbal) communications within a community of practice. (p. 115)

Our graduate students are becoming skillful, through courses like 1107, in helping to create such work environments. Says Helen:

> As I read the transcripts from the taping of class six, I can now see how the class used honesty, balance between task and process, respect for each other, and effective communication (our class norms) to become unstuck and accept the diversity in the class. We moved from the stuck position to a position that valued the benefits of the polarities of task and process. The synergy and enthusiasm within the class was positive and inclusive. We had valued and celebrated both sides of the poles of task and process, and it felt great. (Helen, final paper, course 1107, 2001)

Notes

I gratefully acknowledge the following students[2] from two sections of my graduate course in Fall 2001, "Developing and Leading High Performing Teams: Theory and Practice," who have graciously offered me permission to use ideas and quotes from their final course papers for this chapter. From them and their colleagues in this program, I continue to learn so much: Janet Anderson; Susie Blackstien-Adler; Judith Franks; Terence Frater; Bev Hardy; Ursula Jorch; Myra Kreick; Caitlin Riddolls; Patricia Robinson; Hannah Sauer; Wang Yi; Mark McManus. I also wish to acknowledge all of the participant organizations from our recently completed research on organizational learning (Laiken et al., forthcoming). I particularly thank the ten organizations whose employees generously contributed their time through the completion of questionnaires, and the members of the four case organizations who participated as interviewees, as well as their workplaces that provided support during all phases of the research process.

1. Transformative learning is defined by Patricia Cranton (1994) as "the development of revised assumptions, premises, ways of interpreting experience, or perspectives on the world by means of critical self-reflection" (p. xii).
2. The names in the text have been changed to pseudonyms to protect confidentiality.

References

Argyris, C. (1990). *Overcoming Organizational Defenses: Facilitating Organizational Learning*. Boston: Allyn & Bacon.

Argyris, C. and Schön, D. (1978). *Organizational Learning: A Theory of Action Perspective*. Reading, MA: Addison-Wesley.

Bandura, A, (1974). "Behaviour Theory and the Models of Man." *The American Psychologist* 29, 859–869.

Brenegan, L. (2000). *Dialogue and Process Consulting*. Unpublished Master's thesis. Toronto: Ontario Institute for Studies in Education of the University of Toronto.

Briggs, K. and Myers, I. (1998). *Myers-Briggs Type Indicator*. Palo Alto: Consulting Psychologists Press, Inc.

Capra, F. (2002). *The Hidden Connections: Integrating the Biological, Cognitive, and Social Dimensions of Life into a Science of Sustainability*. New York: Doubleday.

Cranton, P. (1994). *Understanding and Promoting Transformative Learning: A Guide for Educators of Adults*. San Francisco: Jossey-Bass.

Ellinor, L. and Gerard, G. (1998). *Dialogue: Rediscover the Transforming Power of Conversation*. New York: John Wiley & Sons.

Hersey, P. and Blanchard, K. (1988). *Management of Organizational Behaviour: Utilizing Human Resources*. 5th ed. Englewood Cliffs, NJ: Prentice-Hall.

Isaacs, W. (1993). "Taking flight: Dialogue, Collective Thinking and Organizational Learning." *Organizational Dynamics* 22, 24–39.

Johnson, B. (1992). *Polarity Management: Identifying and Managing Unsolvable Problems*. Amherst, MA: HRD Press, Inc.

Kolb, D. (1984). *Experiential Learning: Experience as the Source of Learning and Development*. Englewood Cliffs, NJ: Prentice-Hall.

Laiken, M. (2001). "Models of Organizational Learning: Paradoxes and Best Practices in the Post-Industrial Workplace." In Charles A. Rarick (Ed.), *Conference Proceedings of the 21st OD World Congress, Vienna, Austria July 16–21, 2001* (pp. 1–16).

Laiken, M. (1997). "Collaborative Processes for Collaborative Organizational Design: The Role of Reflection, Dialogue and Polarity Management in Creating an Environment for Organizational Learning." *Organization Development Journal* 15 (4), 35–44.

Laiken, M. (1994). *Conflict in Teams: Problem or Opportunity?* Lectures in Health Promotion Series No. 4, Centre for Health Promotion, University of Toronto.

Laiken, M. (1993). "The Myth of the Self-Managing Team." *Organization Development Journal* 12 (2), 29–34.

Laiken, M., Edge, K., Friedman, S., and West, K. (in press). Formalizing the informal: From Informal to Organizational Learning in the Post-Industrial Workplace. In E. Church Schragge and N. Bascia (Eds.) *Making Sense of Lived Experience in Turbulent Times: Informal Learning.* Wilfred Laurier Press.

Lewin, K. (1951). *Field Theory in Social Science.* New York: Harper & Row.

Luft, J. (1970). *Group Processes: An Introduction to Group Dynamics.* 2nd ed. Palo Alto, CA: National Press.

Mezirow, J. (1991). *Transformative Dimensions of Adult Learning.* San Francisco: Jossey-Bass.

Nonaka, I. and Takeuchi, H. (1995). *The Knowledge-Creating Company.* New York: Oxford University Press.

Senge, P., Kleiner, A., Roberts, C., Ross, R., Roth, G., and Smith, B. (2000). *The Dance of Change: The Challenges to Sustaining Momentum in Learning Organizations.* New York: Doubleday Currency.

Senge, P., Roberts, C., Ross, R., Smith, B., and Kleiner, A. (1994). *The Fifth Discipline Fieldbook: Strategies and Tools for Building a Learning Organization.* New York: Doubleday Currency.

Taylor, M. (2002). *Draft outline of Learning Toward Ecological Consciousness: Selected Transformative Practices.* Unpublished.

PART 2

Learning Through Engagement in the Life World

Prologue

> Putting our own inner houses in order will prove the key to reinventing work for the human species. And not only individuals have inner houses; the inner houses of our communities, our churches and synagogues, our economic and political systems, and our neighborhood and family relationships all need our attention at this critical moment in human and Earth history.
>
> Matthew Fox, *The Reinvention of Work* (1994)

Transformative learning potentially takes place in our most valued spaces and moments. Learning emerges from our experience as our environments "speak to us" and we to each other, where we live and work. The following chapters explore diverse sources of learning in communities and work settings where deep relational work of ecological consciousness is encountered.

This section comprises an illustrative range of places that are challenged to learn relationally—a culture as it evolves through time, a community education setting, a vocation, and the workplace. Each distinctively expresses the nature of learning as full engagement, openness, and participation with one's being.

Indigenous educator Gregory Cajete's essay (chapter 6) expresses this most profoundly, out of his experience as a Tewa Indian of the Pueblo People of New Mexico. In what was a keynote presentation at the Fourth International Conference on Transformative Learning, Cajete recounts the Pueblo myth of origins, which is a foundational story of the emergence of life that gives the reader a sense of the interdependence, interconnection, and relationship of a people with their land and history. The Pueblo guiding story gives a sense of a people's worldview and it sets out clear sets of responsibilities that are meant to be practised from generation to generation. Cajete reflects on the import of the origin story for indigenous educators and draws a comparison between indigenous education and modern Western education.

Feminists Dorothy Ettling and Lulesa Guilian (chapter 7) reflect on their evolving practice and learning in their work as community educators and researchers. In a three-year project with women in transition seeking to become agents of change in their own lives, their purpose was to develop a collaborative methodology of adult education that grew organically out of their work with the community women and is based in theories of transformative learning, feminist poststructural pedagogy, and ecological dimensions of learning. Their work reflects the role and value of relationship and community for women in pursuing personal transformation and taking collective action. A salient feature of the project was the profound learning that the authors, being open, gained personally and professionally through a challenge they experienced during the project. The study speaks through the interwoven links between internal and external factors in sustaining change and makes a compelling argument for collaborative learning and cooperative inquiry in university research. The work reflects on the significance of an integrated approach to women's community education, advocating the integration of theory and practice in curriculum and research.

Jessica Kovan and John Dirkx (chapter 8) explore the inner journey of nine individuals into and through sustained work as environmental activists in nonprofit organizations. They show how "quality of life" factors are essential features in the maintenance of sustained commitment to work of nine professional activists. Their essay deepens our understanding of the role and nature of the learning process in sustaining long-term work commitments to their work. Kovan and Dirkx note that sustained commitment comes through a sense of vocation and calling that involves complex, ongoing relations between the outer world and one's inner self. They call the deep order changes that these activists have to sustain, "soul work" arising from a vocational call.

Finally, Patricia Boverie and Michael Kroth (chapter 9) provide with a perspective based on passion in the workplace, stories from 300 working adults across their life span from diverse backgrounds and representing a broad range of careers from medical doctor to office clerk. Respondents were asked about a time they were passionate about their work, what created that passion, how they maintained it, and if they lost it, why and how they got it back. These stories provided rich descriptions of how people find and keep their passion for work. They provided real-life examples of processes and strategies for developing and maintaining passionate work commitments. From these stories the authors draw several key theories in the areas of passion, learning, transformation, and intimate relationships, offering a model and reflections about practices nurturing passion in, what is now for so many, a de-energizing workplace.

CHAPTER 6

A Pueblo Story for Transformation

Gregory A. Cajete

T his chapter provides an overview of perspectives of "transformational education" that have been informed by my experience as an
indigenous educator and as a Tewa Indian from Santa Clara Pueblo,
New Mexico. Growing up within the context of my community in New
Mexico, I have gained important insights that I have applied to my work as
an Indigenous educator. For the past 30 years, I have been working as a
"front-line" educator exploring and implementing strategies to improve or
otherwise transform Native American education. During this time, I have
gained a basic understanding of the "ecology" or set of essential relationships
and principles that guided Indigenous education and which I believe parallel those of transformational and holistic education. My hope is that in reading this chapter exploring Indigenous education you will find some "seeds"
for thought, some perspectives, some understandings, some insights, some
sense of "face," "heart," and "foundation" that will give you the kinds of
insights into your own work that I have found for mine.

What exactly is meant when we say the "indigenous education?" In the Tewa
language we often refer to the process of gaining an education in the same way
as we refer to "breathing in life" or to "be with life." This inherent linguistic connection of the process of education to life itself is no accident since the very
nature of any true educational process is developmental and transformational.
Indeed, much debate in education today revolves around a struggle between
finding ways to maintain, evolve, enhance, and nourish our life through the
learning process verses its commodification and standardization that often leads
repression of the deeper levels of learning. The understanding of education as

a way of "breathing life" as seen and experienced through traditional indigenous education is reflective of what transformational educators know to be the true nature of learning.

I invite you to gaze through an indigenous window and experience the view as seen from the perspective of the Pueblo people of New Mexico. I invite you to look at the world of indigenous education and begin to reflect upon its transformative orientations. These orientations illustrate the "lived experience" of a traditional Indigenous people's interdependence, interconnection, and relationship with their history, their land, and with each other that is so apparently missing in the context of our modern life today. Envision this journey in an "enchanted place"—along the mountain pathways and the streams, the lakes, the valleys, and deserts of New Mexico. As is true with all indigenous people around the world, Pueblo peoples have a guiding story. This guiding story gives Pueblo people a sense of perspective and also describes some very clear sets of responsibilities that are meant to be practiced from generation to generation.

The Pueblo myth of emergence is a guiding story of origins that I believe metaphorically presents a long-term view of the purpose of "education." The emergence myth presents the idea that Pueblo people have been given guiding thoughts on how to live sustainably and respectfully with the land. It is through their participation with the landscape, with the plants, with the animals, with the natural forces of the earth over many generations that Pueblo people have come to understand their role as caretakers. It is important to emphasize here that the Pueblo story of emergence has many variations. Indeed, it continues to be a "sacred story" told among Pueblo people today. It is a very special story, the details of which can only be fully told in certain prescribed and private ceremonial contexts. In this chapter, I will relate *only* the general thoughts of the story, which are shared by most Pueblos of New Mexico. In relating the lessons of this story, I draw primarily from *various published versions* of the story already related by various anthropologists, archaeologists and historians rather than the any personal or community versions. The sacred aspects of the Pueblo origin story should necessarily remain private and the *intellectual property* of the various Pueblos in which this story still guides the life and vision of the community.

The general Pueblo story relates that human beings have always been evolving within a landscape and in a sense we are in a continual journey of becoming human. This idea of becoming fully human and fully alive is central to the ways in which indigenous education is reflected upon, the way in which it is talked about, the way in which it is storied, danced, sung, and otherwise represented in indigenous communities.

The story tells that there were three worlds before this and in each of these worlds men and women were instructed to learn how to live in a proper relationship within those worlds. It relates that there was a set of understandings and a set of ways of being that people had to come to terms with in order to move or evolve to the next level of being human. In every respect this is a story of transformation. First, the story tells of a time when people existed at a very primal level, then evolved, through various stages of physical, mental, and spiritual development, into the current stage or the fourth world. It is told that the ancestors of Pueblo people emerged into this world from an earth navel. When they emerged they were given instructions and were greeted by plants and animals, by the mountains and waters, by the sun and the moon, and also led along a rainbow path, a pathway of understanding that was to characterize their way of being in this world. It is within the context of these primordial physical, mental, and spiritual forces that this guiding story begins.

"In the eye of the beholder" is a metaphor that describes the idea that the way in which we view the world very much determines how we will treat it. The Indigenous eye looking out into the natural world sees a tapestry of interdependence and relationship between humans, plants, animals, and natural forces of the world. As Indigenous peoples traditionally looked out into the world the ecology interactions and interrelationships formed the context within which their cultures were formed and evolved. It is this all-encompassing ecological perspective that continues to characterize both indigenous science and, more generally, Indigenous knowledge today.

The understandings and the perspectives that native people have about the life process of learning are coded within their stories, their designs and traditions of art and dance, within their languages, communities, and expressions of science and technology.

The "Anasazi" is the popular name given to the pre-Columbian ancestors of the modern day Pueblos. Anasazi culture is thought to have begun about A.D. 700 reaching it height around A.D. 1200 as evidenced in the building of ceremonial complexes such as Chaco Canyon and Mesa Verde. There is a design motif on a 1000-year-old Anasazi plate, which I often use to illustrate the relationship Puebloan people continue to feel for their land, particularly its plants, animals, and birds. On this plate you can see a representation of the sense of connectedness, interrelationship, and integration the Anasazi artist felt for the natural world. The black monochrome motif depicts a human effigy figure intimately intertwined with a form representing a Sand Hill crane, a beautiful graceful bird associated with the Rio Grande river marshes. When you look closely at this motif you cannot see where the Sand

Hill crane figure begins and the human effigy ends. The reason is because they are one design. This is a simple yet profound statement of the deep interconnection felt and expressed by the Anasazi artist in this design. It is a visual representation of a whole philosophy of life.

Who were the first Americans and how long have they been here? Suffice it is to say that the ancestral Puebloan peoples have been in the Southwest for at least 10–15,000 years. It seems that it takes that amount of time to come to really understand how to live sustainably in a "place." Through several hundred generations, Puebloan peoples learned to participate fully within their landscape, within their place. This has been Pueblo people's legacy as Indigenous people of this continent. This example is reflective of the continuity and depth of "traditional ecological knowledge," which forms one of the foundations of Indigenous education.

Storytelling and storytellers form another foundation of the Indigenous way of education. One mythic Southwestern storyteller, Kokopele, has become a symbolic modern icon representing the mystic Southwestern Indigenous cultures. Representations of Kokopele as an iconic symbol of the Southwest appear everywhere from paintings hanging in the posh hotels of Santa Fe, Tucson, and Phoenix to the silver, turquoise, and gold jewellery hanging around the necks of sophisticated East and West coast jet setters, to the neon symbol that beacons tourists to come to one of the many Indian Casinos throughout the Southwest. He has become a ubiquitous symbolic figure that has captured the Western imagination. But, for Pueblo people, he is traditionally a very sacred symbol because he represents the procreative powers of nature. He is a quintessential symbol of fertility and creativity. He is a storyteller, a trader who moved from place to place, trading items from one village to another. He played a special kind of flute music. He is really the archetype of the creative spirit within human beings, embodying our roving spirit and the need to move from place to place in search of understanding, to create ourselves as human beings.

In the general story of Pueblo origins it is said that when the "People" emerged into this world they settled in many places. And evidence of the truth and reality of this is to be found in the thousands of Puebloan ruin sites found throughout the Southwest. This kind of origin story is common to many Indigenous tribes in the United States, Canada, Mexico, Central and South America. The memories, and the stories of the places in which a People have lived, are part of the spoken and the lived earth that Indigenous people recognize as being a part of their legacy and a part of their traditions and history.

It is said that the Puebloan ancestors moved along an actual series of pathways to reach the places where they now live. If one really thinks about what is entailed in the Western concept of education and then tries to describe it in a native language, you would be hard-pressed to find anything that would be equivalent to what we would define as education today. Generally, what you would find in native languages would be words for moving along a pathway or a description of the concept of pathway or road. You would find words that would be connoted with "remembering to remember" something that is important to you. You would encounter words that would describe the process of knowing or coming to know, which includes in the Tewa language, "hah-oh" or "to breathe in." And so, these metaphors, which characterize the process that today is called education, have a very different orientation when you look, hear, and reflect on them in terms of Indigenous tribes. Pathways, as a physical and linguistic metaphor, are what have characterized this foundation of Indigenous knowledge through time, through generations, and through the landscape.

It is said that the ancestors of the Pueblo settled by lakes, streams, springs, and the great river (Rio Grande). In these places they came to know the nature of water and water processes, and through that understanding came to understand why water was so important and such an elemental force within the life of human beings and within the life of the earth itself. Pueblo people evolved at various stages during this long journey of development. The early stages were characterized by hunting and gathering and eventually by the cultivation of corn, which was introduced by Kokopele probably from Mexico. And those understandings again are still remembered in the stories that we continue to tell about the times and the places that we have lived.

As Pueblo ancestors evolved into more complex societies, the issue of how to get along with each other became more acute. Ironically, the two quintessential problems that we face today as educators are both about relationship. The first is how are we going to get along with each other, which is the multicultural dilemma of social ecology, social interaction, and social relationship. And the second is how are we going to deal with our relationship with the natural world, which is in such total disarray. This is the physical ecology, how do we deal with our relationship to the earth and to all that is a part of the earth? These two quintessential problems form the context from which the "seed" of transformative education needs to begin to grow. The thinking and education surrounding the kinds of issues generated by these two problems are what have to be transformed in the context of our work as educators along the lines of transformational education.

For example, Pueblo people have had to deal with issues of social ecology for quite some time. There is evidence of Puebloan groups coming together only to split apart once again. Clan groups that attempted to live together and experienced conflict moved away from each other as this was seen as often the most expedient solution for social conflict. The dilemma of conflict in a social group is always a key dynamic of social ecology. Coming together to form larger groups and learning to understand one another is a long and a very complicated process of building sustainable social relationships. The Pueblo story of emergence along with other Pueblo stories have provided insight into ways to deal with these ongoing issues of social ecology. Community and social relationships then are other foundations of indigenous education.

Many Pueblo communities continue to represent the Indigenous way of structuring the world within the context of the community itself. For example, the adobe apartment buildings of Taos Pueblo and the outline that they form against the sky mirrors in a general way the outline of the mountains in the immediate background of the Pueblo. These mountains form the watersheds and sources of plants and animals, which the Pueblo Taos has depended upon for over a thousand years. The mirroring of the structures of one's community to the sources of that community's life is quite natural and characteristic of a lived, practised community of relationships among many Indigenous people. There are many other examples of such mirroring or attempts to "resonate" with the sources of community life among other Pueblos and other Indigenous communities.

Historically, for Pueblo people, two guiding sets of relationships have been their relationship to plants and their relationship to animals. Two types of dances performed by all Pueblos, the corn dance and the buffalo dance, symbolically represent these two worlds. The two worlds of relationship to plants and relationship to animals in Pueblo life and tradition come together in the performance of these dances.

These dances represent the traditions and the interactions and the perspectives that Indigenous Pueblo people have continued to practice. It is in these early relationships, these early interactions with plants and animals that you find the sources from which traditional cultures draw their sense of place, their sense of relationship, their sense of history. So Pueblo people continue to dance those relationships, they continue to honor the animals, which were the foundations of early Puebloan life and sustenance. Pueblos continue to practice the technologies of farming year in and year out as Pueblo men gather in early springtime to clean the ditches that bring water from the rivers and the mountain watersheds to the Pueblo and to the Pueblo fields, to bring them forward with life once again. Through the traditions associated with the cycles of planting and harvesting, Pueblos continue to commemorate all of the expressions of life their communities have been involved in perpetuating, in each of these important cycles of human life.

One of the things that obviously characterize traditional cultures around the world is that they all follow social and ceremonial cycles timed to natural rhythms. These cycles are synchronized with the environments with which they interact. These cyclic relationships are in turn symbolically represented in the traditional forms of art, song, and dance. For example, the concept of the Earth Mother and human relationship as children of the earth is represented in Pueblo stories as Corn Mother and her two perfect ears of corn. The ears of corn represent the first man and the first woman, which goes back to the Pueblo origin story. This concept of the Corn Mother is then transformed into yet another expression through the form of dance and song. Throughout the growing cycle of corn, the whole of various Pueblo communities come together to dance their relationship to corn. They come together "to remember to remember" who they are as clan members, as community members, to celebrate the life that they have been given during that year and to ask for life to be given to the community in subsequent years. These transformations of a thought, in a sense, are that complex of dynamic and ever transforming relationships evoked by the metaphor "in the eye of the beholder." These are the guiding thoughts of a people's origin myth becoming manifest in the things that people actually do and the things that people actually create in order to bring those thoughts to life.

"We are all kernels of the same corncob" is a saying sometime used by Tewa elders. What this really means is that we are all related and that there is a unity in diversity. When one looks at a cob of traditional Pueblo corn you see that at each kernel is different, it is an individual, it is unique, and it has a different hue, a slightly different shape then other kernel. Each kernel leans against its neighbor. Yet, each kernel leaning against one another form the community that is the corncob. This is the biologically embodied idea that we are all related, "we are all kernels of the same corncob." This is a physical illustration of interdependence and the perspective and that everything that we do is related. Parallels to this Indigenous perspective may be found in the biological perspective underlying the theory of "complex adaptive systems" that views all things as continually and dynamically interacting in interrelationship and interdependence with each other from the micro-level to the macro-level.

Extensions of the metaphor "we are all kernels of the same cob" is found in how we share a common humanity and at the same time are unique and different as individuals and as cultures. As cultures, human beings have approached the task of living a life in very different ways yet we are bonded by the underlying unity of being human.

In Indigenous relationships to food, one again sees the reflection of this idea of interdependence. And so, as is true with Indigenous people all over the world, the essential components of traditional Pueblo life and culture can be traced back to an association with food and other primary sources of human life. There is a maxim shared by Indigenous people all over the world that "you must know where your food comes from and you must honour it." Given this maxim, the use of food in every kind of form of Indigenous celebration, community ritual, has been a foundation of remembering to remember those things that give life, and learning how to be with life. Offering food as a symbol of life becomes another metaphor for interdependence and interconnection as a way of understanding our relationships to each other. So knowing where your food comes from is one of those complexes of understanding that transforms the idea of interrelationship into something immediately tangible and which all of humanity shares.

The role of the elder in the context of a traditional community, the role of a man and a woman and their role as teachers, as people who nurture their community and their families is another component of Indigenous education. There is a role played by Indigenous men and women in traditional society, which is significant. So much so that the way the male and the female complement one another is symbolically represented in all Indigenous societies. There is an embodied realization in Indigenous societies that to make a community, to make a family, to make a world, you have to creatively work these two complementary relationships in harmony with one another. In terms of Indigenous education, this idea of complementarity and mutuality is extended to include concentric rings of essential relationships and responsibilities.

There is a Nahutl poem that reflects on what is a "true and rightful education." The poem states that first one must find one's face or one's identity, one's true sense of self. Then one must find one's heart, which is to find that divine spirit, that source of desire within you that motivates you and moves you to do what you do. Then one must find one's foundation, which is that kind of work or vocation that allows you to most completely express your heart and your face. Then one must find one's relationships, first of all, of oneself to oneself, then one's relationship to the family, to the clan, to the tribe, to the place in which you live, your homeland, then the natural world and finally, to the whole cosmos. These concentric rings of relationship, these practiced responsibilities, these sets of understandings, form a context and also work together to help one find one's face, and one's heart, and one's foundation. Ultimately, the goal of a "right and true" education is to become "complete" as a man or as a woman, to become fully alive and a realized human being in a harmonious relationship with one's inner and outer worlds.

The idea of these concentric rings of relationship working through human communities and also through the human life, the idea of journeying, the idea of working and understanding these relationships is the basis of Indigenous education. The process one goes through within these rings of relationship takes time and leads to becoming not only more complete and full but also forms the foundation for becoming a "teacher and an elder" respected for what one teaches and for the knowledge that one holds and carries. In Indigenous cultures, this is the reason elders are venerated. It is not because one is merely old. Everyone gets old, it is a biological fact that we all face. To become an elder is a whole-making process within the context of a traditional society. The meaning of being an "elder" is to be found in the process of having moved through the circles of knowledge, the relationships and the understandings of an Indigenous society. In the faces of many Pueblo elders one sees, in a sense, the faces of all Indigenous elders and the life and the traditions that they hold and carry with them. They reflect in their face and behavior that they have found face, found heart, and found a foundation within the concentric rings of relationship and responsibility to their community.

The beginning of this Indigenous learning circle is children. Indeed, for every human culture, it is the children who ultimately carry a culture forward into the next generation. Developing the ability of its children to carry its knowledge, culture, and values forward is perceived as the real task of Indigenous education. Indeed, this is the task of any form of "rightful and true" education.

It is in the expressions and behavior of the young where one really begins to gauge whether a teaching process has been successful in conveying these messages, these understandings of life, culture, and relationship. Elders and educators, along with community and parents guide the process of creating happy, healthy, whole individuals in Indigenous communities. When Indigenous elders today speak about education they speak little about courses, curricula, grades, and degrees. Rather, they refer to the wholeness of the process of coming to know who you are, where you have been, and where you may go in the future. It is this mixture of perspective, understandings, and action that come together to form the basis of Indigenous education.

In a modern and increasingly global society the ability to not only honor children, but to bring them "forward" through an ecologically and life-oriented form of education is largely absent. It is something that has to be recaptured if we are to have any real future. Indeed, in order to deal with the kind of complexities involved with addressing the two quintessential problems of global relationship, that of getting along with each other and sustaining ourselves in our physical environments, we will require Whole People. We will require people who have the ability to think at many levels and in multiple contexts.

We will need people who have a kind of emotional stability and spiritual strength that was certainly facilitated through Indigenous education.

The questions that we must reflect on are as follows. Where do we go from here? What kinds of insights does Indigenous education offer Western thinking? What does the exploration and the revitalization of Indigenous educational practices have to offer Indigenous people themselves as a possibility for transformational education and learning in a twenty-first century world?

What I have presented reflects some of the underlying meaning of Indigenous education in terms of Pueblo story and tradition. It is clear that there are profound and powerful foundations of education among indigenous peoples. Today, it is these foundations that Indigenous people are seeking to once again apply in contemporary terms. There are a few Indigenous educational traditions that have remained intact in spite of historical trauma and the trials and tribulations that Indigenous people have gone through since Columbus. Many Pueblo communities have been able to hang on to some part of their traditional culture and to convey that at least to this generation. But, Pueblo people, like all Indigenous people around the world, face tremendous challenges in today's world of continuing those traditions, of holding onto the kinds of land bases that allow these traditions to flourish and evolve. Even maintaining their influence on their own children, which becomes a major challenge in today's society, is becoming more difficult in Pueblo families.

Consciously emerging into a New World of being and thinking through education depicts a kind of transformation that I feel is important in terms of Indigenous education and Indigenous society today. This vision guides my work and the work that other Indigenous educators are doing today. My personal vision is predicated on really going back to my own traditions to bring forward those essential life-oriented ideas and principles set forth in the Pueblo Story of Origin and make them operational in a contemporary sense, and to build and use them as a foundation for a vision that we may have for the future. In order to continue our traditions as Pueblo people we have to ensure that our young people have a sense of identity. We have to ensure that they are given possibilities for finding their face, finding their heart, finding their foundation—in relationship to themselves, their families, their tribes, and the world in which they live, toward becoming complete men and women. So the journey continues as we evolve and as we develop the ideas and the concepts of Indigenous education. These are the thoughts and these are the perspectives that Indigenous people hold and must now move forward in their ongoing journey of transforming themselves into complete human beings.

Where do we go from here? To give a symbolic response to this question, I will give an example that originates from the pre-Columbian Southwest. Among the Anasazi, whole complexes of star knowledge were embodied in their architecture. During the summer solstice sunrise on June 21, sitting in Casa Rinconada, the largest kiva in the complex of Anasazi ruins at Chaco Canyon, you will see the first light of the summer solstice day pierce through a particular window cut in the eastern side of the kiva. This first light of the longest day of the year forms a beam of light that strikes the wall opposite the window and illuminates a strategically placed niche. The rising of the sun as you see it while sitting inside Casa Rinconada is the same sun that was viewed over a thousand years ago by the Anasazi. The alignment of rising sun, kiva window, and niche is no accident. This commemoration through alignment to the rising, noonday, and setting sun of summer solstice is repeated in dozens of ways in structural ruins throughout Chaco Canyon during summer solstice. It is the celebration of life and the attempt of the Anasazi to establish a kind of "sympathetic resonance" between themselves on Earth, the Sun, and the whole Comos. Although the Anasazi have long since left Chaco Canyon, the structures that they left behind continue to herald this center of the yearly cycle of the Earth's movement around the Sun. For me, this special event is a symbolic reminder and an affirmation of an Indigenous way of knowing and being in the world. Many Indigenous people are actively engaged in a transformative quest to understand and apply the legacies and the depth of their own traditions and knowledge through all forms of education, formal and informal. It is time that we collectively acknowledge the importance and profound lessons of Indigenous knowledge and guiding stories to our lives today and to the lives and future of our children. Indeed, paying close attention to the lessons of Indigenous stories may determine if we are to have a future at all. This is the transformational quest and challenge as seen through the "eyes of the beholder." So, "be with life," as we Tewa, say. And may the good spirits guide and keep you on your transformative journey.

Note

This chapter is an edited version of a keynote presentation given by the author at the Fourth International Conference on Transformative Learning, Center for Transformational Education, Ontario Institute for Studies in Education of the University of Toronto.

CHAPTER 7

Midwifing Transformative Change

Dorothy Ettling and Lulesa Guilian

Feminist literature has drawn attention to the lack of diverse voices in women's research (Cook and Fonow, 1990; DeVault, 1990; Harding, 1991; Kaschak, 1992; Gorelick, 1996; Gottfried, 1996). This is especially true of the voices of women representing the diversity of color and class (Anzaldua, 1990; Bing and Reid, 1996; Collins, 1990; Reid, 1993; Reid and Kelly, 1994; Zinn et al., 1986). Even less represented in the literature are the implications of research conducted with groups who are marginalized from the dominant center of the inquiry process. In this chapter, we discuss two outcomes of a three-year project with women in transition seeking to become agents of change in their own lives. One of these outcomes was predicted; the other was total gift. The planned for outcome was the evolution of a collaborative methodology of adult education that grew organically out of our work with the community women and is based in theories of transformative learning, feminist post-structural pedagogy, and ecological dimensions of learning. Here we share three of the basic principles of our methodology, which foster what we describe as the development of an ecological consciousness. The second outcome, unforeseen, was the change experienced in the research team, itself. We will describe aspects of our own personal transformation as we sought to midwife change in others.

Achieving agency in one's life is a challenging task for many women. On the one hand it necessitates that we discover and claim our inner power as a person of worth. On the other hand, it demands that we understand the political implications of powerlessness and find ways to challenge the operations of power to which we have been acculturated. It is essential to recognize both of these aspects as crucial to the concept of personal empowerment (hooks, 1993, 1994; Kitzinger, 1991). For such a transformation to occur "radical changes are needed both inside and outside of the woman" (Young and Padilla, 1990, p. 6). This presupposes a relational wholeness between the individual person and her systemic context (O'Sullivan, 1999). Internally, women need to identify their own feelings of oppression and pain, and gain the strength to confront these experiences. Externally, stereotypical roles and societal patterns need to be disclosed and examined. It is our contention that within an action research study, this process of discovery and confrontation is as applicable to the research team as it is to the participants of the inquiry.

Developing an Educational Methodology

There is a history of adult learning opportunities for women offered through grassroots groups in neighborhoods, churches, political activist groups, and volunteer organizations that encouraged women's role in shaping political action and consciousness (Bookman and Morgen, 1988). Today those occasions are less frequent in countries like the United States. The average U.S. citizen in recent decades spends far less time with friends, neighbors, and civic organizations (Putnam, 2000). This reflects a diminution of many traditional, informal learning situations. Yet simultaneously, persons are living longer, staying healthier, and persistently searching for meaning in their lives. At the same time, advances in technology and communication have made it easier for us to inform and be informed of the possibilities for new knowledge, skills, and opportunities for influencing change across boundaries of geography and socioeconomic status. All this provides stimuli for many universities concerned about social justice and ecological sustainability to reach out and provide empowerment educational programs in community settings. Rooted in both the academy and the community, we began our educational program as a collaborative effort among practitioners, women in the community and adult educators. "Collaboration between women on the inside and on the outside of academia, which is democratic and egalitarian . . . imagines that the way things are is not necessarily the way they have to be." It enables us to discover the "energy and conviction that will put persistence, resistance, emancipation and transformation back on to the agenda of women's education" (Thompson, 2000, p. 105).

We initiated our education process in a personal empowerment program with women in community-based settings: structured transitional housing programs. The women were in transition from homelessness to self-sufficiency and were seeking to become agents of change in their own lives. We named our approach Learning to Learn (LTL) and described it as a process of reflection–action–reflection in which the women were taught the skill of critical reflection on experience in an educational intervention. We also documented the course of personal change through systematic data gathering. Our initial findings testified that the participants in the study benefited from the intervention and many grew in self-awareness and self-determination. Since then we have broadened our involvement to include groups of women survivors of domestic violence, social service agency staff, women in transition from incarceration, and neighborhood groups of women who are seeking greater personal and collective empowerment. We have redescribed our process as transformative education and have begun to recognize and report the connection between transformative change in one's personal life and the commitment to work for social change in the broader community. We now identify our educational goal as facilitating personal leadership growth in socially responsive learning communities (Ettling, 2001). While we emphasize the capacity of uncovering assumptions as basic to transformative change, we honor the role that the "marginal, the liminal, the unconscious and the embodied" contexts play in the transformative learning endeavor (O'Sullivan et al., 2002, p. xvii). Most importantly, we now recognize that a key element of transformative learning in any community-based program is relational. The notion of building community, regardless of the setting, is pivotal in our approach. Thus, a foundation of our model is creating a learning community.

Ecology of Women's Consciousness

Our process is fashioned upon several sources. Jack Mezirow's (1991; Mezirow and Associates, 2000) insightful design for transforming meaning perspectives or habits of mind offers a foundation for the heart of transformative learning. Critical reflection is introduced in numerous ways within our educational programs and forms a kind of foundational competency in our work. The changes and additions we have made to Mezirow's original schema arose through the years as we interwove insights from women's development theory (Miller, 1986; Jordan et al., 1991; Gilligan, 1993; Goldberger et al., 1996), feminist pedagogy models (Lather, 1991; Taylor and Marienau, 1995; Hayes and Flannery, 2000), the critiques of his conceptual design (Cranton, 1994; Tennant and Pogson, 1995; Taylor, 1998, 2000; Brookfield, 2000), and the expansion of transformative learning theory to include an ecological consciousness and perspective (O'Sullivan, 1999; O'Sullivan et al., 2002; O'Neill and O'Sullivan, 2002). In presenting our methodology, we attempt to demonstrate how we have benefited from those insights as well as our own experience. We describe transformative learning as a process that can be difficult to track and clearly cannot be captured in systematic steps (Ettling and Thurston, 2001). Personal and collective wisdom emerges from various sources and in its own time in the body–mind–spirit field. External observation might document two steps forward and three steps backward in both a person's insight and her ability to act on that insight. Yet the process of change is occurring. Other studies concur with our perspective (Coffman, 1989; Dewane, 1993; Pope, 1996) that the nature of transformative change is more like an incremental and cumulative journey rather than an immediate awareness. While we honor the cyclical nature of transformative change, we also are committed to educational processes that facilitate that change. Therefore, we offer three aspects of our methodology that we have determined essential in our educational approach: social construction of identity, context of relationship, and accessing multiple ways of knowing.

Social Construction of Identity
The first is the principle that transformation is fostered by understanding oneself and by becoming conscious of and examining the social construction of one's identity. This learning principle can be categorized as post-structural (Tisdell, 2000) as it implies a focus on how the social structures of gender, race, and class inform individual identity and includes an analysis of these structures while fostering personal change. As women uncover assumptions, perceptions can radically shift. It is at this moment that a woman knows she indeed can change her reality and choose to engage in the critical reflection that can alter the meaning of an experience. This is an empowering moment. Elizabeth Tisdell (2000) affirms this. "As learners examine how social systems of privilege and oppression have affected their own identity, including their beliefs and values, their understanding and thus their identity begins to change. They also increase their capacity for agency—the capacity to have more control over their lives" (p. 171). Our educational approach, therefore, starts with a validation of a woman's experiences, ideas, and needs.

This contextualization also applies to our strategies of inquiry. Emphasis is placed on the manner of explanation and meaning given to the experience by each individual. Grounding in personal, individual experience confronts writing from the position of a universal human being, a writing that is disrespectful and irrespective of a woman's life story. Contextualization is often absent in research analysis. "Upholders of the traditions argue that the subjective, in the sense of the personal, anecdotal and the individual, has been thought to detract from the certainty, reliability and usefulness of knowledge" (Griffiths, 1995, p. 56). "The search for dailiness of women's lives is a method of work that allows us to the take the patterns women create and the meanings women invent and learn from them...we begin to lay out a different way of seeing reality" (Apthekar, 1989, p. 53). This subjectivity also then informs our development of theory. Knowledge that emanates from varied settings and populations replete with diversity offers the reader the opportunity to learn from that diversity and be enriched by its complexity.

Context of Relationship
The second premise of our approach is that transformative learning is facilitated within the context of relationship, a learning community. Our project participants identify building bonds of friendship and support as a significant aspect of sustaining the capacity to uncover and alter deeply seated assumptions about oneself and reality. The presence of others who "hear one into speech" (Morton, 1985, p. 55) is experienced as essential to claiming oneself and one's beliefs. Hayes (2000, p. 92) speaks of women "giving voice" as the process of naming previously unarticulated parts of ourselves. Therefore, we place primary importance on building a relationship within the learning group and realize that this emphasis necessitates both time and support.

Women's writings (Anzaldua, 1990; Collins, 1990; hooks, 1994; Goldberger et al., 1996; Hayes and Flannery, 2000) attest to the centrality of relationship in women's lives regardless of race, ethnicity, or socioeconomic status. The literature increasingly reflects that relational context greatly influences the process of women transforming not only cognitively, but also emotionally, spiritually, and physically.

Accessing Multiple Ways of Knowing
An underlying assumption about mutual engagement is that participants are more likely to contribute when invited to show up wholly, in mind, body, and spirit. Whole participation is encouraged when spaciousness for unhurried listening and different ways of knowing are engaged (Ettling and Gozawa, 2000). Thus a third principle of our educational approach is accessing multiple ways of knowing. Different ways of knowing push us beyond rationality and engage us both subjectively and objectively. Such knowing is evoked through imagery, movement, song, poetry, and attention to dreams as well as stories, to both the deep listening and the telling of them. It is often the nonrational, intuitive knowing that intimately connects the knower to that which is known and cultivates an ecological consciousness.

Honoring multiple epistemological sources, in our inquiry, insists on the expanding nature of knowledge and decries a singular paradigm of knowledge construction. Approaches such as symbolic, intuitive, hermeneutic, organic, and cultural inquiry all transport us as inquirers into realms where we must attend to all the facets of the research participant's awareness and reality as well as our own. As researchers, it requires that we write, think, and feel with our entire bodies rather than only with our minds (Minh-ha, 1989).

Stories are a way to access both the context and meaning of experience. By proposing processes that invite storytelling and spaciousness, encouraging whole person participation and striving to act in an interdependent and inclusive ways, we attempt to invite inner conflict and paradox to the conscious level. In this, we imply a vital role not only for intra-subjectivity but also for intersubjectivity in regard to transformative change. Two methodologies, action inquiry and organic inquiry, served us well with this research intention. Action inquiry (Brooks and Watkins, 1994) focuses on experiential learning and systematizes it into theoretical or practical knowledge, privileging action and informal theory and using reflection on action as the basis for knowledge development. Organic inquiry (Clements et al., 1998; Stromstead, 2001) authorizes personal experience and utilizes both the researchers' and participants' narratives. Thus, we were consistently compelled as researchers to reflect upon our own personal stories of change as well as document those of our research participants.

Mutual Midwifery

The second theme of this chapter is a glimpse into the experience of the research team over a period of three years as we facilitated the educational processes, gathered research data, and collaboratively developed the transformative approach described earlier. The team was composed of the initiating researchers and doctoral students from two different Ph.D. programs.

Each graduate student who joined the research project chose to participate as a part of a year-long research practicum expecting to develop her skills as a practitioner both in methods of inquiry and as a facilitator of change. While we accomplished these initial goals, what occurred at a deeper level for everyone was a new self-awareness and an increased capacity for reflexivity, described by Patti Lather (1991) as the ability "to reflect on how our value commitments insert themselves into our empirical work" (p. 80).

The project initiators were two mid-life women, a professor in transformative change studies and a practitioner working with homeless women. Two of the doctoral students were involved in the research for the entire three years. Four students joined the group in years two and three. Two joined in the final year of the project, for a total of ten in the research team. The students in the team ranged in age from early forties to late fifties. Three of the women were African American; one was from the Dominican Republic; one was Chinese American from Hawaii; one a native of Vietnam; one identified as multiracial, African American, Native American, and Asian-Indian; and one was Euro-American. Both the professor and the practitioner were white, one a native of the United States, and one a native of Ireland. As documented later, this rich diversity of heritage proved to be a significant factor in our learning process.

Throughout the project we worked in teams to conduct the educational process, collect and analyze the data. As social researchers, we believed it important to examine and understand our relationship with and impact on the participants in the study. To this end, we met twice a month for half a day as a total group with the intention of processing our work together. These meetings were a crucial part of our commitment to collaboration.

Our discussions surfaced concerns about the meaning of collaboration as members of the group questioned roles and responsibilities. Recurring deliberations emerged about the degree of investment, meaning of delegation, and clarification of roles. But our most significant revelations came as a result of the diversity of our research group that provided us with unique opportunities to examine our own prejudices and scotomas regarding race and class.

Researching Research Team Experience

Midway through year two, the team formally identified and addressed the significant issues that we encountered while crossing boundaries of race and class among ourselves and with the participants. At that time, five issues were named as challenges and dilemmas to be faced.

Confronting Our Own Boundaries and Prejudices

Early in the research team development, we had to address feelings of dominance and prejudice in working with women who were currently living in poverty. We stated these issues in different ways: as the concern of "not understanding the women," as "reluctance to go to the sites of our sessions," or as fear of being perceived as a person of privilege in being able to choose graduate studies or this work. Sometimes, the fear of identification triggered our own personal issues regarding class. Group reflection gave the opportunity to dig more deeply into assumptions and beliefs, to relook and make choices about our attitudes and behaviors. We unearthed buried fears and prejudices about neighborhoods, violence, and the pain associated with memories. Personal experiences of poverty or near-poverty in childhood gave rise to issues of shame and insecurity. The need to "take care of" or "protect" instinctively arose for some members of the group. We were constantly confronted with our own frustration and powerlessness in hearing the stories of disrespect or dismissal that are so common in the lives of the disenfranchised. Team members vacillated between prioritizing personal empowerment or systemic change. All of this forced us to confront our perceptions and our use of personal and institutional power.

Understanding and Dealing with White Privilege

One description of guilt is the internalization of the oppressiveness of the dominating system. In our team reflections, we often struggled with how to deal with our internalization. We began to see how issues of race and class shape all of our lives. We understood white privilege as a location of structural advantage (Frankenberg, 1993; Hurtado, 1996; Fine et al., 1997).

A deeper comprehension of race/class privilege came from the frustration and outrage that team members experienced when having to deal with the arbitrariness of so much of our national social policy. Self-discovery of our intolerance for injustice and the dysfunctional systems designed to be of service to people broke open a new awareness of unrecognized privilege afforded by our middle-class status. Greene (1994) has noted that an unwillingness to notice this "locus of privilege" prevents us from understanding how this position seeps into every aspect of our life as researchers and collaborators with one another. One of our team members was confronted with this reality during our project. Through unexpected financial circumstances, she was forced to use public medical aid. Her experiences of dismissal, disregard, and powerlessness to effect a response from the doctors with simple, legitimate claims were revealing and disturbing. As a woman of color who has worked extensively with diversity issues, she became more aware of her identification with class privilege within the research context. Mies (1983, p. 123) calls this identification "conscious partiality" in contrast to "spectator knowledge" that emphasizes neutrality and indifference toward the participants' lives.

Researching Another's Life While Inviting Her to Collaborate in the Process

A constant preoccupation in feminist action research is to unite the false separation between the research participant and the researcher (Gergen, 1988; Naples and Clark, 1996). Although our intention was clearly to challenge the norm of objectivity and distance within the research context (Cook and Fonow, 1991; Acker et al., 1996), we still wrestled with the dilemmas of how to strengthen collaboration with the participants. In trying to build bridges of relationship, we could not dismiss the effects of social location or unequal opportunities. Participation in our study was voluntary and we constantly attempted to create the means for mutuality. But as researchers, we came with a planned agenda no matter how meaningful we may have perceived it to be. Our team reflections unearthed the predicament: "I have no right to come and talk to them." "This is not mutual." "They know more than I, they are stronger than I." Moving beyond these first blocks to recognize a need for control, and the importance of feeling and being perceived as both competent and compassionate opened the way to learn flexibility and reciprocity in the research context. Lather states that reciprocity "implies give and take, a mutual negotiation of meaning and power" (1991, p. 57). We found this refers not only to the research design, but the way we think about ourselves in the research relationship.

Analyzing Women's Stories and Capturing the Intended Meanings

Our research methodology focused on women's perceptions of their own change. This allowed us to hear the particular meanings that they gave to their experiences. We attempted to stay true to the words and the situations our participants shared with us by quoting with context and checking back with them when possible for verification. Yet it was always a challenge not to leap to interpretations suggested by prevailing theories. The concern of the team members was: "our lenses are so strong, can we really understand the other?" (Anderson et al., 1990).

We conducted our study within settings familiar to the participants, generally meeting in areas provided by the transitional housing program. Thus, we often had to deal with the everyday realities of childcare, noise, interruptions, and agency organizational issues. This kept our feet close to the scene of our project, yet sometimes prompted concerns from the team about whether we were gathering "reliable data." It forced us to place the women and their survival at the center of our analysis and to emphasize the dialectic between researcher and researched throughout the process. As the team's consciousness grew, so did the desire to maintain fidelity to the women's voices. It is noteworthy that we found relatively little in the literature to guide our analysis in a way that remained true to this intention.

Ethics of Inquiry

As we began to present our findings in the public arena through articles, presentations, and advocacy efforts, we were cautious about appearing to be speaking on behalf of a marginalized group, while reproducing dominant discourses in an unthinking way (Poland, 1990; Ribbens and Edwards, 1998). Committed to keeping the participants' voices alive, we searched with them for creative ways to represent their stories through narratives, poetry, and video productions. For us, the researchers, ethics of inquiry took on new meaning and resonance, and became the challenge of presenting our findings while seeking ways for the women to speak for themselves.

Eighteen Months Later

At the end of the third year, we revisited our experience as the research team. Interestingly enough, rather than reporting our experience in the framework of dilemmas, we now named them group learnings. Although some of the same issues were being discussed, the group's understanding and ability to work with the issues had dramatically changed. In this second inquiry, we grouped the findings into five areas.

Understanding Collaboration

We repeatedly addressed issues of ownership, responsibility, and authority. We came to a clear distinction between what we called "efficiency with tasks" and collaboration. Collaboration did not always look most efficient in the short run. Yet we experienced it as a far more effective and meaningful way to work together. It became obvious that we were reaping significant rewards both for the project and for ourselves by maintaining and growing in our collaborative practice.

As the intensity of work and responsibility grew in the study, some difficulty and contention arose within the team regarding differences in investment in the project. With discussion, we realized that this was quite natural. Student members had participated in the study for differing amounts of time. Those who joined the team in this final year had little history, no involvement in the original data gathering, and a limited sense of continuity in the study. This prompted an important learning about collaboration; there is a normalcy and validity in a differing sense of commitment within the collaborative group. We began to value even more the varied perspectives that differences in commitment could offer. This realization also offered a learning opportunity for the primary initiators. The yearly change in the composition of the research team necessitated adequate and meaningful orientation for the new members and demanded much flexibility and openness in the work together. Differing degrees of investment had to be accommodated within a meaningful experience of collaboration.

Insights About a Learning Community

We saw that we had incorporated a very sophisticated form of reflection into our work together. It grew naturally but clearly with intention. Time to listen and dialogue in our bi-weekly gatherings developed trust and relationship. The climate had been set for a space to "grow in" personally and as a group. The willingness to look at oneself, uncover assumptions, and alter beliefs was nurtured through our interactions and discussions. Group reflection as an essential element in collaboration was evident to the entire group. Strengthening this capacity was imperative to our development as a team.

Awareness of Race and Class

The cultural diversity of both our participant groups and the research team offered rich ground to seed new understandings of the impositions of race and class. As a research team, we believed that we must maintain a constant awareness of our own biases, rubrics, and ways of interacting, in order to understand, accept, and negotiate with the culture of the participants. The study highlighted the need for cultural sensitivity regarding applying research methodologies and strategies in diverse groups.

We recognized that educational and psychological theory is primarily based on European acculturation. Applying these Euro-American frameworks does a disservice to participants if our methods only serve to affirm whiteness. While all members of the research team generally agreed that the LTL process is a valuable tool to elicit self-reflection, we recognized the importance of cultural sensitivity in its application and context. We acknowledged the potential damage we can do if our well-intentioned process does not reflect an awareness of the culture of the participants. This realization evoked feelings of internalized oppression in some of the white team members, as they became increasingly aware of the effects of imposing white norms. One member expressed this by saying, "Sometimes I just hate being white. I feel so ashamed." We tried to honor this feeling and recognize that it could enable a white person to understand better the internalized shame of many people of color when forced to fit white paradigms. An increased awareness of oppression gave rise to new understandings about voice. How can we facilitate the participants to speak in their own voice and have that voice heard in its fullness? One team member of the team revealed her own dilemma around finding voice, "When I try to change my voice to be heard, it doesn't work either."

The research team recognized that they had come to a deeper understanding of what it means to participate in a multicultural group that attempts to equally honor the culture of each member in the group. Each one realized that this commitment is a life-long task. We gained an important insight about seeing our work as part of a larger mission in life. Realizing this vision gave both the white members and members of color the strength and desire to engage in self-exploration of how "white" norms function and impact ourselves and others. The collective mission of the group added strength to engage in the inevitable intrapersonal and interpersonal conflict that accompanies such exploration.

Applications of Insights to Work and Personal Life

Our project affected not only the team's interactions within the context of the research project, but also had a profound effect on other aspects of our lives. Multiple perspectives on particular situations enhanced our understanding of power, racial, and cultural barriers in our day-to-day lives and gave us an ability to identify and openly discuss issues of dominance. During our meetings, a member would often relate a story of dealing with one of these issues in family, school, or the workplace and found strength and support in the telling.

Integrating and Applying Multicultural Consciousness

In our initial reflection, cultural awareness was considered a barrier or a dilemma. By the second review it was experienced as liberating to hold this expanded multicultural awareness. One of the most important lessons we learned was the significance of listening from the speaker's cultural context. An anecdote illustrates the import of this capacity. In a group of Asian participants, one woman came to a second LTL session and stated that she would not be able to attend any more of the meetings because she had to prepare dinner for her family. The researchers, one white and one Asian, immediately started to problem-solve for the woman, asking her if she could have someone else prepare the meal or order pizza on those days. She continued to say it was very important for her to prepare the meals and that she would not be able to attend. Upon reflection in our research meeting, our Asian team member noted that the participant was probably upset about disclosing too much information at the previous meeting. She did not want to continue, but stating that she was uncomfortable about the previous week's process would not have been acceptable because it would have implied that she was not respecting the researcher's work. Even the Asian researcher stated that she has been so acculturated that only after some reflection did this become apparent to her.

We also acknowledged that listening from the perceived cultural context of another can be dangerous. There is the potential trap of stereotyping participants based upon our own assumptions about their cultural context.

More than anything, we recognized the value of being authentic with one another. Authenticity about our motives for entering the research, our interests, and our comfort in working with women in poverty was the key to our ability to work creatively and collaboratively.

We began this journey with academic and service aspirations. We sought to learn the art of collaboration while engaging in a research project that held value and meaning for each of us. We hoped to provide a context and an experience for the participants that would be beneficial. We did not dream that we would transform our lives in the process.

Conclusion and Beyond

Our project brings to light the role and value of relationship and community for women in pursuing personal transformation and taking collective action. It attests to the interwoven links between internal and external factors in sustaining change. It also strengthens the argument for collaborative learning and cooperative inquiry in university settings. Finally it stresses the significance of an integrated approach to women's community education, advocating the marriage of theory and practice in curriculum and research.

Finally, we recognize the LTL methodology, as critical self-reflection, is one means of uncovering beliefs and assumptions. It is one way of developing an ecological consciousness. We imagine there are other ways of accomplishing this important aspect of transformative change. What we have discovered, however, is that LTL serves to strengthen the core aspect of our educational goal, that of building a socially responsive learning community. As the women expand their consciousness to see their own beliefs and assumptions with new eyes, they increase their awareness of the assumptions and beliefs that dominate our society. Feminist literature has long put forth the axiom that the person is political and that women will consistently look to the needs of the community as well as to their own (Collins, 1990; hooks, 1993; Gottfried, 1996; Naples, 1998; Gittell et al., 1999). In the end, this is our educational aim: to help create communities of learners that aspire to work for personal and social transformation in our world.

References

Anzaldua, G. (1990). *Hacienda caras: Making face, Making Soul.* San Francisco: Aunt Lute Press.

Acker, J., Barry, K., and Esseveld, J. (1996). "Objectivity and Truth: Problems in Doing Feminist research." In H. Gottfried (Ed.), *Feminism and Social Change* (pp. 60–87). Chicago: University of Illinois Press.

Anderson, K., Armitage, S., Jack, D., and Wittner, J. (1990). "Beginning Where We Are." In J. M. Nielsen (Ed.), *Feminist Research Methods* (pp. 94–112). Boulder: Westview Press.

Anzaldua, G. (1990). *Hacienda caras: Making Face, Making Soul.* San Francisco: Aunt Lute Press.

Aptheker, B. (1989). *Tapestries of Life: Women's Work, Women's Consciousness and the Meaning of Daily Experience.* Amherst, MA: University of Massachusetts Press.

Bing, V. and Reid, P. T. (1996). "Unknown Women and Unknown Research: Consequences of Color and Class in Feminist Psychology." In N. Goldberger, J. Tarule, B. Clinchy, and M. Belenky (Eds.), *Knowledge, Difference and Power* (pp. 175–202). New York: Harper Collins.

Bookman, A. and Morgen, S. (Eds.) (1988). *Women and the Politics of Empowerment.* Philadelphia: Temple University Press.

Brookfield, S. (2000). "Transformative Learning as Ideological Critique." In J. Mezirow and Associates, *Learning as Transformation* (pp. 125–148). San Francisco: Jossey-Bass.

Brooks, A. and Watkins, K. (1994). *The Emerging Power of Action Inquiry Technologies.* San Francisco: Jossey-Bass.

Clements, J., Ettling, D., Jenett, D., and Shields, L. (1998). "Organic Research: Feminine Spirituality Meets Transpersonal Research." In W. Braud and R. Anderson (Eds.), *Transpersonal Research Methods for the Social Sciences: Honoring Human Experience* (pp. 114–127). Thousand Oaks, CA: Sage.

Coffman. P. M. (1989). *Inclusive Language as a Means of Resisting Hegemony in Theological Education: a Phenomenology of Transformation and Empowerment of Persons in Adult Higher Education.* Unpublished doctoral dissertation, Northern Illinois University.

Collins, P. H. (1990). *Black Feminist Thought.* New York: Routledge.

Cook, J. and Fonow, M. M. (1990). "Knowledge and Women's Interests: Issues of Epistemology and Methodology in Feminist Sociological Research." In J. M. Nielsen (Ed.), *Feminist Research Methods* (pp. 69–73). Boulder: Westview Press.

Cook, J. and Fonow, M. M. (Eds.) (1991). *Beyond Methodology: Feminist Scholarship as Lived Research.* Indianapolis: Indiana University Press.

Cranton, P. (1994). *Understanding and Promoting Transformative Learning: A Guide for Educators of Adults.* San Francisco: Jossey-Bass.

DeVault, M. (1990). "Talking and Listening from Women's Standpoint: Feminist Strategies for Interviewing and Analysis." *Social Problems* 37 (1), 96–116.

Dewane, C. M. (1993). *Self-Help Groups and Adult Learning.* Unpublished doctoral dissertation, Pennsylvania State University.

Ettling, D. (2001). The Praxis of Sustaining Transformative Change. Unpublished manuscript.

Ettling, D. and Gozawa, J. (2000). "Morphogenic Fields: A Call for Radical Thinking and Being." In K. Klenke (Ed.), *2000 Aom/IAom Proceedings Project 2005 18: 4* (pp. 61–71). Chesapeake: Maximilian Press.

Ettling, D. and Thurston, M. (January 2001). *Voices from the Margins.* Paper presented at the 14th Annual Conference on Interdisciplinary Qualitative Studies, Athens, Georgia.

Fine, M., Weis, L., Powell, L., and Wong, L. Mun. (1997). *Off White.* New York: Routledge.

Frankenberg, R. (1993). *The Social Construction of Whiteness.* Minneapolis: University of Minnesota Press.

Gergen, M. M. (Ed.) (1988). *Feminist Thought and the Structure of Knowledge.* New York: University Press.

Gilligan, C. (1993). *In a Different Voice.* 2nd ed. Cambridge: Harvard University Press.

Gittell, M., Ortega-Bustamante, I., and Steffy, T. (1999). *Women Creating Social Capital and Social Change.* New York: Howard Samuels State Management and Policy Center, The University Center, The City University of New York.

Goldberger, N., Tarule, J., Clinchy, B., and Belenky, M. (1996). *Knowledge, Difference and Power.* New York: Harper Collins.

Gorelick, S. (1996). "Contradictions of Feminist Methodology." In H. Gottfried (Ed.), *Feminism and Social Change* (pp. 23–45). Chicago: University of Illinois Press.

Gottfried, H. (Ed.) (1996). *Feminism and Social Change.* Chicago: University of Illinois Press.

Greene, B. (1994). "Diversity and Difference: Race and Feminist Psychotherapy." In M. P. Mirkin (Ed.), *Women in Context: Toward a Feminist Reconstruction of Psychotherapy* (pp. 333–351). New York: Guilford Press.

Griffiths, M. (1995). *Feminisms and the Self: The Web of Identity.* London: Routledge.

Harding, S. (1991). *Whose Science? Whose Knowledge?* Ithaca: Cornell University Press.

Hayes, E. (2000). "Social Contexts." In E. Hayes and D. Flannery (Eds.), *Women as Learners: The Significance of Gender in Learning* (pp. 23–52). San Francisco: Jossey-Bass.

Hayes, E. and Flannery, D. (2000). *Women as Learners: The Significance of Gender in Learning.* San Francisco: Jossey-Bass.

hooks, b. (1993). *Sisters of the Yam.* New York: Routledge.

hooks, b. (1994). *Teaching to Transgress: Education as the Practice of Freedom.* New York: Routledge.

Hurtado, A. (1996). *The Color of Privilege.* Ann Arbor: University of Michigan Press.

Jordan, J., Kaplan, A., Miller, J., Stiver, I., and Surrey, J. (1991). *Women's Growth in Connection.* New York: Guilford Press.

Kaschak, E. (1992). *Engendered Lives.* New York: Harper Collins.

Kitzinger, C. (1991). *Feminism and Psychology.* London: Sage.

Lather, P. (1991). *Getting Smart.* New York: Routledge.

Mezirow, J. (1991). *Transformative Dimensions of Adult Learning.* San Francisco: Jossey-Bass.

Mezirow, J. and Associates. (2000). *Learning as Transformation.* San Francisco: Jossey-Bass.

Mies, M. (1983). "Towards a Methodology for Feminist Research." In G. Bowles and R. Klien (Eds.), *Theories of Women's Studies* (pp. 60–84). Boston: Routledge.

Miller, J. B. (1986). *Toward a New Psychology of Women.* 2nd ed. Boston: Beacon Press.

Minh-ha, T. (1989). *Woman, Native, Other.* Indianopolis: Indiana University Press.

Morton, N. (1985). *The Journey is Home.* Boston: Beacon Press.

Naples, N. (1998). *Grassroots Warriors.* New York: Routledge.

Napels, N. and Clark, E. (1996). "Feminist Participatory Research and Empowerment: Going Public as Survivors of Childhood Sexual Abuse." In H. Gottfried (Ed.), *Feminism and Social Change* (pp. 160–186). Chicago: University of Illinois Press.

O'Neill, E. and O'Sullivan, E. (2002). "Transforming the Ecology of Violence: Ecology, War, Patriarchy, and the Institutionalization of Violence." In E. O'Sullivan, A. Morrell, and M. A. O'Connor (Eds.), *Expanding the Boundaries of Transformative Learning* (pp. 173–184). New York: Palgrave.

O'Sulllivan, E. (1999). *Transformative Learning: Educational Vision for the 21st Century.* London: Zed Books.

O'Sullivan E., Morrell, A., and O'Connor, M. A. (Eds.) (2002). *Expanding the Boundaries of Transformative Learning.* New York: Palgrave.

Poland, F. (1990). "Breaking the Rules: Assessing the Assessment of a Girls' Project." In L. Stanley (Ed.), *Feminist Praxis* (pp. 80–88). New York: Routledge.

Pope, S. (1996). *Wanting to be Something More: Transformation in Ethnically Diverse Working-Class Women Through the Process of Education.* Unpublished doctoral dissertation, Los Angeles: Fielding Institute.

Putnam, R. (2000). *Bowling Alone.* New York: Simon and Schuster.

Reid, P. T. (1993). "Poor Women in Psychological Research." *Psychology of Women Quarterly* 17, 133–150.

Reid, P. T. and Kelly, P. (1994). "Research on Women of Color: From Ignorance to Awareness." *Psychology of Women Quarterly* 18, 377–486.

Ribbens, J. and Edwards, R. (Eds.) (1998). *Feminist Dilemmas in Qualitative Research.* London: Sage.

Stromstead, T. (2001). "Re-inhabiting the Female Body: Authentic Movement as a Gateway to Transformation." *The Arts in Psychotherapy* 28, 39–55.

Taylor, E. (1998). *The Theory and Practice of Transformative Learning: A Critical Review.* Information Series, 374 Ohio State University Columbus, Ohio: ERIC Clearinghouse on Adult Career and Vocational Education.

Taylor, E. (2000). "Analyzing Research on Transformative Learning Theory." In J. Mezirow and Associates, *Learning as Transformation* (pp. 285–328). San Francisco: Jossey-Bass.

Taylor, K. and Marienau, C. (1995). *Learning Environments for Women's Adult Development: Bridges Toward Change.* San Francisco: Jossey-Bass.

Tennant, M. and Pogson, P. (1995). *Learning and Change in Adult Years.* San Francisco: Jossey-Bass.

Thompson, J. (2000). *Women, Class and Education.* London: Routledge.

Tisdell, E. J. (2000). "Feminist Pedagogies." In E. Hayes and D. Flannery (Eds.), *Women as Learners: The Significance of Gender in Adult Learning* (pp. 155–183). San Francisco: Jossey-Bass.

Young, E. and Padilla, M. (1990). "Mujeres unidas en acion: A Popular Education Process." *Harvard Educational Review* 60 (1), 1–18.

Zinn, M., Baca, J., Cannon, L. W., Higginbotham, E., and Dill, B. (1986). "The Cost of Exclusionary Practices in Women's Studies." *Signs: Journal of Women and Culture in Society* 11, 290–303.

CHAPTER 8

Nurturing the Internal Flame: Sustained Commitment to Environmental Work

Jessica T. Kovan and John M. Dirkx

Whoever you are, no matter how lonely,
the world offers itself to your imagination,
calls to you like the wild geese, harsh and exciting—
over and over announcing your place
in the family of things.

Mary Oliver (1992)

In this chapter, we explore the inner journeys of nine individuals who for many years have been very much a part of the outer world, working as environmental activists. Our purpose here is to better understand how long-term environmental activists sustain commitment to their work. To help set the stage for this discussion, we open with a brief sketch of one of these individuals.

Since she was a little kid, Helen always wanted to help the world in some capacity. Upon graduating from college with a general liberal arts degree, Helen took a long anticipated fly-fishing trip that crystalized her future direction. Arriving at the river's edge, she was confronted with a sign declaring, "Do not eat the fish out of this river." Clouds of silt swelled around her feet with each step she took in the water. As she approached a bend in the river, she encountered a large clear cut bordering the banks of the river. Suddenly she realized that for all of its power and beauty and wonder, the river did not have a voice in society. Having spent her college years working for many different social causes, Helen decided she wanted to lend her talents and skills to help give the river, and all water, a voice.

Twenty years have passed since that fishing trip. Helen is currently the executive director of a small environmental organization. She considers herself a seasoned environmental activist and is viewed by her peers as one of the leading environmentalists in her state. Ironically, she has never thought of her work as a career. When she grew up children wanted to be doctors or lawyers, she says, not environmentalists. In following her passions, Helen has found herself in a career she loves. She is actually surprised by her own commitment and conviction to her work. She feels lucky that she has found her work and her work has found her. At the same time, however, she notes the work is not easy. It is profoundly difficult for Helen to say "no" when she is asked to work on an issue. When she gets a call from someone who says "help me," it is automatic to say "yes." Getting into an issue and really wrestling with it is something Helen finds compelling. She almost cannot *not* do it. Yet, because she personally and professionally cares so deeply about the issues, the inevitable compromises and defeats feel horrendous.

Helen's love for her work is unmistakable. In quiet moments, however, she speaks of times of severe burnout, of feeling overwhelmed by the immensity of the tasks, and the graveness of the issues surrounding her. She offers words of wisdom for others working in similar positions: it is important to remember to have fun, and to keep the faith that you are right in your actions when the world around you is trying to tell you that you are wrong. She also suggests embracing a sense of spirit, directing specific attention to the connections between people and the earth. She has found that to sustain her passion she has to balance her love for the world and her outrage at the injustices. She feels strongly love is what must drive her work and love is what drives the work in the people that she most admires. She has always wanted to work toward making the world a better place. This is her life commitment.

Helen's story provides an important glimpse into the world of the environmentalists, about their entrance into environmental activism, and their continued commitment to the work. Many environmental professionals and others who work for nonprofit organizations feel increasingly discouraged, disillusioned, and ineffective (Snow, 1992; Berry and Gordon, 1993; Thomashow, 1995; ICL, 1996). The average tenure of executive directors of nonprofit organizations is approximately six years, with burnout being one of the highest-ranking reasons for choosing to leave one's job (Wolfred et al., 1999; Singleton and Cunningham, 2000; Peters and Wolfred, 2001). High turnover rates directly impact organizational effectiveness. Seen in the larger context of social change, many of the leading ideas, advocacy, policies, and programs to protect environmental quality emerge from the nonprofit sector (Snow, 1992; Doyle, 1999). Being financially independent with a direct adherence to a cause and constituents, nonprofit organizations play a unique and crucial role in the environmental movement. Yet, as recent studies indicate, the frantic pace of life and the stress of nonprofit work are taking a heavy toll on those working in this sector.

To retain executives, nonprofit organizations should be proactive in finding opportunities for professional growth (Wolfred et al., 1999). They need to be "strong, refreshed, spiritually active, and overwhelmingly positive in their outlook" in order to achieve their greatest levels of effectiveness (Snow, 1992, p. 190). Yet, we understand very little about the nature of the learning process involved in sustaining one's commitment for environmental work. Information about the nonprofit sector emerges as fragmented and poorly defined (Weisbrod, 1988; Wilson, 1994) and little empirical investigation has been conducted of paid staff in these organizations (Herman and Heimovics, 1989; Wilensky, 1995), hence ways to help support and strengthen individuals choosing nonprofit careers remains vague.

Learning from Committed Activists

Helen was a participant in a study in which long-term environmental leaders working in small nonprofit organizations shared with us their experiences of environmental activism. The purpose of our study was to better understand the role and nature of the learning process in sustaining commitment to nonprofit work, with specific emphasis placed on environmental professionals in small nonprofit organizations. We wanted to know about what these stories represent, how passion is sustained, what can be learned from their journeys about maintaining and sustaining commitment to one's work, and how these stories can inform our work as adult educators.

We interviewed six women and three men ranging in ages from 34 to 54. Each person was nominated by their peers as having sustained long-term commitment and passion to their work. Each person also had to have worked for at least ten years in nonprofit organizations with a staff size of ten or less full-time employees. Of the nominated participants, all were white, representing a lack of diversity in the environmental field in general; six were married or in long-term partnerships, two were divorced, one never married; six had children, of which five still had children at home at the time of our interviews. They were a well-educated group with all of the participants possessing a minimum of an undergraduate degree and eight out of nine holding advanced degrees. Two were trained to be lawyers, the other graduate degrees were all in natural resources fields.

We were drawn to this study from our own personal backgrounds. Jessica worked for several years in philanthropy as a grantor for community-based environmental projects, as well as serving as an executive director of a small nonprofit environmental organization, and continues to work on local environmental issues. John has spent his career in the professional development of educators who work with adult learners, seeking to better understand what their work means to them and how they frame and make sense of it. We both brought to the study a strong desire to be able to observe, discuss, and understand more fully the interrelationships between environmental activism, education, and sustaining commitment within the context of people working for the common good.

To probe deeply into their experiences as long-term environmental professionals, we conducted two in-depth interviews with each participant and a full-day group interview with seven of the nine. The stories of these nine activists reflect a profound form of learning, involving recognition and understanding of one's work as calling or vocation, and exemplifying the kind of transformation reflected in Carl Jung's notion of individuation (Whitmont, 1969). These aspects of individuation, however, are not reflected in discrete, epiphanic episodes. Rather, they are experienced within the fabric and weave of their everyday experiences as activists, exemplifying the continuous and ongoing tensions and struggles that characterize the process of individuation. The following is an in-depth account of the activists' stories that lead us to this conclusion.

Doing What You Love

Helen express a deep interconnection between the meaningfulness of her life and the world she has chosen, a theme reflected in all of the participants' stories. They consistently blend personal and professional identities within their work, a merger that is both welcomed and desired. They revealed a deep love and caring for humanity as a core value, with a strong sense of work filling a need to be directly connected to the world. Abigail, for example, whose educational background is in political sciences accepted her job with an environmental advocacy group over twenty years ago. She reasons, "I needed to do something like this in order to feel fulfilled personally. For me, that is probably the main reason that I am in this for the long haul." Sasha, the youngest of the participants, states, "I'm about this whole slew of things...and my interest and passion has become manifested in environmental work." Megan offers, "I am not career motivated. It's not as a career, you know. I am an environmental protection person." This blurring of the lines between personal and professional is also reflected in Peter's statement about choosing environmental work. He notes, "It's not about, you know, it's not a calculation, it's a bit of home."

The activists view their work as critical to their sense of leading meaningful and authentic lives. Their work is directly linked to their passions, to the very being of their sense of identity or self. This intimate connection helps provide a grounding to sustain their commitment. Dara, now in her twenty-second year as an environmental advocate, observes, "In that soul searching that I've done, this has felt really right and good for me.... It hasn't felt like, oh, there are other rungs of the ladder that I want to continue to climb." As the activists told their stories it became evident that many were surprised to find themselves years later still in environmental work. Choosing a path that does not meet societal expectations requires a strong understanding of what drives them in order to push forward. Helen laments, "There isn't much respect for it. I think that remains a crisis. You know, what is the public recognition for this kind of [work]?" She suggests the underlying motivations for an environmental career are not money, power, or prestige. Instead, she reflects, "Where can one have the most impact? In this job, I think I can have a big impact. It's just that no one knows or understands."

The activists' work springs fundamentally from the heart. In their work, they experience a strong connection to the physical world. Through this connection, they receive comfort and are motivated by their work. Peter notes, "I just believe that we have a duty to the earth and that there is a right and a wrong in relation to the earth." He describes this reaction as one's heart opening to the issues. At times, this upsurging of the heart in their work seems to catch the activists by surprise. Abigail exhorts, "When I get passionate... it surprises me because it's coming from a different place than the intellect. I mean when people are talking about heart or soul or whatever, it's like your whole being is saying-yeah, this matters!... It's much more gut level than actually intellectual." They describe these powerful, almost autonomous forces in their lives as passion. Steven, whose career started as an advocate for union workers, remarks, "What passion that I do have about my work comes from those fundamental values that sort of bring to it my understanding and desire to be on this path." Peter defines passion as:

> The ability to invest emotionally in what you're doing. It's not just an abstract duty or obligation, but a feeling that this is good and you really believe in it from the heart. Passion is, you know, the fuel, whether it's from anger or love that makes the work possible.

In the group interview, the activists collectively defined passion as "being engaged with more than your mind—being engaged with your body, your heart and your spirit . . . sort of having a fire." In trying to make sense of this powerful force in their lives, Ben hints at its autonomous nature, "I don't sustain [passion]," he states flatly, "It's like the internal flame."

Being Open to Learning

Woven tightly together with the power of passion in the lives of the environmentalists, a humility and openness to that which remains unknown could be carefully observed. While portraying a strong depth of knowledge about their own needs, core values, and strong connections to the world, the participants also reflected an openness to continually learn about themselves and their work. This form of learning is important in their overall commitment to environmental work and demonstrates a deep desire to engage head, heart, and spirit. Rather than something they consciously direct, however, these activists describe a process that seems to unfold within their lives of its own accord. Dara observes, "It's kind of a fundamental wiring inside me that just says this is the right way to go about stuff." Emily, one of the most veteran environmentalists of the study, comments, "I think there is the notion of being open to learning . . . knowing that you are just always in that and you are never done. It's a process. You're learning all the time. It's not like you're not learning. So it's about being aware and forcing myself to consciously be open to the learning." Learning is not so much about mastering new knowledge and skills as it is about struggling to stay open to and be aware of this movement in their lives. Ben advises,

> [Learning] can be a messy process. I mean learning is not concrete, sequential. Those lessons and flashes of insight come where you least expect it and when you least expect it. . . . To be comfortable knowing that you don't know but being open to that and trusting yourself, that's okay. That's really powerful.

The activists clearly express a willingness to acknowledge not knowing answers. Learning to listen to what is sometimes not readily evident—to what might be below the surface or beyond conscious awareness—arises from and characterizes their deep commitment and passion to their work. As part of the second interview, we asked the participants to draw the cover illustration for a handbook focused on working in small environmental organizations. The drawings and subsequent discussions brought out powerful additional insights. Sasha's picture specifically focused on learning.

She drew a ven diagram with five brightly colored circles abstractly representing, in her words, the big picture, the process, people, fun, and learning. In discussing why the learning aspect was a separate circle, she observes,

> I think sometimes in order to learn really well, you need to step out of your own big picture. In general, we don't build in enough time for reflection . . . just really thinking about what works and what doesn't . . . . I learn in a lot of different ways. I probably learn best from other people. I feel like it's an ongoing thing. I don't know that I've realized when I've learned because it's happening all the time.

The activists describe using reflection, thinking, and other rational processes extensively to get things done, representing an ongoing commitment to self-knowing and a willingness to change. But this conscious, reflective process seems clearly in the service of more powerful, underlying forces, reflected in their commitment to deep emotional and spiritual connections with the work. They view this process as a spiritual quest, saying that people who do not merge values, action, and hope, "live lesser lives." This openness to learning involves a strong sense of the inner life passionately seeking its realization in and connection with aspects of the outer world. Emily astutely suggests that working in the environmental field is not going to make a person popular, famous or wealthy, rather her motivation is "a spiritual value. It's fulfilling . . . that's what keeps me charged."

Hitting and Moving Through the Wall

Doing what you love and being open to the powerful messages emanating from one's inner self, however, often evoke difficult and challenging experiences for the activists. Their work is punctuated with dark moments, episodes that leave them questioning their efforts, doubting themselves, feeling like there is no more to give. In the ongoing challenges, they often feel alone in their struggles, noting with assuredness that what they are voicing is probably different than what is being felt by the others. They looked almost enviously at their peers as having more energy, passion, and commitment. Ironically, often these individuals were also part of this study, people expressing the same sentiments. Abigail describes a period of severe burnout as:

> A time period of absolute overwhelming stress. Anxiety at all times. Nonstop insomnia. And feeling like you could Never Get Anything Done. That the important things could never happen. I mean just classic depression

symptoms. Everything. Just really bad. The worst part again is the sense that this stuff mattered. It wasn't stuff that you could let go.

Dara describes burnout as "a feeling of being just totally buried and feeling that there is no way out and it's hopeless, so it's a pretty deep depression." Peter suggests,

> You can't get excited about stopping bad things from happening. You want to see good things happen and they weren't. So . . . I thought I just can't do this anymore. I am going to either have a heart attack or a nervous breakdown and I just needed something that was more fulfilling spiritually.

In Helen's words, "I was just tired. I felt tired. You know the hours we work and a lot of weekends and evenings and I was tired. I got to the point where I didn't want to even drive by work when I wasn't at work." Ben suggests that the reason burnout among environmentalists is so pervasive is due to the inability to both say no and to really take care of one's self. "It can lead to leaving the field. That's when the other ten alternative career paths start looking really good."

At the time of the interviews, the participants all talked about their burnout in past tense while cautioning that future periods were always looming. They spoke of coping mechanisms used to survive and grow from these time periods, including imposing a pause in their lives, removing themselves from the environment, and reflecting on how to move forward. These were periods in their lives when they seemed to intuitively recognize that they were too much with the world and they needed to reconnect with what was close and deeply personal. Dara calls it "taking time to dig yourself out." Abigail describes such a time period in detail.

> I knew that I didn't want to quit, and I knew that if I quit, all it would do is mean I would have to go find another job. And I doubted I would find one that I liked as much. And the goods were important enough to keep. But, it was essential to go back and recover. . . . I learned a lot of the importance of developing that space, getting back to where you are able to do what you want to do, without always feeling anxious. . . . After three months, I went back to work, and I was much better. Things had really gone back into a better perspective. . . . I think everybody needs to recognize there are limits. . . . When you're in an intense business like this, you cannot get away from it. So it's going to build and build, until there's a point where you cannot stay, you just have to stop. You have to figure out how to get back.

The activists learn to live through these dark moments in their lives by changing jobs, changing responsibilities within their organizations, taking leave for extended periods of time with or without pay, and looking for outside learning opportunities. In stark contrast to running from their burnout or trying desperately to avoid it, the activists seem to actively enter into it, trying to understand what the burnout is indicating, making changes or taking the necessary time away, and moving forward. Part of moving forward entails a level of acceptance of the enormity of the tasks ahead and a recognition that their own needs are important and valid. Megan laments, "[It's] negative to have work that you really care about because then it's an emotional investment. The same thing relates to marriages and to relationships.... You don't just leave [when] you hit the wall." By staying with the pain, embracing the suffering, and holding the tensions, the activists are able to move through these dark periods to a new awareness of themselves and their relationships with their work.

Environmental Activism as Soul Work

The stories shared in this study suggest that sustained commitment arises from a complex and ongoing relationship between the outer world and one's inner self. In this relationship, we can see the recognition of and response to a call, and the continuous struggle and deep, transformative learning that is involved in answering the call. As we shall see, their descriptions mirror the complex and profound dynamics that Jung attributed to the process of individuation (Whitmont, 1969) and what Thomas Moore (1992) refers to as "soul work."

Realizing the Sense of Vocation or Call

The environmentalists of this study have found themselves drawn to their work while continually discovering new depths and mystery in themselves and in their world. While they readily recognize their conscious participation in the direction their lives have taken, their stories also reveal a sense of a deepening understanding of a fundamentally unknown, yet acceptable, force at work that helps to define who they are. Their stories reveal the notion of vocation or "calling," with vocation referring to an intersection of the deeply personal with that which is socially purposeful, meaningful, or necessary (Rehm, 1990; Hansen, 1995), or the "place where your deep gladness and the world's deep hunger meet" (Buechner, 1973). A calling suggests a deep interconnection between the meaningfulness of our lives and the meaningfulness of the work we do (Whyte, 2001). The activists' work is a natural expression of the self.

The idea of environmental activism as a vocation or calling helps deepen our understanding of how activists sustain commitment to their work. In this sense, commitment and vocation are closely intertwined, implying that it is not necessarily an individualistic choice to act. At its deepest level, vocation, "is something I can't not do, for reasons I'm unable to explain to anyone else and don't fully understand myself but that are nonetheless compelling" (Palmer, 2000, p. 25). Being guided by vocation involves learning to listen to the deep but powerful messages that life sends us, representing a form of ongoing learning and inner work. In describing their work as a simultaneous engagement of head, heart, and spirit, the activists suggest an evolving integration of their inner selves with the work of environmentalism. What they do seems like a natural extension of who, in their heart of hearts, they feel they are called to be. They are often at a loss to clearly explain how this sense of calling has come to dominate their lives in such a central and forceful way, but they remain convinced that this is something they were meant to do. A close alignment exists between the deep values they bring to their work and the hope they feel when aligning their work tightly with those values.

The activists' stories also help us understand another aspect of sustaining commitment. While a sense of vocation or calling may be at the core of sustaining commitment, recognizing and answering a call within one's life is anything but easy. Caring deeply about one's work brings with it the risk of feeling overwhelmed and discouraged. Their work and their commitment are often riddled with doubt and uncertainty, even dark periods of depression and despair. At the same time, they perceive both the deep sense of calling and the doubt, uncertainty, and struggle as if they are parts of the same cloth, joined together through some existential mystery.

Thus, bound up with this sense of vocation or calling is a deep and ongoing form of learning to understand who they are within their work. It represents a difficult and often painful journey to integrate conscious and unconscious dimensions of their lives, to embrace this mystery and enter fully into it. Answering the call and sustaining commitment and passion to it involves the inner work of the self, the work of soul (Moore, 1992). As work brings the person in deep and intimate relationship with the outer world, it becomes a location for a type of learning that involves the search for and construction of inner meaning. The stories of the activists participating in this study reveal the ways in which the inner self expresses itself in their work. They are fundamentally stories of individuation and transformation.

Sustaining Commitment Through Transformative Learning

Mitchell Thomashow (1995) found that for people working on environmental issues the most critical component in nurturing their environmentalism is the ability and willingness to look deeply within themselves, to understand their motivations and aspirations, to clearly articulate values, and know how to apply them to professional and personal decisions. Such processes often involve deep shifts in the ways in which one views the world and the self in relation to the world. This form of learning has been described by Jack Mezirow (1991) and others as transformative and has become a widely popular focus for both research and practice in adult education.

The stories of the activists participating in this study reflect the importance of inner work as suggested by Thomashow (1995). To sustain commitment and passion, the environmental activists engage in an ongoing process of transformative learning. Similar to Mezirow's theory, the forms of transformative learning reflected in the inner work of these activists suggest deep shifts in their frames of reference. The activists also stress the importance of reflection in helping them work through some of the difficult times.

But their stories also suggest aspects of transformative learning that seem underdeveloped or largely ignored in Mezirow's theory of perspective transformation. Rather than the dramatic or ephiphanic shifts described by Stephen Brookfield (2000), the activists demonstrated processes that seemed more gradual and occurred over an extended period of time. This view of transformative learning parallels the perspective advanced by Laurent Daloz (2000) who suggests this "change or shift was long in coming and its possibility prepared for in myriad ways, generally across years" (p. 106).

While the deep engagement in learning described by the activists may result in various "disorienting dilemmas" or catalytic events, these seem more the result of an attitude or a stance toward one's life, rather than provoking change itself (Dirkx, 2000). The processes of transformation reflected in their stories are not start and stop events, bounded by a "trigger" at one end and a remarkable conversion at the other. Rather, their struggles to sustain commitment and passion for their work reflect an active engagement with the everydayness of their lives, a challenge to answer the call within their work. It is intimately bound up with and embedded in the historical, developmental, and social contexts of their lives.

The activists' stories rarely indicate a strong reliance on critical reflection and self-analysis, processes that are suggested to be at the heart of transformative learning (Mezirow, 1991). In fact, their narratives often downplay the role that reason and reflection play in these processes. The activists accept the power of inner work as coming to "know and understand the self and to be able to interact with the outer world and the collective" (Dei, 2002, p. 125) while also understanding emotions as an important source of knowledge. Commitment is sustained among these individuals through a holistic understanding of knowing and learning, one that intimately involves "head, heart, and spirit." In their stories, we see forms of transformative learning characterized more by sitting, observing, and listening to the images that come to populate one's consciousness (Scott, 1997). The activists' experiences of transformation suggest a lived stance toward a sense of call, a form of practice reflective of deep spiritual commitments (Teasdale, 2002), and a gradual unfolding of the self. Their stories affirm a kind of spiritual pilgrimage through which they come to see and understand deeper and different aspects of themselves. They speak of a kind of spiritual knowing similar to the African views of spirituality described by George Dei (2002, p. 124), in which the self is recognized as "a complex, integrated being with multiple layers of meaning." The stories point to the complex social, emotional, and spiritual processes involved in deep inner work and the processes of transformative learning (O'Sullivan et al., 2002).

Nurturing the Soul

These aspects of the journey and transformation of the self are consistent with what Jung described as the process of individuation (Whitmont, 1969). Grounded in depth psychology, this view suggests that transformative learning reflects the profound and lifelong struggle of the person to be who he or she is called to be (Whitmont, 1969). According to Jung, development of individuality is inherent to being human, and the process is stimulated and guided by a genuine, natural striving for individuation—becoming who we truly are. Individuation stresses the formation and differentiation of individual beings, apart from yet intimately connected with the broader collective (Jacobi, 1990). It refers to the process by which a person becomes "whole," through recognition and integration of conscious and unconscious elements of oneself. It is a process of learning who one is apart from, yet intimately interconnected with, the collective in which one's life is embedded. Characteristic of the process of individuation, the activists in this study learned to be in the world but not of it. Despite their deep commitment to the world and the environment, they saw themselves as different, apart from the collective. Their experiences suggest that transformative learning and the process of individuation in which this form of learning is embedded, arise from a deep, dialectical engagement both with the world and one's self. There is something about being an activist that touches these individuals at a very deep level and environmentalism becomes the context through which this calling gains its voice.

In many respects, the activists realize at some level that they are not the "captains of their ship," that their lives receive direction from a source other than their conscious waking selves. In the processes of individuation, the inner world of the self seems to have its own agenda, which may be different or even at odds with what we consciously think is our mission in life. As Andrew Samuels (1989) suggests, "...in the soul's depths, things are not necessarily what we think or feel they are. Nor what we desire them to be" (p. xii).

Transformative learning involves recognizing and connecting with those aspects of the self that remain largely unknown to our conscious waking selves. The activists' stories reflect the continuous struggle and conflict between their external and internal worlds, both important and deeply valued. They often feel a deep sense of being bogged down in the mire of their own existence and see no immediate way out. In this place, there is pain, emotion, and strong affect. In enduring these tensions, they become increasingly aware of those aspects of the self of which they were previously unaware. As these aspects become conscious, their overall sense of who they are as a person changes and transforms. By recognizing the expressions of this inner world in everyday experience, the activists are able to further consciousness in a largely unconscious world.

The activists' descriptions of their experience also implicitly portray a multiplistic sense of self. They talked metaphorically about the head, the heart, and the spirit, how each of these entities were present in their lives and work in different ways, how each aspect of their being has to be a recognized piece of who they are in the world in order to feel whole, to gain some degree of integration and sense of wholeness, and to be able to continually push forward. They define this aspect of their experience as "dangerous," the part that is not well accepted in a culture that idolizes unitary identity and technical rationality. In the process of individuation, humans strive to fully differentiate the multiple selves that make up the inner self, and to come to know and integrate these different selves within a greater sense of inner wholeness (Whitmont, 1969). Such an endeavor is marked by difficulty and challenges, evoking a deep and profound sense of ambivalence with confronting the dark, unknown, multiplistic, and often unwanted aspects of one's self (Whitmont, 1969; Jacobi, 1990).

The activists' descriptions of hitting the wall and working through these periods in their lives are consistent with what some have referred to as the "dark night of the soul" (Ulanov, 2001). This period refers to those experiences associated with the process of individuation that are characterized by emotional and often difficult and wrenching conflict and turmoil. It feels as though there is nowhere to turn, nowhere to go for help, nothing that can be done. The activists' description of burnout resembles this dark night of the soul. For example, the activists suggested that their personal needs are not the priority, paralleling the findings of other studies looking closely at people working for the common good (Daloz et al., 1996). When they "hit the wall," however, they are suddenly forced to put the self first and figure out how to pull themselves back up or through. This is deeply painful, in part, because to be so self-focused goes against their values and visions. Such periods of overwhelming stress, however, often become moments of deep and potentially transformative learning. In falling apart, the activists experience meaningful change. Passing through this paradox of stress, or what Jung refers to as a cycle of alienation and inflation (Whitmont, 1969), increases the activists' knowledge about themselves and their ability to continue in their work with a sense of vocation. In this period of despair, letting go allows them to paradoxically experience hope and often find their way out. As they come to learn, "care of the soul" is a continuous process that will not make life problem-free. Rather, it is focused on cultivating a more meaningful life (Moore, 1992).

Sustained commitment and passion reflects a willingness to grow during times of deep stress. The activists have been forced to confront inner work, to recognize their own needs, to understand who they are in their work, and have grown from the experience. And, as has been suggested by the activists, they have come away even stronger in their convictions and their understanding of self.

References

Berry, J. and Gordon, J. (Eds.) (1993). *Environmental Leadership: Developing Effective Skills and Styles*. Washington, D.C.: Island Press.

Brookfield, S. (2000). "Transformative Learning as Ideology Critique." In J. Mezirow and Associates (Eds.), *Learning as Transformation: Critical Perspectives as a Theory in Progress* (pp. 125–148). San Francisco: Jossey-Bass.

Buechner, F. (1973). *Wishful Thinking: A Seeker's ABC*. San Francisco: HarperCollins.

Daloz, L. (2000). "Transformative Learning for the Common Good." In J. Mezirow (Ed.), *Learning as Transformation* (pp. 103–121). San Francisco: Jossey-Bass.

Daloz, L., Keen, C., Keen, J., and Parks, S. (1996). *Common Fire: Leading Lives of Commitment in a Complex World*. Boston: Beacon Press.

Dei, G. (2002). "Spiritual Knowing and Transformative Learning." In E. O'Sullivan, A. Morrell, and M. A. O'Connor (Eds.), *Expanding the Boundaries of*

Transformative Learning: Essays on Theory and Praxis (pp. 121–134). New York, Paygrade.

Dirkx, J. (2000). "After the Burning Bush: Transformative Learning as Imaginative Engagement with Everyday Experience." In C. Wiessner, S. Meyer, and D. Fuller (Eds.), *Challenges of Practice: Transformative Learning in Action: The Proceedings of the Third International Conference on Transformative Learning* (pp. 247–252). New York: Teachers College.

Doyle, K. (1999). *The Complete Guide to Environmental Careers in the 21st Century.* Washington, D.C.: Island Press.

Hansen, D. (1995). *The Call to Teach.* New York: Teachers College Press.

Herman, R. and Heimovics, R. (1989). "Critical Events in the Management of Nonprofit Organizations: Initial Evidence." *Nonprofit and Voluntary Sector Quarterly* 18 (2): 119–132.

Institute for Conversion Leadership (ICL). (1996). *Great Lakes, Great Stakes: The Environmental Movement in Reflection.* Flint, M.I.: C. S. Mott Foundation.

Jacobi, M. (1990). *Individuation and Narcissism: The Psychology of the Self in Jung and Kohut.* New York: Routledge.

Mezirow, J. (1991). *Transformative Dimensions of Adult Learning.* San Francisco: Jossey-Bass.

Moore, T. (1992). *Care of the Soul: A Guide for Cultivating Depth and Sacredness in Everyday Life.* New York: HarperCollins.

Oliver, M. (1992). *New and Selected Poems.* Boston: Beacon Press.

O'Sullivan, E., Morrell, A., and O'Connor, M. A. (Eds.) (2002). *Expanding the Boundaries of Transformative Learning: Essays on Theory and Praxis.* New York: Palgrave.

Palmer, P. (2000). *Let Your Life Speak: Listening for the Voice of Vocation.* San Francisco: Jossey-Bass Publishers.

Peters, J. and Wolfred, T. (2001). *Daring to Lead: Nonprofit Executive Directors and their Work Experience.* San Francisco: CompassPoint Nonprofit Services.

Rehm, M. (1990). "Vocation as Personal Calling: A Question for Education." *Journal of Educational Thought* 24 (2): 114–125.

Samuels, A. (1989). *The Plural Psyche: Personality, Morality, and the Father.* London: Routledge.

Scott, S. (1997). "The Grieving Soul in the Transformation Process." In P. Cranton (Ed.), *Transformative Learning in Action: Insights from Practice* (pp. 41–50). San Francisco: Jossey-Bass.

Singleton, M. and Cunningham, R. (2000). *Executive Director Experience and Tenure Survey.* Seattle, W.A.: The Volunteer Center, United Way of King County.

Snow, D. (1992). *Inside the Environmental Movement: Meeting the Leadership Challenge.* Washington D.C.: Island Press.

Teasdale, W. (2002). *A Monk in the World: Cultivating a Spiritual Life.* Novato, C.A.: New World Library.

Thomashow, M. (1995). *Ecological Identity: Becoming a Reflective Environmentalist.* Cambridge, M.A.: The MIT Press.

Ulanov, A. B. (2001). *Finding Space: Winnicott, God, and Psychic Reality.* Louisville, K.Y.: Westminister John Knox Press.

Weisbrod, B. (1988). *The Nonprofit Economy.* Cambridge, M.A.: Harvard University Press.

Whitmont, E. (1969). *The Symbolic Quest.* Princeton, N.J.: Princeton University Press.

Whyte, D. (2001). *Crossing the Unknown Sea: Work as a Pilgrimage of Identity.* New York: Riverhead Books.

Wilensky, A. S. (1995). "Understanding the Culture of Nonprofit Executives Through Stories: A Qualitative Investigation." *Educational Policy Studies* (p. 252) Atlanta, G.A.: Georgia State University.

Wilson, M. (1994). *The State of Nonprofit Michigan.* E. Lansing, NonProfit Michigan Project, IPPSR. Lansing: MSU Press.

Wolfred, T., Allison, M., and Masaoka, J. (1999). *Leadership Lost: A Study of Executive Director Tenure and Experience.* San Francisco: Support Center for Nonprofit Management.

CHAPTER 9

A Transformation Model for Passion in the Workplace

Patricia E. Boverie and Michael Kroth

The more we know about the world, the more that we know that we cannot separate the physical from the social, the biological from the spiritual, or the historical from the present or future. Everything is interconnected. Stanley Milgram's "six degrees of separation" research of the 1960s has developed into highly sophisticated studies of networks (Buchanan, 2002). It turns out that there are deeply similar network structures in areas as complex and diverse as the World Wide Web, the food webs of any ecological system, and the networks linking the economic activity of any nation (Buchanan, 2002).

Organizations are also systems of interconnections and relationships. Margaret Wheatley (1992) says "We are beginning to recognize organizations as systems, construing them as 'learning organizations' and crediting them with some type of self-renewing capacity" (p. 13). This self-producing, or autopoetic (Maturana and Varela, 1992; Wheatley, 1992), quality is something organizations share with living organizations and natural systems.

To describe the analogy between organizations and natural systems even more specifically, reflect upon what it is like to walk into any organizational setting. Within that organizational "environment" there is a cycle of life and death. There are natural, often reciprocal, relationships between sustenance and growth, reproduction and birth, breaking and healing. There is a process for gaining membership and for dealing with those who do not fit. External factors that impinge upon this environment change the dynamics, but the organizational environment, being self-producing, adapts to continue its existence.

As discussed in chapter 1, organizations, over time, developed a more mechanistic metaphor that moved the emphasis of natural order to an unnatural system that devalued humane processes and systems. This resulted in organizations with a strong instrumental consciousness, which led to a de-emphasis of caring for the whole person in our workplaces.

Organizations are central to individuals' lives. In our current society these institutions have become communities in themselves and the various communities in which we live have blurred boundaries. For example, over twenty years ago, Dorothy Tennov (1979) described what he called the new family—the Association. Associations are composed of people, unrelated by family ties, who talk to each other regularly, share their ups and downs, assemble for minor holidays and celebrations. They care for each other when in need. Our mobile society and our specialized workplaces have created these new "family" structures. The nurturing we once received primarily from our families now comes in part from our workplaces.

Technological, demographical, and cultural change occurs at an ever-increasing pace in our organizations. This is indicative of the "turbulent environment" described in chapter 1, that is "highly dynamic and complex such that the constituent systems are unable to predict and must deal with constant uncertainty". Organizations, in their attempt to meet these demands and to evolve quickly, have often done so at the expense of the employees. This constant and often unplanned change has a direct and often a detrimental effect on the individuals who make up the organization.

Today's organizations need to have an ecological perspective—to view themselves as environments that facilitate human potential. An ecological perspective requires that attention must be paid to the interaction between the organization and the individuals who make up the organization. Highly successful companies have proven that when there is a good fit between organizational and individual needs, both prosper and grow. Robert H. Waterman's (1994) book, *What America Does Right*, is focused on the relationship between organizations and people. Successful companies, he says, tend to view the organization as a family made up of individuals who have needs, feelings, biases, talents, and personalities. He contends that we need to pay attention to the needs of the individuals in the organization as well as to the needs of the organization. This reinforces an organizational imperative to tap into the multiplicity of passions that reside in workers of all persuasions and experiences.

Our research has focused on finding the qualities of work that people can feel passionate about. The days when organizations can ignore the human aspects of their employees are over. This has led toward the recognition and importance of the emotional and spiritual aspects of us.

As individuals, we seek intimacy as a basic need and drive. Intimate relationships make us feel cared for, needed, loved, and connected with others. This need for intimacy is central to the concept of our ecological self, that is, seeing ourselves as relational totalities. An innate need such as this is inherent in what it means to be human. Just as individuals seek intimacy and emotional connectedness with others, in organizations, employees seek connections with their fellow employees and to their work. They want to feel needed and cared for, just as they do in their private lives. When this happens, employees are apt to have more loyalty, greater motivation, and a true commitment to what the organization is trying to accomplish.

What is Passion?

We all experience passion by virtue of being human. Passion evokes images of deep commitment to another person, to an idea, or to a cause. Every person has the capacity for passion and yet many do not lead passionate lives. The origin of the word passion comes from *passio*, or suffering (*Webster's New Collegiate Dictionary*, 1979). Suffering, or pain, is a very real part of passion and one of the reasons many people, either consciously or unconsciously, are not willing to expose themselves to it. Society contributes to this dehumanization. In chapter 1, it was noted that the modernist context in which we live forces a rationalistic, detached, and dispassionate framework that sacrifices an understanding of ourselves as an embodied, engaged, and connected society.

Passion is at the root of creative genius, personal transformation, and notable events. Passion is emotional energy that stimulates life, and energizes individuals to work toward a goal. New products, new ideas, creative new ways to deliver services, inventions, and scientific discoveries are created because someone or some organization is passionate. "People who love their work exhibit enormous energy, a positive state of mind, and a sense of vision and purpose. They realized that what they are doing fits into a larger picture and can see how what they do makes a difference in the world as a whole" (Jaffe and Scott, 1988, p. 69).

Yet over time we have tried to make the workplace an arena without emotion. The industrial revolution with its mechanistic, instrumental view of people, changed the workplace into one where individuals were seen as mere cogs in the machinery of the business, and reduced them to silent, obedient employees. In recent years, we have seen many changes in the workplace to make it more humane, but we still have far to go, especially in terms of looking at the emotional and spiritual needs of individuals. We want the outcome of passionate work, but we don't want employees to have emotions at work. Taking the passion, the love of work, and the meaningfulness of work out of the workplace creates halls of despair, the corridors of the living dead.

We need a new conception of the workplace. Instead of vanquishing emotions, we need to channel them. Instead of chastising the passion in employees, we need to help people to understand and use what they love to do. We need to have a workplace where employees are not confused when we say we want them to be loyal and hardworking, and yet have asked them to check their desire, their humanity, at the door. For individuals, passion resides internally and may be expressed to others. For organizations, passion is the cumulative, emotional effect of every employee interacting with his or her work and with each other. This ecological view of individuals in a relational totality follows closely Warwick Fox's (1990) idea of cosmological identification, whereby our worlds must be realized as one unfolding reality.

Passion contains two, interrelated, qualities: (1) the pure joy and excitement of doing something that is enjoyable to do, and (2) meaningfulness, or caring deeply about something. Passion can be found in either, but to be fully engaged requires both (Boverie and Kroth, 2001).

Enjoyment

For work to be passionate it must also be fun, exciting, and joyful. Many people have lost this, and with it their capacity for passionate work. Understanding what it is we love to do and then finding ways to pursue that work is an important part of living passionately. Over the years, fun and work have been considered mutually exclusive terms. Again, this is related to historical influences such as Taylor's "scientific method" of creating efficient organizations at the cost of de-emphasizing our natural human desires (Kast and Rosenzweig, 1970).

Meaningfulness and Spirituality

Individuals seek fulfillment by doing work they view as important. We want work to make a difference. We feel strongly about the things we do that will change people's lives, improve the world, and leave a legacy for others. For many, spirituality is a necessary component of meaningfulness. Spiritual leaders from earliest times have taught that work is a manifestation of our inner or spiritual selves. Matthew Fox (1994), in his book *The Reinvention of Work*, says that "Work comes from inside out; work is the expression of our soul, our inner being…it is the expression of the Spirit at work in the world through us" (p. 5). Today, many are engaged not just in finding the meaning of work, but in finding the meaning of life itself.

John Scherer (1993), in *Work and the Human Spirit*, describes spirit as a critical element of future success. "The huge challenges facing the workplace today are not going to be overcome with new management theories or motivational tips and techniques. I happen to believe that we are in a crisis which must be approached as something so profound, so fundamental, so universal, that it can only be resolved at the level of the human spirit" (p. 7). Scherer says "…What it takes for *companies* to survive is also what it takes for *individuals* who make them up to survive. The highest goals of any business can best be realized by awakening and nurturing the human spirit of the people who comprise it—its leaders, its employees, and even its customers" (pp. 5–6).

And yet, organizations either overlook or trivialize this inner need. Lee G. Bolman and Terrence E. Deal (1995), in *Leading with Soul*, say "Most management and leadership programs ignore or demean spirit. They desperately need an infusion of poetry, literature, music, art, theater, history, philosophy, dance and other forms that are full of spirit" (pp. 167–168). Leaders who recognize this human need tap into core human qualities that revitalize lives and organizations. "Leading with soul returns us to ancient spiritual basics—reclaiming the enduring human capacity that gives our lives passion and purpose" (p. 6).

In our research we found that work without joy or meaning results in burnout, lifelessness, lack of creativity, and a dearth of initiative. From the individual's perspective, going to work each day in this mode is an attempt each day to survive. The goal is just make it through eight hours until the clock says it's time to go. From the organization's perspective, huge amounts of productivity are left on the table, as worker ingenuity, drive, and collaborative spirit remain untapped.

Many organizations overtly or covertly discourage passion at work. They prefer to live or die by "reason." The mind is all-powerful for these groups, and the heart of little importance. Many organizations are dominated by rationality, the desire for "bottom-line" results, linear thinking, and dispassionate decision-making, even though most new businesses are built on someone's dream, on a major risk, on an intense desire to succeed in helping people, on making a great product, or creating something new. This way of doing business inhibits us from moving forward to healthier value systems and toward a flourishing organizational ecology.

Some organizations carry an underlying belief that people are mere objects. This is an unstated (usually) conviction that individuals are just input and output systems and that if the right incentive structure and systems are created that they will react like any other well-oiled machine. You can sense when people are viewed as things when they are referred to as "assets," or "intellectual capital," or when leaders talk about throwing "resources" at a problem. When organizations view people as objects it makes sense that they would try to structure emotion out of the system.

Learned helplessness is "the giving-up reaction, the quitting response that follows from the belief that whatever you do doesn't matter" (Seligman, 1990, p. 15). It is different than unconscious censoring—just never thinking of something—in that it is a conditioned way of negative thinking. Social norms can suppress the natural human tendency to learn and discover. Mom and Dad tell us not to follow our dream of becoming a poet because there's no money in it. A teacher tells us that we ought to think about becoming a teacher and not a mechanic (or vice versa) because we don't really have the talent to do one or the other. After a while we censor our dreams. It is frightening to think that the dreams of whole classes of people are censored before they even graduate from high school, and often many years before that. People with learned helplessness don't even try anymore.

Organizations often promote learned helplessness in their employees. Tacit understandings about who will and will not succeed tell employees in sometimes-subtle ways that no matter how hard they try they can only go so far. There may be unspoken rules, for example, about what the ceiling is for a person without a college degree. Sooner or later these cause people to seek avenues for success outside the company or to just give up. Policies, procedures, and reward systems that stifle initiative may create an employee population that simply gives up.

Every organization has a unique culture, comprised of a set of unwritten assumptions about the past, present, and future. Like every paradigm, these assumptions are often considered valid even when the environment changes. To the extent organizations reinforce unhealthy assumptions about the workforce, they inhibit growth. The research on organizational culture tells us that it is the leaders' values and beliefs that drive the culture (Schein, 1992). But it is the employees who must work and live within the culture. Most organizational cultures were not created systematically or with a specific design in mind. Because of this, many cultures have dysfunctional aspects that inhibit employee development and passion for work. Surfacing unspoken assumptions is a way of overcoming ignorance about how people are treated the way they are, and why. One of the most liberating acts is to create a climate in which critical thinking is the norm. Paulo Friere (1970) proposed that liberation is a result of transforming one's consciousness, a process he called "conscientization." The conscientization process is one, "in which men, not as recipients, but as knowing subjects, achieve a deepening awareness both of the sociocultural reality which shapes their lives and the capacity to transform that reality" (p. 27).

Transforming Work: Our Findings and Model

Organizational, educational, and clinical psychologists have long studied motivation. There have been many different theories put forth to describe how to develop motivation within individuals, organizations, and systems. Despite the host of papers and books on the subject, motivation continues to be a real concern.

The basis of our model for developing and maintaining motivation for work was initially drawn from the research in the psychological field of love, attraction, and relationships. What makes our approach unique is that we started with the theories of interpersonal passion and used those ideas to view passion for work. The development of our model began with a search for what makes people love their work. What makes a passionate employee? Why do passionate employees lose their passion?

Our Passion Transformation Model (Boverie and Kroth, 2001) was then validated and elaborated upon based on the results of a qualitative research study influenced by several key theories in the areas of passion, learning, transformation, and intimate relationships. We asked over 300 working adults to share critical incidents regarding their experiences with passion and work. These interviewees, mostly living in the United States, came from diverse backgrounds and occupations. They ranged from individuals in their twenties to those in their late sixties, from medical doctors to office clerks. We asked our interviewees to tell us about a time they were passionate about their work, what created that passion, how they maintained it, and if they lost it, why and how they got it back. These stories provided rich descriptions of how people find and keep their passion for work. They provided real-life examples of processes and strategies for developing and maintaining passionate work. These processes fell into five areas we have labeled as the keys to helping individuals who have lost their way or who find their passion waning to regain a love for work.

Occupational Intimacy

The ultimate goal of our Passion Transformation Model is the development of what we call Occupational Intimacy. Occupational Intimacy is a term we developed to represent the closeness, or relationship, that passionate people feel about their work. Like two passionate lovers, people in love with their work feel that it is inseparable; it is a part of who they are. They feel a sense of personal commitment to what they do. They are emotional about it, they have strong feelings of dedication, care, support, and desire associated with it. Recognition and rewards often stimulate passion for work, but many times people are so in love with their work that they would do it for the pure joy of it. Another aspect of Occupational Intimacy is the relationship one has with the people who work in the organization. Intimacy is high when the organization, the leaders, the managers, and coworkers truly care about each other and about how they do their work.

When we asked our interviewees what Occupational Intimacy meant, their answers fell into three categories: having a nurturing environment, being able to do meaningful and significant work, and having fun and enjoying what you do. A 32-year-old training manager said Occupational Intimacy is, "Developing a relationship with your job, trying to better yourself and your job situation so that you can have a long-term relationship with your job."

Nurturing Environments

Nurture comes from the Latin word for nursing. To nurse is to provide nourishment, to care or provide for tenderly, and to cherish. To nurture is to nourish, to feed, to educate, and to rear. Environments that foster passionate employees, nourish, feed, and develop them.

Bolman and Deal (1995), in their book, *Leading with Soul*, say the following about caring workplaces:

> Pressures of immediate tasks and the bottom line often crowd out personal needs that people bring into the workplace. Every organization is a family, whether caring or dysfunctional. Caring begins with knowing about others—it requires listening, understanding, and accepting. It progresses through a deepening sense of appreciation, respect, and ultimately, love. Love is a willingness to reach out and open one's heart. An open heart is vulnerable. Accepting vulnerability allows us to drop our masks, meet heart to heart, and be present for one another. We experience a sense of unity and delight in voluntary, human exchanges that mold the "soul of community." (p. 103)

Meaningful Work

When asked what Occupational Intimacy was, approximately one-third of the responses indicated it was a place where they were doing work that was meaningful to themselves, the organization, and society. One of our interviewees said, "I have a hard time getting involved in activities when I cannot see their purpose or usefulness."

Morris Rosenberg, a sociologist, first coined the term, "mattering" (Schlossberg et al., 1989). According to Rosenberg, mattering refers to the beliefs people have that they matter to someone else. He found that a feeling of mattering made the difference in people's motivation to stay engaged in learning. Doing work that one feels "matters" is important to keeping one's passion alive.

Enjoying Your Work

When asked what Occupational Intimacy was, again about one-third of the responses indicated it was doing work they loved and having fun. A 25-year-old retail manager said, "Occupational intimacy is actually loving your job. Looking forward to going to work and knowing exactly what you do and how you effect others through what you do."

When we are doing work we love time seems to fly and we are totally involved in what we are doing. Mihaly Csikszentmihalyi (1990) describes this as Flow. Flow is experienced when we are doing work we know we can accomplish, for which we have the time and space to complete, that we know exactly what we are doing, and we receive immediate feedback. We are so engrossed in this work that our troubles and preoccupation with ourselves disappear. When we are in Flow, time seems to become altered and we lose track of it. People who love their work find themselves in a state of Flow more often than those who are watching the clock, and waiting for the day to end.

Nurturing, meaningfulness, and enjoyment create a sense of intimacy with our work. One of our interviewees said, "I think to the extent that we foster a sense of wide-awareness and mindfulness, we can rejuvenate people about their work and about their sense of intimacy and the work place.... In very powerful ways, [we] can make a difference in how connected you feel and how excited you are about that work."

Passion Transformation Model

Our model is based on transformational learning theory and we have found evidence to support it in the stories that working adults have related to us. Our model shows the sources underlying passion as inputs to a systematic process of Discovering, Designing, and Developing, with the output resulting in greater passion and what we define as Occupational Intimacy. This same process can be used to develop passion for work, for relationships, or for life in general. Within the Discovering, Designing, and Developing processes are Enablers for each process. Individuals can use the process to develop personal passion, and organizations can use the process to design programs and practices for making the workplace more supportive of passionate employees. This developmental, transformational model, if used by either individuals or organizations, can help to sustain the energy and interest of employees in the workplace.

For organizational transformation to occur, all members of the organization must (1) be free to question assumptions and beliefs and (2) work together to create a new system based on clear assumptions, values, and beliefs. Our study identifies key factors that explain how passion develops and is sustained. These keys make up the three processes of our Passion Transformation Model.

The Discovering Process

Passionate people have discovered work that excites them. For individuals, the first key is discovering what excites you. Looking back to times in your life when you felt passionate about something, doing self-analyses, and figuring out what is really important to you, and asking yourself how you would like to spend your time are all ways of discovering your passion. Likewise, smart, forward-looking organizations find ways to help their employees discover their passion. Organizations can provide career counseling, vocational and personality testing, or opportunities for employees to develop a career path in the company.

Discovering can be an *evolutionary* process as one learns more and more about the world and about his or herself; or it can be a *revolutionary*, sudden, powerful, mind-and-heart-changing experience. Discovery can be *intentional*—occurring via purposeful contemplation, reflection, or experiential testing; or it can happen to us, be *imposed* when events such divorce, death of a loved one, a new baby, health problem, or being fired from a job cause us to think about life differently.

Even if a person has "seen the light" and seems to know what really excites her about work, continual inner work intended to maintain awareness is critical to sustain that passion. Ongoing critical reflection and study must continue in order to understand the sources of one's passion, to recognize when it is waning, and to explore either the incremental or quantum changes required sustaining or increasing it. This vigilance is required lest over a lifetime the perceived passion slowly, often unconsciously, devolves into just surviving.

The ultimate goal of Discovering for organizations is to have employees who know what they love to do and who are doing it. Discovering for organizations means providing ways for employees to determine the kind of work that produces their best efforts, their most creativity, and the highest quality of work. To be effective, an organization must first have a very clear idea of its own mission, vision, and culture—in other words to Discover its own passion; and second to find, hire, motivate, develop, and retain key talent by helping *them* attain and sustain passion for the organization and its work over time.

The Designing Process

Passionate people find ways to make their lives exciting, meaningful, and special. Taking what they've discovered about themselves, they shape their own lives to fit it. The Designing process involves setting goals, and then finding the environments that encourage passionate work.

For individuals, the overarching goal of the designing process is to develop strategies to begin living your purpose. Part of the designing process includes all the preparations—mental, social, spiritual, physical—necessary to embark upon passionate work. As an individual, that includes planning strategically and practically how you will achieve the goal of passionate work. For organizations, the overarching goal of the designing process is to create a passionate work environment for your employees. For both individuals and organizations, the purpose is to be intentional about creating the means to achieve passionate work.

Organizations can be creative about job responsibilities, look for ways to provide variety in the work, link employees with customers so that they can see results, cross-train employees, provide recognition and rewards, find sources of fun and play, make the mission and vision of the organization inspiring and the goals challenging. Many organizations can reduce the risk of employees leaving their jobs by encouraging them to change jobs within the organization and providing opportunities to do it. Especially early in a career, organizations can help employees test new jobs, take on new tasks, go to different courses, provide mentors or coaching in new situations, so that trying new responsibilities become normal rather than exceptional. The larger the employee's knowledge base, the more valuable the employee, and therefore the more willing she or he will be to change jobs if the organization thinks there might be a fit between company and employee needs.

The Developing Process—Risking, Learning, and Building Self-Efficacy

Risk is an important part of living passionately. Those living passionately invariably have taken risks. To do otherwise is to play it safe, sit on your heels, and regret opportunities missed. But one must be thoughtful and intentional about risk-taking. It is taking risks that moves one toward passion and allows one to grow. Organizations can be very helpful in providing opportunities for individuals to take on new projects, to work in different areas, to try new skills.

People who take reasonable risks are constantly Learning—about themselves and about their work. Passionate people are always learning, reinventing themselves, and exploring new things. Individuals must be continually learning in their jobs in order to have passion. If they aren't challenged in their job, they should find new things to learn or move on to something new. People who are constantly learning are more likely to be passionate, and to feel confident about their abilities. Employees who continually grow help organizations to prosper.

Self-efficacy is the belief that we have about our ability to do something. The concept of self-efficacy was developed by Albert Bandura (1977) to describe the personal beliefs we have about our ability to perform. According to Bandura, expectations of self-efficacy are the most powerful determinants of behavioral change because self-efficacy expectancies determine the initial decision to perform a behavior, the effort expended, and persistence in the face of adversity.

Self-efficacy powerfully affects our behavior. We may have the skills and talent to take on more challenging jobs, but if we believe that we are incapable of being successful, we are unlikely to apply for new positions. Positive self-efficacy is developed by trying new things and then evaluating how you did. People with low self-efficacy are unlikely to try new things, and hence may lead less passionate lives. One of the most important aspects of self-efficacy is that we *can* change it from low to high. Often, taking small steps builds self-efficacy over time.

By taking little or big steps, we are taking *risks*, as we risk we *learn*, and as we learn we develop higher *self-efficacy*, our belief in ourselves, and that we can accomplish what we set out to do. All three, working together as the *Developing* process, advance our quest for a more passionate life.

Implications for Individuals and Organizations

For the Living Dead—those employees who are burned out, hate to get up in the morning, are depressed, or find they have lost their lust for life—using the Passion Transformation Model can mean a complete turnaround in their lives. It can help them to discover what truly makes them happy and energized, and help them to actually follow through and make changes in their lives. These changes could be within the same organization or, if they are not well suited for that employer or work, it can help them to find the work they should be doing.

Passion suggests strong feelings, feelings that reside deep within ourselves. We are passionate about those people and things that stir those feelings, that touch our basic values and beliefs. When we connect, reflect, and are in touch with those basic values and beliefs, then we can transform our lives. We can make the choices that before seemed hard or impossible to do. When we discover, truly discover, what is important to us, then we can formulate the plans to live the lives that are meaningful to ourselves. When we are doing meaningful, interesting work, in organizations that care about that work, then we become capable of steering our own course, and living passionate lives.

If, as proposed in chapter 1, we must consider the ecological content as essential to a flourishing and sustainable humanity, true leaders have a special role to play. Leaders can construct workplaces where not only the environments and benefits are good, where jobs are challenging and interesting, and where employees know why they are important, but also where they have opportunities to learn and develop. Learning, taking risks, and the subsequent effect that it has upon employee self-efficacy is what keeps them on the payroll, keeps them passionate, and keeps the organization learning, growing, and prospering. Constructing these workplaces requires nothing short of transforming work. Leadership is where the transformation process must start.

Transforming work can mean changing the work itself, so that it can be more enjoyable, meaningful, and productive. Alternatively, transforming work can mean work that changes the individual. In this instance, the work environment or the tasks involved in completing the work act upon the individual to transform him or her into someone, preferably, who is increasingly growing, learning, and enthusiastic. Sometimes it involves transforming the work to meet your needs, and sometimes it means transforming yourself to reach the work you love. As we seek work that we can be passionate about we will be transformed. The very process of seeking, changes us from what we were to something else.

Organizational transformation is also a complex undertaking that requires the people in the organization to change, as well as the organization itself. Many of our organizational cultures are currently based on assumptions that have gone unquestioned since the early part of the twentieth century. "In the workplace, stagnant and oppressive organizational conditions persist simply because of the unquestioning acceptance of traditional organizational norms" (Brookfield, 1990, p. 147). These very assumptions are the starting place for organizational transformation.

In the Passion Transformation Model, the Discovery Process provides for systematic exploration of organizational assumptions, values, beliefs, and barriers that are the foundation of the current culture. It is in examining these basic systems of belief that an organization can begin the process for transforming work. Currently, the Passion Transformation Model is being used in a variety of settings to guide leadership development and improve employee morale. In these organizations the Discovering process has helped to disclose barriers and constraints to employee motivation. It is this nexus of organizational nurturing and employee need for sustenance, where the ecological self thrives.

Understanding the barriers to a passionate workplace is only the beginning step. Once dysfunctional assumptions or beliefs are uncovered, leaders must work with their employees to create new or more developed organizational cultures. Working with employees to transform the organization will help to insure that the new workplace is one where the employees can develop and grow.

Because learning is so vital to passionate employees, opportunities for learning must be carefully and systemically integrated into the organizational structure, processes, and procedures. Mentorship programs, adequate training for all job skills, leadership succession, formalized employee feedback, career development, tuition reimbursement and applications such as just-in-time training are but a few ways to help ensure that employees have opportunities for continual learning. Not only must individual learning be accommodated, but also systems for organizational learning must be determined. Annual review of programs, opportunities for dialogue, knowledge preservation, and knowledge management systems are just a few systemic means for enhancing organizational learning.

Summary

In the workplace, the task is to examine our environment and begin the process of deep, transformational change. If we are to foster our learning toward an ecological consciousness, a new conception of interacting and valuing each other is required. Understanding that we exist in fluid systems that are comprised of complex, diverse individuals is critical to examining the underlying assumptions that confine growth. Beginning with a clearer sense of values and mission, the iterative transformational process we developed can facilitate this examination. No longer can we merely change a product, process, or employee to create sustainable change. We must work with the complexity of the system, helping both the employees and the organization realize greater depths of passion and motivation. Providing work that employees can feel passionate about, and an environment where they feel cared for and have built strong interpersonal relationships, will build commitments that are mutually beneficial.

References

Bandura, A. (1977). "Self-Efficacy Mechanism in Human Agency." *American Psychologist* 37, 122–147.

Bolman, L. G. and Terrence E. Deal. (1995). *Leading with Soul: An Uncommon Journey of Spirit*. San Francisco, CA: Jossey-Bass.

Boverie, P. and Kroth, M. (2001). *Transforming Work: The Five Keys to Achieving Trust, Commitment, and Passion in the Workplace*. Cambridge, MA: Perseus Publishing.

Brookfield, S. D. (1990). *The Skillful Teacher*. San Francisco: Jossey-Bass.

Buchanan, M. (2002). *Nexus: Small Worlds and the Groundbreaking Science of Networks*. New York: W. W. Norton and Company.

Csikszentmihalyi, M. (1990). *Flow: The Psychology of Optimal Experience*. New York: Harper Perennial.

Fox, M. (1994). *The Reinvention of Work: A New Vision of Livelihood for Our Time*. San Francisco: Harper.

Fox, W. (1990). *Toward Transpersonal Ecology*. Boston: Shambala Press.

Friere, P. (1970). *Pedagogy of the Oppressed*. New York: Continuum.

Jaffe, D. T. and Scott, C. D. (1988). *Take this Job and Love it: How to Change your Work Without Changing your Job*. New York: Simon and Schuster.

Kast, Fremont E. and Rosenzwig, James E. (1970). *Organization and Management: A Systems and Contingency Approach*. 4th ed. New York: McGraw-Hill, Inc.

Maturana, H. R. and Varela, F. J. (1992). *The Tree of Knowledge: The Biological Roots of Human Understanding*. Boston: Shambhala.

Schein, E. H. (1992). *Organizational Culture and Leadership*. 2nd ed. San Francisco: Jossey-Bass.

Scherer, J. (1993). *Work and the Human Spirit*. Spokane: The Paulsen Center.

Schlossber, N. K., Lynch, A. Q., and Chickering, A. W. (1989). *Improving Higher Education Environments for Adults*. San Francisco: Jossey-Bass Publishers.

Seligman, M. E. (1990). *Learned Optimism: How to Change Your Mind and Your Life*. New York: Pocket Books.

Tennov, D. (1979). *Love and Limerence: The Experience of Being in Love*. New York: Stein and Day.

Waterman, R. H, Jr. (1994). *What America does Right: Learning from Companies that Put People First*. New York: Norton.

Webster's New Collegiate Dictionary. (1979). Springfield, MA: G&C Merriam Company.

Wheatley, M. (1992). *Leadership and the New Science: Discovering Order in a Chaotic World*. San Francisco: Berrett-Koehler Publishers.

PART 3

The Dynamic Relation of Personal Agency in Community Context

Prologue

> The view of nature which predominated in the west down to the
> eve of the Scientific Revolution was that of an enchanted world.
> Rocks, trees, rivers and clouds were all seen as wondrous, alive, and
> beings felt at home in the environment. The cosmos, in short, was
> a place of *belonging*. A member of this cosmos was not an alienated
> observer of but a direct participant in the drama.
>
> Morris Berman, *The Reenchantment of the World* (1981)

As we have suggested in our introductory chapter the development of
the "modernist project" is a world based on an orientation of instrumental rationality and truth as object that is de-contextualized. The
exclusive emphasis on objective knowledge has undermined the role of story
and narrative in knowledge making the place of embodied participation of
story forms problematic. The readings in this section bring to the forefront
themes and practices of embodiment, participation, and narrative as inherent in nurturing an ecological consciousness.

The chapters in this section represent a diversity of starting points
for journeys toward embodiment, integrity, and connection—the ecological
self. However, all begin with adversity and brokenness reminding us that
darkness and difficulty are inherent in the unfolding of the living universe.
All express the profound, emergent understanding that our personal flourishing and the well-being of the wider world are mutually dependent.

To experience life's fullness, it is necessary for us to engage with generosity and compassion in the wider world; caring for our world begins with self-respect and self-compassion.

Yuka Takahashi (chapter 10) illuminates the reciprocity between personal well-being and concern for ecological survival, personal, and social transformation, in her story of personal learning from her committed career as an ecological educator. Hashimoto beautifully presents the inside-out perspective of what Jessica Kovan and John Dirkx describe as the challenges of environmental activists. She traces her own experience through the challenges of making environmental issues matter to youth in Japan, through her work with marginalized children in Thailand and Cambodia, and takes us into the pain of suffering children, poverty, violence, and injustice. She opens to us her moments of hopelessness, anger, and guilt, but also her turning point in being able to reinterpret and reenter her work with hope, courage, and renewed commitment.

Eimear O'Neill's work (chapter 11), framed in a feminist perspective, explores the foundational importance of participatory relational knowledge-making. She develops themes around personal transformation through her community art installation entitled "Holding Flames." The lantern exhibit and each lantern-maker collectively symbolize a community of women knowers integrating the work of active knowledge-makers artistically expressing their own particular journeys of transformation—journeys through what the author calls small "t" and capital "T" trauma. Vividly illustrating artful inquiry with her own experience, the author powerfully expresses the parallel of each of the participant's personal transformation and the larger project of women consciousness in our present historical juncture. O'Neill articulates the current urgent project of transforming of human consciousness toward the participatory and ecological.

Barbara Dewar and Sandra Campbell (chapter 12) examine an emergent practice that has enabled them and other members of Esprit Association to break out of personal limitations and constraints to personal strength, integrity and proactive participation in the wider social world. They trace their journey of embodied learning through an appreciation of vulnerability and the importance of story. Drawing on the thoughts of physicist David Bohm and a constructivist perspective in intersubjective psychotherapy, they explore the depths of dialogical methods and the significance of context in developing "participatory consciousness" and appreciation of difference in a social world. Dewar and Campbell explicate Esprit's extension of their own learning journey including a wider set of relationships through networking on the Internet where personal narratives are shared in a dialogical encounter with numerous participants. In these unique personal encounters through dialogue work on the Internet, sharing of personal stories is seen as a way to add to the context of a larger collective story to enter and deepen ecological consciousness.

Valerie Petrie (chapter 13) describes how her identity as an agent of change was the starting point in the development of what she names a "Way-of-Giving" model that arises out of an ecological consciousness that has as its core element the "gift-giving." In her essay she develops a model of giving in community settings that supports everyday practices of living and giving, which supports and affirms citizens, consultants, volunteers, and family members in community. In an ecological context, she develops the idea of "landscapes-of-giving," which represent distinct economic environments and community networks simultaneously. The chapter encourages the potential that exists to foster a variety of ways of giving that anticipate the deeper orders of awareness and understanding that is involved in the development of ecological consciousness as it enhances community living.

Finally, Merriam Bleyl and Patricia Boverie (Chapter 14) explore the nature and development of "elder wisdom" in the experiences of people from five different cultures. They provide a model called the "Wisdom Ladder" to articulate similarities in the journeys of wise elders and their contributions to their cultures. The stories that are embodied in wise elders are seen as instructive to the larger world of today's complex cultures. They are also suggestive of practices that foster the development of wisdom over a lifetime.

CHAPTER 10

Personal and Social Transformation: A Complementary Process Toward Ecological Consciousness

Yuka Takahashi

> Any recovery of the natural world will require... a conversion experience deep in the psychic structure of the human.
>
> Thomas Berry (1998)

Introduction

As described in chapter 1 of this book, we are at a critical moment in history where we are not only facing ecological and other social crises of an unprecedented scale, but we are also challenging the destructive forces that give rise to these crises and attempting to create new possibilities. All around the world, there are individuals, groups of individuals, and organizations participating in the process of creating ecologically sustainable and just societies.

At the same time, the modern world as it has been configured by instrumental consciousness constrains' us in many ways, including through "the grip of the culture on constituents consciousness" (Chapter 1, p. 5). Thus, even as we participate in the process of seeking new visions and creating the new society, we may find that we carry with us the instrumental consciousness we have internalized.

In this chapter, I will attempt to illuminate the importance of personal transformation to the process of creating new possibilities, drawing on critical reflections of my participation in social transformation, and the insights I have gained from my encounters with people who are engaged in this process. I will also explore what personal transformation entails, the nature of the process, and how it relates to social transformation.

Recovering the Realm of the Personal

I first became fully aware of the importance of personal transformation as a foundation of social transformation while I was working as an environmental educator in a nongovernmental organization (NGO) in Tokyo in the mid-1990s. A popular approach to environmental education at that time in Japan[1] was merely to present facts indicating the seriousness of the ecological crisis—how much of the forest on the planet was lost, the number of species endangered, and so on. This approach often fails to touch and motivate students from within. The emphasis on facts about the symptoms of environmental destruction can give students the notion that environmental issues are something that are "out there" and remote from them. Concerns about environment issues, therefore, tend to be forgotten outside the classroom. Additionally, this approach had a disempowering effect on students by giving them a sense of powerlessness and despair.

An elementary school teacher of my acquaintance shared with me his frustration at attempting to introduce environmental education into the curriculum. He told me that many of his students were exhausted by the competitive mode of schooling, feeling disconnected from the world and from themselves. He said, "These children don't feel that they matter, that they are important. How can they possibly feel that the planet matters?" His dilemma exemplifies the problem faced by environmental education, and more broadly, of any attempts to transform the society that neglects personal and inner transformation. If we are to teach peace, justice, and ecological sustainability, we not only need to teach it, but we must also enable students to hold such values and create them within themselves.

I could relate to this problem on a personal level. My colleagues and I were often so caught up in trying to make changes in the external world that we had little time or energy to nourish and take care of ourselves. We pushed ourselves to the extreme to compensate for the shortage of staff and funding, often sacrificing our personal lives. While trying to convey the appreciation of nature to others, we hardly had time to appreciate the wonders of nature ourselves. At the time of my conversation with the teacher mentioned here, a major construction project that had a devastating effect on the environment was given a final approval in spite of a decade of protest by the activists and community groups that eventually became a nationwide movement in Japan. A sense of futility and burnout enveloped all of us. For self-protection, we had to be "tough" and often suppress our emotions and sense of compassions. Bitter arguments broke out during meetings. Two of my colleagues eventually suffered nervous breakdowns and had to leave work. Another relied on medication to continue.

I became increasingly aware of the gap that existed between my daily practices and what I was advocating. I began to question how I could empower others when I was feeling so disempowered myself. It was evident that I needed to think about the personal empowerment that comes from within, not only to aid my search for better ways to implement environmental education—which is my way of participating in the process of social transformation—but also for my own continuation in that process. Thus began my journey to pursue personal transformation. This led me to eventually leave my work and pursue graduate studies in Canada, where I became acquainted with Edmund O'Sullivan's (1999) earlier works on transformative learning. This provided me with a conceptual framework for my understanding of personal transformation. The journey continued as I took a post for two years in the Asia Pacific regional office of a UN agency located in Bangkok. There, I worked in various countries in the region on projects involving inclusive education and education for a sustainable future.

Personal Transformation as Embedded in the Process of Social Transformation

I learned from Brian Murphy's book, *Transforming Ourselves, Transforming the World* (1999), that the personal disempowerment I felt within the process of social transformation was not unique. Murphy, an activist himself, points out that people who are engaged in social transformation tend to devote little time to the realm of the personal, even though this is the source of our actions and what most affects us. He argues that there is a need "to share our private thoughts, the personal reality that moves us beyond ideals of struggle, or change, or justice, to transformative action" (p. 5).

Yet, the focus on personal transformation may be regarded with certain skepticism within some movements, since ecological and social issues have too often been reduced to mere problems of individual attitudes, behavior, or lifestyles that can be rectified without disturbing the status quo. My argument for personal transformation, however, by no means undermines the importance of the need to critically examine and fundamentally change existing political, economic, and social structures and systems. The personal transformation to which I refer is a process that needs to be embedded in our daily resistance to destructive forces of the modern world. I maintain that such individual personal transformation builds the foundation for our collective, broader social movements. As Erich Fromm (1976) warns us, the political revolution that neglects to change how people think will defeat its own purpose as revolution since the new sociopolitical institution will recreate the conditions of the old society.[2]

In the following section, I will explore the four major aspects of the personal transformation that are embedded in our daily struggle for social transformation. I will illustrate how such personal transformation motivates us to participate in social transformation, and further guides, sustains, and empowers us in our participation.

The Process of Personal Transformation

Movement Beyond Modernist Worldview

One of the major tasks of personal transformation is to break free and challenge the modern instrumental consciousness that creates destructive forces. This task requires what O'Sullivan calls *critique*, becoming aware of the "ontology that underlies our current discourse and recognize(ing) our immersion in it" (Introduction, p. 3).

Some of the characteristics of the modern industrial society important to this and the following discussion (Bohm, 1976; Capra, 1982; R. Miller, 1991; Durning, 1992; Alley et al., 1995; Mies and Bennholdt-Thomsen, 1999) are:

(1) belief in limitless material growth;
(2) success and happiness seen as the acquisition of material wealth as well as achievement of "higher" social status;
(3) human beings seen as primarily economic beings whose purpose is to produce and to consume;
(4) society seen as a competitive marketplace;
(5) mechanistic, atomistic view of the universe that gives rise to fragmented thinking;
(6) divisions between people, family, profession, nation, race, gender, and religion seen as overriding our common humanity;
(7) nature seen as having only instrumental value, a resource to be exploited;
(8) patriarchal views and principles;
(9) dualistic view of mind/body, mind/spirit, reason/emotion, reason/intuition with mind, and reason valued over other.

As exemplified by the gap between my own visions and practices, it seems we do internalize the modern consciousness even as we participate in the process of transformation. We need to continue to critically reflect on the values that we hold, our ways of living, and how we engage in the process of social transformation to ensure that we do not replicate the very consciousness and the systems we are challenging.

The critical questioning of our world and of ourselves is the starting point in participation toward social transformation. At the same time, this process can also generate a sense of guilt as we begin to see more clearly the modern consciousness that is internalized within us and in our way of life, and its consequences. To a certain extent, this is a natural part of the process, but being guided by guilt in our participation toward social transformation is both disempowering and misguided. Social transformation is not about suppressing our own personal needs or happiness for a greater goal. That perception of social transformation is based on a juxtaposition of our personal happiness with the well-being of the larger world and is, therefore, also an off-shoot of the modern consciousness.

One of the underlying beliefs of the modern world that we need to challenge and move beyond is the myth of personal happiness—that the continuation and expansion of the industrial economy will eventually lead to material wealth for the majority of the people, and will thus ensure our personal well-being and happiness. Everyday, we are exposed to commercial messages that define happiness in terms of material goods. If we accept this myth, efforts to fundamentally challenge current socioeconomic structures would be seen as contradictory to the pursuit our personal happiness.

This myth is doubly faulty. First, as seen in chapter 1 of this book, the growth of the economy has resulted in material gains for only a very small percentage of the world's population. The vastly larger percentage has seen their living situation worsen. The failure of the industrial economy to provide material wealth for all is not, as popularly believed, due to insufficient growth or individual failures. Maria Mies (1998; Mies and Bennholdt-Thomsen, 1999) contends that exploitation of marginalized people (the majority of the world's population) and nature is the precondition of the industrial economy. For example, accumulation of the huge profits of transnational corporations are based on the exploitation of people (primarily women) working in Export Processing Zones[3] (EPZs or maquiladoras) in the Third World who provide cheap labor under unsafe and unhealthy working conditions. Even this employment is not long-term as factories move into other countries in search of even cheaper labor. Meanwhile, in overdeveloped countries, "jobless growth" has become a normal phenomenon (Mies and Benholdt-Thomsen, 1999, p. 48).

Second, even if material wealth for all was achievable, research shows that there is no obvious relationship between material wealth and perceived personal happiness. Despite near-doubling of both the GNP and personal consumption expenditures per capita since 1957 in the United States, the number of Americans who report that they are "very happy" has not increased (Durning, 1992). There are also few differences in the levels of reported happiness between citizens of affluent and very "poor" countries (Argyle, 1987). Alan Durning and Michael Argyle both conclude that conditions of happiness do not depend much on wealth or the material conditions of life. Durning (1992) states:

> ... to the contrary, life's most meaningful and pleasant activities are often paragons of environmental virtue. The preponderance of things that people name as their most rewarding pastimes—and interestingly, the things terminally ill individuals choose to do with their remaining months—are infinitely sustainable. Religious practices, conversation, family and community gatherings, theater, music, dance, literature, sports, poetry, artistic and creative pursuits, education, and appreciation of nature all fit readily into a culture of permanence—a way of life that can endure through countless generations. (p. 138)

It is ironic and outrageous, then, that our personal happiness is used as a justification to support the modern industrial economy, which in fact is destroying the very things—including nature, health,[4] communities—that are truly meaningful to us. Yet, trapped in the modern worldview as we are, most of us have not questioned ourselves as to what really makes us happy and what is truly meaningful in our life. As Fromm (1941) astutely observed more than fifty years ago, "modern man [sic] lives under the illusion that he knows what he wants, while he actually wants what he is supposed to want" (p. 252).

In breaking free from this myth of happiness, we see the process of social transformation for what it is. It is not a process through which we suppress or sacrifice our personal needs and happiness. It is a process through which we seek happiness, albeit at a deeper level.

Awakening Our Whole Persons

As discussed in the chapter 1, the modern world impedes us from developing our authentic selves. In particular, a strong rationalistic dualism underlies our modern societies where what is regarded as belonging to the realm of reason is separated from and seen as superior to that of the realm of "nonrational." We are conditioned to suppress the latter that includes the sense of wonder, the sense of the sacred, emotion, intuition, the body's ways of knowing, and life-sustaining values such as care and respect. Some eco-feminists (Plumwood, 1998; Warren, 1998) have pointed out such rationalistic dualism forms the justification for various forms of oppression, including the domination of nature, of women, and of ethnic minorities.

The process of challenging various forms of oppression and creating new visions for society is also a process of reaffirming life-sustaining values and awakening our whole person. Thomas Berry (1998) writes: "The entire earth is a gorgeous celebration of existence in all its forms. Each living thing participates in the celebration as the proper fulfillment of its powers of expression" (p. 187). Often social transformation is regarded as a sombre and solemn process. Nevertheless, as discussed earlier, it ought to be about the pursuit of deep happiness—it is the celebration of our existence.

It is significant that many who have long been engaged in the process of transformation seem to embrace a deep-rooted joy of life, this celebration of existence. Murphy (1999) recalls his experience of drowning in despair in war-torn El Salvador. An old woman in a settlement for displaced people told him to enjoy life for they did not need his sorrow, but rather, wanted to share his joy. Murphy calls the insight he gained from this woman a "gift of life." In spite of the horrors and atrocities, the flame of deep joy can burn within, encouraging us and sustaining us through hardships.

I also received this "gift of life" from the people with whom I worked when I was engaged in educational projects for marginalized children in the Asian region with one of the UN agencies. The director of nonformal education in Thailand once told me that to be a nonformal educator one must be able to sing, dance, and tell jokes. Indeed, I saw how songs, music, drama, and other forms of art, and sometimes even just "talking and laughing" became such a powerful media in learning for social transformation. Many of the nonformal educators/activists, in spite of the hardships they were facing, had the amazing knack of celebrating the joy of life with their whole beings. When I joined them in their singing, dancing, and laughing, I felt whole and alive, and I learned the joy of living.

Reconnecting ourselves with the natural world also helps us to awaken our senses and our sense of wonder. However, mere physical presence in nature is not sufficient. Once, I took a group of children from an urban area for a walk through a magnificent primary forest on one of the islands of Japan. Later, I asked the children to describe what they heard as we went through the forest. "Nothing," and "It was just quiet there," were the kind of replies I received. I realized that even as we walked through the forest, the children had hardly been taken in their surroundings, immersed in talking and playing games with one another. They had remained closed and separated from the rest of nature. Next time, before the walk, I handed them a "letter from the forest," inviting the children to come and listen to the "concert" performed by nature. In the forest, we each found our special "seat" and sat down to listen to the music of nature. This time, the children heard and enjoyed the sounds of tree leaves rustling, the far-off rumbling of the waves, and the songs of insects. This experience made me realize that conscious engagement is sometimes required in order to awaken ourselves. Even after realizing how closed and fragmented I was becoming during my hectic time working for an NGO in Japan, it also took me some time before I was able to "open" myself. John Miller (1988) suggests that awareness of movement, what he calls "mindfulness" (p. 92), helps us reconnect our mind and body. I began meditation, dance, and taiko (Japanese drum—a very spiritual instrument) and found these activities very helpful in opening, reconnecting, and centering myself.

Reconnecting Ourselves with the Rest of the World

As O'Sullivan points out in chapter 1, in the modern world configured by instrumental consciousness, we become isolated and alienated from the rest of the world thereby "fostering the minimal self." O'Sullivan argues that for the creation of the new possibilities we need to reaffirm our connection with the world that includes, but is not only limited to, the rest of the human community. "We are creatures of the wider earth community and the very universe itself" (p. 13). The relationships discussed here are qualitatively different from the ones based on the instrumental consciousness that prevails in this world. Recovery of our connection with the rest of the universe entails full recognition of each others' inherent worth, including that of ourselves.

Affirmation of our relationship with the world affects the way we approach social transformation. For example, our commitment to the well-being of the environment shifts from mere "protection of our natural resources" to a more ecocentric approach of caring about the environment for its own inherent value. Similarly, we begin to see environmental and other social issues not as something external to us, but about us. Actions that we take to address these issues are for ourselves.

Engaging in transformation to move beyond our minimal self to recover our connection with the world is also essential to building up worldwide movements to create new possibilities. There are unfortunate examples where the emergence of oppressive hierarchies and practices, distrust, internal disputes, and human-chauvinistic behaviors posed barriers to the realization of common goals.

The movements that involve people reaching across differences to form solidarity for the creation of just, caring, and life-sustaining societies in turn create space and opportunities for us to directly and indirectly connect with others and form noninstrumental relationships. Connecting with the people who are working for the same goals, sharing concerns and frustrations, but more importantly, hopes and visions, is one of the major sources of empowerment that sustain us as we participate in the process of social transformation.

Affirmation of Ourselves in the Process of Social Transformation

One of the major impediments to the realization of our visions for society is the feeling of powerlessness and despair, which engulfs and immobilizes individuals. As we engage in the process of personal transformation, paradoxically, we can also become vulnerable to despair, for awakening our whole person on the one hand allow us to recover our connections, but on the other it also opens us up to the pain that we had been suppressing. Therefore, the process of reaffirming ourselves in our deep connection to the rest of the universe becomes an important part of personal transformation and social transformation.

As mentioned earlier, I began to engage in the same practices to recover my whole person while I was in Canada. I continued similar practices when I later went to Bangkok. Nevertheless, there came a time when opening up myself became too painful to continue. One part of my job involved monitoring the primary schools for the inclusion (or, more to the point, the exclusion) of disabled and other marginalized children (those affected by HIV/AIDS or those living on the streets). My involvement extended to other areas of these children's lives and, although intellectually I knew about the plight of these children, it was extremely painful to actually experience the harsh realities of their existence. I became deeply depressed as I witnessed more and more of their hardships.

The peak of my despair came following my visit to Phnom Penh, Cambodia. There, I encountered many children who had become blind due to the lack of vitamins in their diet. I could not help but think of the food we take for granted and the vitamin pills in the cupboard of my house that could have prevented the blindness of these children. I tried to imagine what life must be like for these children. Some of Phnom Penh's unpaved roads with their holes and bumps were hard for me to walk on with my vision. But, at least, the roads were free of the numerous land mines still scattered throughout that country.

In one of the boarding schools run by a Christian organization on the outskirts of Phnom Penh, I met a young girl who had been rescued from a human trafficking operation. She had been sold and smuggled to Bangkok where she was forced to beg on the streets. Her face and body were disfigured from the acid poured over her so that she would attract more pity and make more money by the gang who "owned" her. She smiled shyly at me, her face contorting from the effort. Even the small boarding school that had become her haven had recently been attacked by a group of soldiers intent on raping the girls within. The danger is always present for these vulnerable girls.

After this trip to Cambodia all I could think about was the needless suffering I had witnessed. I could not make sense of it. Was this human nature? Was there really any meaning in the universe after all? My faith in the innate goodness of people and my hope for a better future was ebbing away. I was consumed by the anger I felt toward the extent of inequity and injustice in the world, my sense of helplessness, and the guilt of knowing that I benefited from the privilege generated from that very oppressive system. I struggled not to numb the pain by building walls around myself. During this time I could not engage in the practices that helped me to center myself in Canada. I was unable to sit still and meditate because in doing so I risked opening myself up to the images of all the suffering that I had seen.

What lifted me out of this dark hole was my encounter with some people in Dhaka, Bangladesh, which I visited two months later. During a workshop, one of the participants invited me to her school. This school, a nonformal institution for children living in the slums, was run by an NGO. At the time of my visit, the funding had been suspended for this NGO because of a scandal involving its director.[5] The school was being run by the teachers who were working without pay in order to continue educating the children. I was impressed by the innovative programs run in this modest wooden building with its damp dirt floor, the only source of light coming from a small window. The students were engaged in their learning with obvious enjoyment and enthusiasm. I read some of their writings that had been translated into English. In one, a little boy described how he and his sister had come across a man the boy described as being "like a child even though he was old." The man had no home so the boy and his sister took him home. Their parents gave him some food, and from that day, the man lived with this family and became one of them. The boy liked this man very much and they played and sang together. But one day, the old man wandered off. The boy wrote that his family was very sad and worried about the man. I was deeply moved by this writing. How many families in "rich" countries would share their home and food with a man from the street?

Many other writings showed similar love and care directed toward their families, friends, and others. These children were not oblivious to the harsh realities of the world—the writings displayed a remarkable understanding of how the world worked—the divide between rich and poor, and how the affluence of the rest of the world resulted in their oppression. Although these writings showed some resentment about their condition, far stronger was their spirit of resilience against adversity and their deep compassion for others.

The teachers and the children in this school taught me to see marginalized people not as the victims of social injustice, but as individuals who are in the process of social transformation. Where before I had seen only despair, now I saw hope, courage, and resistance. This shift in my perspective, in turn, allowed me to focus on the potential within myself and in all others as well.

During the two years I worked in the Asian region, I saw some of humanity's worst aspects, but also some of the best. The best were not great acts of leaders of social transformation, as I might have once expected, but rather glimpses of the unconquerable human spirit of people in their everyday existence. I still come across these "best" aspects of humanity and it is these occasions that give me the impetus to participate in the "momentous project of reversing the destructive trends of across our world" (Introduction, p. 12).

Personal and Social Transformation

As seen in the previous section, the four major aspects of personal transformation—movement beyond modernist worldview; awakening our whole persons; reconnecting ourselves with the rest of the world; and affirmation of ourselves in the process of social transformation—are interrelated and mutually reinforce one another. Together, these interrelated elements create a process through which individuals move beyond their minimal self to embrace "ecological consciousness."

This personal transformation is a process by which individuals challenge the modern consciousness and create new possibilities within them, and in their everyday lives, including their participation in broader social movements. The values and visions embraced by these individuals will be reflected in, and eventually shape the direction of, the process of social transformation. At the same time, it is through participation in the process of social transformation that personal transformation is able to unfold. Our personal transformation, in many ways, is constrained by the existing systems and structures of modern society. Although we negotiate and change external conditions at the personal level, the changes in the systems that are achieved through social transformation will create a much more conducive environment for personal transformation. Thus, personal transformation and social transformation are inseparable and complementary parts of the whole. As we move toward ecological consciousness, we develop a notion of self where "the self is the world, and the world is self" (O'Sullivan, 1999). From this selfhood the divide between social and personal transformation becomes false: personal transformation is social transformation, and social transformation is personal transformation.

The Journey Toward Personal Transformation: A Work in Progress

My journey toward personal transformation has taught me to celebrate the joy of life. It has given me hope, and strengthened my commitment to the process of reversing the destructive forces and creating new possibilities. I now see my participation in the process of social transformation as a process of affirmation of both my own self and of the world to which I am deeply connected.

At the same time, my process of personal transformation is very much still a work in progress. As external situations—ranging from my personal relationships to wider movements in society—fluctuate, I continuously seek to maintain and further develop my connection to the world, life-sustaining values, hope, and strength in everyday life. The meditative practices in which I engage help give me awareness of my current state and conditions, and to make adjustments I listen to my inner voice that tells me when I am going too quickly, or when I am losing my perspective. There are times, however, when I do lose my balance and stumble (and sometimes crash!), but I have been able to pick myself up and carry on.

I am beginning to suspect that I am engaged in a never-ending journey, that I must continuously strive to nurture, further develop, and translate in my everyday life, the perspectives I have gained. In fact, perhaps it is the constant engagement required in this process that leads me to healthy questioning of myself, my practices, and of broader movements. I also believe it is the constant challenge that makes me fully appreciate those wonderful moments when I am able to experience, not just conceptually understand, my deep connection to the rest of a world that is full of possibilities.

Notes

1. Today, a broader range of environmental education is more commonly practiced in Japan, including that which gives more focus on empowerment from within.

2. On the other hand, Fromm (1976) also points out, "purely physical change has always remained in the private sphere and been restricted to small oases, or has been completely ineffective when the preaching of spiritual values was combined with the practice of the opposite values" (p. 134). His observations adds to the argument of this paper, that we need both social and personal transformation that mutually complement each other and are, actually, parts of the whole.

3. For detailed accounts on the exploitation of women in EPZ, see Runyan (1996).

4. For accounts of the health hazards caused by the activities of the modern industrial economy see "Close to home: Women Reconnect Ecology, Health Development" edited by Vandana Shiva (1994).

5. I am happy to report that the management of the NGO that runs the school has been replaced and funding has been restored. Recognition of the quality of the education being provided by the teachers in this school contributed to the decision to restore funding.

References

Alley, K., Bailey, C., Faupel, C., and Solheim, C. (1995). "Environmental Justice and the Professional." In B. Brayant (Ed.), *Environmental Justice: Issues, Policies and Solutions* (pp. 35–44). Washington, D.C.: Island Press.

Argyle, M. (1987). *The Psychology of Happiness*. London: Methuen.

Berry, T. (1998). "The Viable Human." In M. Zimmerman, J. Baird Callicott, G. Sessions, K. Warren, and J. Clark (Eds.), *Environmental Philosophy* (2nd ed.) (pp. 183–192). New Jersey: Prentice-Hall.

Bohm, D. (1976). *Fragmentation and Wholeness*. Jerusalem: Van Leer Jerusalem Foundation.

Capra, F. (1982). *The Turning Point: Science, Society, and the Rising Culture*. New York: Simon and Schuster.

Durning, A. T. (1992). *How Much is Enough?: The Consumer Society and the Future of the Earth* (1st ed.). New York: Norton.

Fromm, E. (1941). *Escape from Freedom*. New York: Toronto: Farrar & Rinehart.

Fromm, E. (1976). *To Have or to Be?* (1st ed.). New York: Harper & Row.

Mies, M. (1998). *Patriarchy and Accumulation on a World Scale: Women in the International Division of Labour* (New ed.). London: Zed.

Mies, M., and Bennholdt-Thomsen, V. (1999). *The Subsistence Perspective: Beyond the Globalized Economy*. Victoria, Australia: Spinifex Press.

Miller, J. (1988). *The Holistic Curriculum*. Toronto: OISE Press.

Miller, R. (1991). *New Directions in Education: Selections from Holistic Education Review*. Brandon, Vt.: Holistic Education Press.

Murphy, B. K. (1999). *Transforming Ourselves, Transforming the World: An Open Conspiracy for Social Change*. Ottawa: Inter Pares.

O'Sullivan, E. (1999). *Transformative Learning: Educational Vision for the 21st Century*. Toronto: University of Toronto Press.

Plumwood, V. (1998). "Nature, Self and Gender: Feminism, Environmental Philosophy, and the Critique of Rationalism." In M. Zimmerman, J. B. Callicott, G. Sessions, K. Warren, and J. Clark (Eds.), *Environmental Philosophy: From Animal Rights to Radical Ecology* (2nd ed.) (pp. 291–314). New Jersey: Prentice-Hall.

Runyan, A. S. (1996). "The Places of Women in Trading Places: Gendered Global/Regional Regimes and Inter-nationalized Feminist Resistance." In E. Kofman and G. Young (Eds.), *Globalization: Theory and Practice.* New York: Pinter.

Shiva, V. (1994). *Close to Home: Women Reconnect Ecology, Health and Development.* London: Earthscan Publications Ltd.

Warren, K. (1998). "The Power and the Promise of Ecological Feminism." In M. Zimmerman, J. B. Callicott, G. Sessions, K. Warren, and J. Clark (Eds.), *Environmental Philosophy: From Animal Rights to Radical Ecology* (2nd ed.) (pp. 325–344). New Jersey: Prentice Hall.

CHAPTER 11

Holding Flames: Women Illuminating Knowledge of s/Self-Transformation

Eimear O'Neill

Art
Reveals heart
Goes under head
To what matters

A Dream: Sparks into Flames

In January 2000, I was still struggling with a densely and painfully written dissertation in clinical psychology on what women found transformative in the psychotherapy process, when I dreamt that the exposed brick wall of my verandah-sized therapy office was hung with many tiny hearth-places. These firelit miniature openings were humming with vivid moving figures. I knew I was looking into the lives of the women I work with, the chattering "community in my head" of clients, colleagues, and women friends whose experiences shape my own awareness and, through my daily praxis, each other's.

I had already begun to reconceptualize therapy as a form of transformative learning when a week later, in my local supermarket, wooden box lanterns with cutout images of seasonal renewal, butterflies, flowers, bunnies, frogs, and dragonflies, caught my eye. I bought 30 on the tacit recognition that I had found small installation spaces reminiscent of the hundreds of hearth-places in my dream. I put a few different lanterns on the shelves in my office. When several clients said they might like to "do something" with them, the idea emerged of asking anyone who wished to use them to capture some immediate sense of their own journey of self-transformation.

From that intuitive spark emerged the community art installation, "Holding Flames," at the core of my research on women's knowledge of the participatory nature of s/Self-transformation.[1] "Holding Flames" is both the title of the installation and of the larger project. Fire carries the complexity of transformational dynamics, being both life-giving and consuming. Flame is the symbol, the heuristic, used by many wisdom traditions and by general systems theory to capture "the way an open system, like ourselves, consumes the matter that passes through it, burning it, so metaphorically does it process information ever breaking down and building up again, renewed" (Macy, 1991, p. 28). "Holding Flames" also describes the deep psychotherapeutic and alchemical process of staying with disconnected painful experiences long enough to have them reintegrated into the broader contexts of our current understandings.

The focus of this chapter being the praxis of artful inquiry, the process of the lantern project as a whole is discussed briefly. The installation contains pieces from women (colleagues, friends, and fellow students as well as clients) all of whom self identify as having undergone personal transformation (see figure 11.1). It also includes a lantern holding core aspects of my own transformation. The story of my own lantern is used to exemplify the processes through which artful inquiry raises participatory consciousness.

Figure 11.1 Holding Flames.

The call to participate in the project was posted broadly. Emphasis was made on the invitation that the pieces were not so much about making art as about making something truly reflective of each woman's own transformative journey. The only limitations put on what participants might do with the wooden box base supplied were that the finished pieces be less than three cubic feet in area and safely usable as lanterns. Both these stipulations were related to the stated intention to display the gathered pieces publicly in a community accessible space. Group display was the only way, given individual confidentiality, that lanterns could be shared with each other and the community at large rather than remaining somehow the "property" of the researcher. Participants were encouraged not to include obviously identifying information on the lanterns. Every lantern handed in was displayed. Artist statements were optional. I did not provide an artist's statement, nor was my lantern privileged in placement within the display. Lanterns were made privately, in each participant's own space and time, within the four-month limit. As the artist statements indicate, the process of making the lanterns was in itself transformative for many.

In the end, all participants made themselves known to me over the course of four displays. I was in turn forthright with known participants about which lantern was mine, without comment on its significance. Because they chose to reveal themselves and their lanterns to me, it was possible to get some sense of the diversity of the women involved. The women participating range in age from their early twenties to their late sixties. They are mainly white women, though not all North American; some are European. There is racial and ethnic diversity echoing that of Toronto's population, that is, at least 30 percent were women outside of the dominant culture. Indigenous women, women from Africa, the Caribbean, and Latin America participated. Most of the women were educated (postsecondary school), and clearly self-reflective. However, participants varied widely in terms of class and privilege. Some are reliant on student loans, mothers' allowance and welfare, others on earned and even on inherited wealth. They are from a wide variety of spiritual traditions, Native, Buddhist, Jewish, Eck, Muslim, and Pagan, to mention a few other than Christian. Several of the women had disabilities, mostly invisible, for example arthritis, heart conditions, cancer, and fibromyalgia. There were women from a continuum of sexual identifications. Although a few participants are professional artists, the majority range in artistic experience from previous inactivity to lively arts engagement. Almost all had participated in some form of therapy. Others had participated in spiritual retreats or less Eurocentric forms of transformation such as work with native elders or mindfulness training. All had sought some process of personal transformation in relationship with another.

When the installation was complete, there was a sense of community, of separate forms in relationship to each other in ways where no one stands out and each is distinctive, a sense of the particular linked by unseen connections that comes through even in the photographs. Apart from the extraordinary diversity of response to a similar box shape, what was evident as soon as the lanterns began to come in was that each required some honoring of its own place. Not all could be hung. Some needed careful balancing or a larger base area than others. The idea of making a double-hinged, flexible wooden screen to both hold them all in community and to give each its own pedestal or hanger, emerged intuitively just prior to the first spring Solstice showing. This timing of the first exhibit was deliberate, echoing our earth connection in cycles of transformation. I drew a flames template for the top of the screen to have it "hold flames" in real and symbolic ways. Like the human embodied self, all materials are biodegradable or recyclable. Sanded and shaped coat hangers in unique forms hold lanterns in tension away from the flammable screen. The supports were ready-made post toppers and variable sized logs from a local garden center. Some of the participants (over 100 colleagues, family, and friends) who came to the opening ceremony tucked spring flowers around the base and spontaneously contributed songs, music, poetry, and blessings. Together, the lanterns give some sense of the embodied presence, creative diversity, and many places from which each and all of us, as a community of knowers and members of earth community, understand the personal transformation needed for human change.

In Touch with Creation: Participatory Consciousness and Artful Inquiry

Artful inquiry generates and exemplifies a deeply relational and participatory worldview. "A participatory worldview allows us as human persons to know that we are a part of the whole rather than separated as mind over and against matter, or placed here in the relatively separate creation of a transcendent god" (Heron and Reason, 1997, p. 275). As such, a participatory worldview "places us back in relation with a living world—and we note that to be in relation means that we live with the rest of creation as relatives, with all the rights and obligations that implies" (Heron and Reason, 1997, p. 276). Thus, in psychotherapy, in artful inquiry, and in daily living, I see an ethical stance and practice of respect for all earth-connected life as the basis for a participatory way of knowing. Given its multi-centricity, such a worldview includes a sense of knowing we can never fully know, or rather that we can know only from the depths of our own embodied contextualized experience.

Inclusion of others' knowledge in their capacity for ecological self-regulation expands what we know. It is such respect as an embodied practice that then enables the world and other beings to make themselves known to the seeker (Cheney, 2002). For psychotherapy, recovering participatory consciousness implies respectful attention to the embodied spirit in each and attention to connections and disconnections within the whole at multiple levels, whole person, whole community, whole earth.

This sense of mattering in the larger arc of the cosmos, this knowing that we are all participant, active and responsible in shaping the world, is our source of meaning. Despite his exclusionary language, Albert Einstein (1949) captures the problematic and the path toward recovery of this denied deeply relational awareness:

> A human being is a part of the whole called by us "the universe," a part limited in time and space. He experiences himself, his thoughts and feelings as something separate from the rest, a kind of optical delusion of consciousness. This delusion is a kind of prison for us, restricting us to our personal desires and affections for a few persons nearest to us. Our task must be to free ourselves from this prison by widening the circle of understanding and compassion to embrace all living creatures and the whole of nature in its beauty. (p. 125)

To feel compassion for all that lives and to be reconnected to the whole of the natural world in all its aesthetic and erotic wildness is more than reconnecting with the collective unconscious. Participatory consciousness encompasses our conscious lived awareness of our particular place and moment in the cosmological web of life at multiple levels in continuum with our embodied unconscious. It necessarily moves us toward emancipatory compassion for wholeness in the natural world, in others, and in the self.

When the lantern installation, and each of the lantern-makers, are seen within this participatory paradigm, we can see "Holding Flames" as the representations of a community of women knowledge-makers showing something of what matters in their own particular journeys of transformation. These pieces are artful representations of each women's embodied, placed, and political transformation. Given that women's consciousness is core to the current urgent project of transforming of human consciousness toward the participatory and ecological, they offer much to shift traditional processes of consciousness-raising (Tarnas, 1991; Goodman, 2003). For example, even in responding to the strictures of the box form, the lantern-makers reveal the paradox of containment in therapy and in systems of oppression. This limitation provided "a small enough space to be safe and non-threatening for self expression" and "the opportunity to burn up the box and, put the ashes in a jar and keep only what is useful, the handle," to quote two co-participants.

The fullness of symbolic, reflective, imaginal, developmental, critical, and thematic learnings from the lanterns can only be hinted at in this piece. Even in the larger project, what one will have is one lantern-maker's account of her involvement in the lantern installation, though admittedly I am the one who has the privilege and responsibility to hold the pieces to be put together. Imagine, as you read this, the very different, vivid, and telling stories of each of the other lantern-makers. Some glimpses of these can be found in another lantern-maker's words, "At meaningful thresholds of my life, 'I' am not the box/body/mass at all, it is just a doorway, an entrance, an end trance."

Making Shadows Visible

In the lantern project, there are representations of what is self-disruptive, that is, of what these women are transforming from as well as toward. What the participatory worldview developed here suggests is that these are Self as well as self-transformative journeys. The personal self resonates with what is happening at collective and transpersonal levels. Just as multiple-nested contexts of family, community, peoples, lands, and Earth shape our personal self, we in turn co-constitute them within fragile ecological systems of change. One's personal dynamics resonate with those of one's multiple nested contexts. Hence trauma at the level of Earth's biosphere shapes the human personal embodied self and vice versa.

In the lanterns there are signs of what I would term big "T" trauma, that is, of the wounds caused by specific events of violation in situations that are inescapable and those that overwhelm one's usual resilience. There are also signs of the insidious daily small collective "t" traumas of racism, colonization, anti-Semitism, or misogyny such as the violent repression of women's sexuality or cultural expectations around women's body image. There is an image of a Gulf War tank with blood on its tracks, broken children's alphabet pieces, a gun shell, Earth sundered, a woman's naked body tied to a clock face, the words "slut," "Bill C31" (also known as the Indian Act). There are many hints of trauma that are both individual and collective. Thus the removal and abuse of a whole generation of aboriginal children in the name of education under colonization, has particular personal and intergenerational effects as one lantern shows. Child abuse is intimated on many. Trauma at the public level, like the Gulf Wars and September 11, 2001 terrorist attack, leads to and resonates with other personal and community traumas as we will see in more detail when exploring my own lantern. To paraphrase Carl Jung (1961), the issue here in terms of self-transformation is to make the shadows visible and not to naively believe we can remove them.

Other researchers indicate what tends to initiate lantern-makers' movement toward self-transformation, toward seeing those shadows, and the effects on their lives. These include wanting to matter where continually devalued, feeling support and connection after isolation, and beginning to experience one's capabilities or creativities in situations such as returning to school (Ettling, 2000). Issues of children's safety, community unrest, oppression and internalized oppression, recovery from violence, and addictions also spark change (Ettling, 2000).

The lanterns suggest that whatever the impetus, the transformative movement is emancipatory and toward the more participatory or deeply relational. The boxes are broken apart, cut open, built over, climbed out of, burnt to ashes, transformed into a garden. They weave personal, community, social, and planetary disruption as they integrate personal and community transformation and healing.

How Women's Artful Inquiry Illuminates s/Self Consciousness

Art, and artful inquiry, is more than a way of knowing. Berthold Brecht's metaphor that "art is not a mirror of reality but a hammer with which to shape it" speaks to the expository and shaping power of art. Art reveals to others and to ourselves something of each human being's sense of their lifeworld, some manifest expression of their distinctive experience and perspective on the participatory continuum of consciousness and unconsciousness. As Rosie McLaren (2001) states, art "uses structural expression to give felt meaning to lived experience."

Public showings of women's art are a powerful active challenge to dominant epistemologies that privilege certain forms and makers of knowledge. Seen in community, women's artful inquiry increases epistemological equity personally and culturally. Women expressing nondiscursive experience in artistic forms provide a collective experience of great power, an ontological ground zero that is not just socially constituted but embodied, sensory, geographically placed. Art is a potentially emancipatory alternative to formal accepted epistemologies, subverting man-made language and established patriarchal and imperialistic academic traditions. It opens up shared space and voice for those marginalized. bell hooks (1995), writing on black women's personal and political transformation through art, comments; "It occurred to me that if one could make a people lose touch with their capacity to create, lose sight of their will and their power to make art, then the work of subjugation, of colonization, is complete. Such work can be undone only by concrete acts of reclamation" (p. xv). It is not coincidence that artful expression is active in social justice, revolutionary, and liberation movements and that popular education and participatory action research value theater, cartooning, and community art projects. Art counters the kind of epistemological violence that values only certain kinds of knowledge. It opens up the possibility of a more inclusive knowledge-making community, one that can include those traumatized, for example. For women and children, this is important, given their over-representation amongst those abused, violated, displaced, and dominated.

Mary Ann O'Connor (1999) suggests that women's creativity does not fit with the autonomous suffering "genius" standing outside the culture, the solo, generally male, model of Western cultures; that women's creativity is indeed more participatory, culturally embedded and contextualized, and an important avenue for self-differentiation within attachments. Like Lynn Margolis and Dorion Sagan, she sees the link between creativity and cooperation and that all creativity, like creative evolution in the natural world, is built on cooperative rather than competing dynamics (O'Connor, 1999; Margolis and Sagan, 2001). As Audre Lorde (1984) suggests, the significance of creative expression, is its importance as "a source of power and information within our lives that arises from our deepest and non-rational knowledge, which offers a well of replenishing and provocative force to the woman who does not fear its revelation, nor succumb to the belief that sensation is enough." O'Connor (1999) echoes my own belief and that of other feminist therapists that cutting off creative expression is linked to "silencing the self" and depression in women (Jacks, 1991), and that regular practice of creative expression is an effective way to gain self-empathy and empathy for others. We are mutually constituting. Creative expression enables us to become more aware of the sensory, emotional, and imaginative as well as the rational aspects of that reciprocal process.

Early experiences, those before or beyond words, are often revealed through art. In the lantern project, we can see many children peering through the lanterns, enticing the child in the observer. Small crayon-colored pets, reversed alphabet letters, teddy bear beads found strung across cribs are glimpsed as we look at the pieces. When the lanterns are lit, there is a numinescent appeal. One viewer writing in the guest book comments, All of the lights remind me of my childhood visits to the side altar of St. Vincent's church where a light in front of the Baby Jesus statue drew me. I brought my child to this place. I sense the lanterns are a space for the "sacred child."

Words seldom convey what a child knows. Early childhood learning is sensory and multimodal. According to researchers like Daniel Stern (1985), children experience themselves not as merged but as distinctly themselves in their own sensory rhythms and intensities within the whole, as a self always in relation. With schooling into predominantly verbal/scientific/mathematical knowing and cultural models of identity, that multimodal childhood knowing is split, fragmented, made less whole. In the case of early childhood trauma, what was inexpressible can be unearthed by art. In her book, *Banished Knowledge*, psychoanalyst Alice Miller (1990) writes of the dramatic effects of art therapy in releasing what was for her personally unspeakable about her own childhood experiences even after two full analyses.

The processes of art-making and of artful inquiry thus enrich and enliven therapy. They "go under," even subvert, the binary and dichotimized nature of most Western meaning-making structures. The arts are integrative, not only in honoring body–mind–spirit relationships, but also by being transdisciplinary in their creation, presentation, and embodied content. Artful expression, in paintings, poetry, dance, or theatre, can allow for contradiction and paradox to be held together without collapsing into reductionism. When what is being expressed are aspects of the personal or collective self, the arts can be more fully representative of the self's complexities and layers. The swirling currents and flows of the interpersonal world can be seen by the art-maker herself. As one lantern-maker states; "I see myself in a steel box that while protecting me from vulnerability also stopped me from feeling or reaching out. I began with the help of a therapist, to open up little doors into myself and out of the steel box."

The process of art-making requires us to slow down and pay attention in the moment. Like mindfulness or meditation, it can be a way to bring the expressive embodied self more fully into the now. It necessitates attention and interaction with what is actually there, not with what one wishes was there. What is "there" is neither inside nor outside the skin-bounded self but liminal to both. With less linear representation, what is "there" artfully is less caught in time or space. What is there includes one's materials and context, one's personal embodied history, and one's expressive imagination in the moment. Thus, in the lantern project, what we made was shaped to some degree by the strength required to cut through the compressed layers of the plywood forming the original box—shaped by the "box" of our own perceptions. The very process of the moment could transform the meaning of the piece. For example, the glass jar used to exemplify one lantern-maker's personal transformation, contained the ashes of the structure of the box, keeping only the handle to hang the jar with its tea-light. The shattering of my own lantern structure during the later stages required an acceptance of the flaws and a revisioning of where to place pieces that in itself woke new understandings of the underlying experience, as we will see later.

What artful inquiry provides is an engagement with material realities while also engaging the imaginal. What we cannot envision we are less likely to move toward. Transformative learning theorists like John Dirkx (2000) and John Heron (Heron and Reason, 1997) support the view that the ways we come to perceive and apprehend ourselves-in-the-world, in that more participatory sense, are fundamentally emotional and imaginative rather than rational, conceptual, or linguistic. And it is within the ecology of the imagination that sustainable rebalancing can occur and lead to action. One lantern-maker conceived her lantern as a three-part piece, a removable semi-transparent rounded cocoon or chrysalis in which rested the box collaged with photos, words, and images, some of childhood trauma. Both of these sat in a nest of red dogwood branches. Only when the piece was displayed, did she and others see the egg in the nest that glowed with the life within. Since the initial installation, this woman has moved out of a financially supportive but creatively constraining marriage, written a short novel and several short stories for publication, and begun moving more openly into a network of more mutual relationships.

An Illustration of Artful Inquiry as Personal Revelation

Moving closer to my own lantern, exploring this and summarizing experience with subsequent art pieces is intended to give a more embodied sense of the unfolding process and integrating power of artful inquiry described earlier. See figure 11.2.

The little girl is seen through the remnants, the opened-up reminders of the original man-made wooden box. I am four and a half here, and my world is about to change. I am a very white-haired little girl, curls bleached by years of sun in Cape Coast, a village in Ghana, West Africa, where my father had come as a teacher with the White Fathers, arranging for my reluctant mother, six-week-old brother, and my toddler self to follow. This is a vivid teeming wild place with few white people. It is my homeplace until 12. The monkey in whose gaze and full body hug I am reveling, is a holding matrix and comforter in the glorious intensity and danger of my life-world. The photograph, one of hundreds taken and developed by my creative but art-disparaging father, is set in a wall of stones, shells, and coral pieces from Ghana, Ireland, the Greek islands, Mexico, Costa Rica, and Ontario, all the wild and cultured places shaping me. The wall is handmade, fit together like the stone

Figure 11.2 My lantern, "Sanctuary".

walls still common as boundary markers in my birthplace, Northern Ireland, and in Ontario's pre-Cambrian shield lake lands where I spend time. The original wooden box is cut open into a garden-like sanctuary, the light sunk into the earth. The remaining wooden structure is wound with growing thyme. The barely recognizable box is set in an earthenware pot that has hung on the wall of my therapy office since I started my practice there ten years ago. It hung in the center of the wall where I envisioned those hearthplaces. I have painted the pot like Earth seen from space, holding some sense of the cosmological, of self in the universe, and universe in the self.

Visible high on the stone wall is a guardian angel, a protective ever-present friend from my Catholic childhood. What she guards is my heart. A slightly more ambiguous impish figure, a curvaceous erotic porcelain fairy, is also visible. Creatures capable of flight, whether mythopoetic or in the natural world, hold magic and hope for me, for many cultures. The dragonfly touching down honors the natural world as well as echoing the symbol of renewal cut out from the original box, like memory. The small brass container full of the colored flight feathers of wild birds may be recognizable to some as a Winchester shell, one large enough to kill a human being. It would seem there are long-lasting signs of something less than safe in this sanctuary, when one moves in close.

In front of the sanctuary structure, concealing the fracture that happened as I bore out space for the light, is a hand-carved bone sheila-na-gig. "Sheila-na-gig" means "woman of the opening" in my Gaelic mother tongue. It is the name for the hundreds of trickster-like female figures with self-opened labial folds found carved above ancient church doors and on fortress walls all over Ireland and parts of the British mainland. There is scholarly debate on whether these figures warn of the evils of female sexuality or honor women as the opening to life. Modern Irish feminists have reclaimed the figures as symbols of women's place in the sacred. Only the curious might notice the wound in this particular figure's sex, a tiny vulval redness. The bone figure has been almost impossible to secure in place and has fallen and broken several times. All of the lantern, except the bullet, is of natural materials and will eventually return to the earth like myself.

There were many clues of something awry shortly after the time the photo I use in the lantern was taken. I smashed my nose, split my forehead, and broke my pelvis in the following year, all accidents, the only ones in my life before or since. Then there was my odd response to dangerous situations, apparently fearless, during the bombings and shootings that marked my university years. Given my first job was as a welfare officer in both the Catholic and Protestant districts alight with violence, this was interpreted as a strength. It was only after marital separation and several years of therapy that the four-year-old in my lantern burst back into consciousness. Triggered by a newspaper article about a father who had tried to murder his toddler's sexual abuser in the courtroom, I fell into grief, unsure what had happened but dreaming nightly of my dismembered body rushing from the ground into vivid life. In images and sensations, I began to recover memories of being sexually abused by the steward boy who was my caregiver during childhood in West Africa. My only memories of that period were written in my body, in the bones. Only through the spiraling layered process of recovery over the next five years did I begin to make the complex connections between my mother's emotional absence through depression, that time of increased racism as Ghana became independent, and my own anguished silence about my adolescent black male abuser. He disappeared abruptly after a row with my explosive father and by the time I had been sent away to school in Ireland at eight, the memory was gone.

Thirty years of dissociation should have been another clue that this was not yet the full story, despite the revelations uncovered in that first therapy. Dissociation is the compartmentalization of memories so that they are inaccessible, held apart from the rest of one's consciousness. It is an effective coping strategy for intense pain, especially when embodied. Recovering some of those memories and working through the healing process with a wise, warm, and creative therapist, did transform my life and all my relationships. It also transformed my framework for therapy and my daily praxis more than any of my concurrent graduate school training and placements. What it did not fully transform was my relationship with my self, my own theory-making, and ways of knowing.

The clues in my lantern, made in spring 2001, were enough to begin to stir again the ghosts of almost 50 years buried in my body. By the summer I was in pain. My back, hips, and shoulders ached deeply. I could not support myself for long. I had battled fibromyalgia for years but this was more intense. I had deep body tension and bone pain. The tension increased during a summer course that I taught on strategies for stopping violence against women and children. By now I recognized what was happening so, while very uncomfortable, I was not as terrified as in the past. I knew I was back in a traumatized state, sleeping poorly, waking frequently with my mind racing. Driven to write, I was unable to do so. Hundreds of scattered notes on bits of paper accumulated. Attempts to integrate the notes led to chaotic thinking and self-loathing.

Making and looking at my lantern, unearthed further concrete information. I could see there were still walls there under the thyme, still something to do with armed violence and flight that was expressed but unclear. I knew intuitively it had something to do with the sexual abuse and with my bones too. The most obvious clue to what was still so disruptive was the way I treated myself as I made the lantern and dealt with others' exhilarated responses to the installation. I was driven and not in pleasant ways. Nothing I was doing was right. My lantern would never be finished. I was too slow, too awkward, too impatient, too intense; it was too personal, too revealing. In the antiviolence course I was teaching, I was not communicating what needed to be said, not responsive enough to the pain and tensions of my students stirred by the materials. It went on and on, a stream of roofbrain chatter that heightened the body tension and made it difficult to enjoy my recognizably wondrous life.

It was August when I realized what my body already knew. I had been immobilized by a jarring accident. I had run away from my abuser up an iron ladder that rose 16 feet straight up the outside of a water tank perched on the hill behind our bungalow. The rusty ladder came away as I reached the top. I was slammed to the ground with the ladder across me. The steward boy had pulled me out from under the ladder when my father arrived and tried to raise me to my feet. My pelvis was broken. I was unable to walk. I remained strapped to a surfboard for about two months. I was immobilized, my body wrapped in cloth like a mummy to prevent my motion. My monkey was gone, eaten overnight by the soldier ants as she slept tied to a box in a tree near the compound. I was without comfort and unable to comfort myself. During that time the sexual abuse continued. I was reliant on my abuser for even the most basic of care, toileting. I did not speak. My distress was presumably seen as due to my injuries. Eventually I had to relearn to walk ... toe–heel, toe–heel, toe–heel ... like a robot. I was not in my body. I could not bear to stay.

Human inhumanity, whether as childhood sexual abuse, systemic racism or colonization, environmental degradation or enforced poverty, wounds and fragments at the mind–body–spirit level. It becomes traumatic when we are caught inescapably in a painful situation that overwhelms our usual coping strategies. Our sense of the whole, of the participatory, of our place in life's meaning, is shattered. Deeply imprinted in our cells, the effect of trauma remains with us long after the events (Van der Kolk, 1988).

Beginning not only to use, but to honor, the deeply held knowing that emerges in forms of artful expression, my own and others, opened up in me tender areas, old wounds that, like necrotic tissue, needed probing and clearing out for healing. The lantern project and the making of my own piece reintroduced me to an earlier grounded child self whose whole being was attuned to the feel, touch, smell, sights, rhythms, intensity of what was going on around her including the terror and anxiety of others. She/I was a being who needed comfort. I bought myself a soft toy monkey and began to address the arthritic damage evident on a bone scan that revealed activity along my spine, hips, and shoulders that formed the shadowy shape of an enlarged ladder segment. The art put me in a different place, painful, often deeply sad, but less heady and more able to be actively present in the moment.

The practice of artful inquiry has had a continuing significance for me, suggesting that it may for others also. The devastating disruption of personal and cultural security brought about by the September 11 terrorist attack and subsequent "war against terrorism" led by the United States and Britain, reopened old wounds and led to a deeper integration of what I had begun recognizing through personal artful inquiry. It resonated with my earlier traumatic experiences in times of armed conflict, as a child and as a young woman. Subsequent art pieces have been a way of capturing the shifts in my own sense of self that tie the traumatic events together. They have helped me express and then see my own fears and needs around bringing down earlier structures of meaning, challenged in my therapy praxis and social activism but only now addressed in myself and in my scholarly work. The ancient stone walls of my training are crumbling. My four-year-old talks. I listen.

Conclusion

My lantern, like each of the lanterns in the community, speak of the need for boundaried sacred spaces like therapy where consuming intensities of the personal self can be experienced in the contexts of all our relations. They hold some sense of a multi-centric universe where each being or form is manifest in the context of resonating communion with others. And they reveal processes of change that are transformative, breaking down and going beyond current meaning-making structures in ways that are highly creative.

Transforming therapy practices begins not with mythical neutrality, but with therapists' active and evident respect and advocacy for the participatory interconnected nature of all life. This is a stance that is curious and exploratory rather than righteous or judgmental of any aspect of self or relationship. It means therapists need to do their own in-depth healing and have a commitment to ongoing self-reflection that is more than abstract. Our own work includes critical literacy and continuing development of ways to recognize and address power differences in relationships. In particular we need to increase mutuality within the bounds of the therapeutic relationship, actively increasing our cultural competencies and drawing on differences as resources to enrich personal and community life.

Not only is fostering our personal participatory consciousness a clear necessity, so too is our involvement in ongoing peer supervision and community with other therapists involved in commitment to social activism, to bearing public witness in varying ways to what is heard in the sacred boundaried places of therapy. It would be impossible for me to be openhearted, innovative, and hopeful in the work I do without the support, respectful challenge, and resourcing of those from a variety of disciplines who have shared monthly peer supervision with me over the last five years. Community building from a diversity of perspectives needs to be built into therapist training, cutting across the boxes of professionalism. We need knowledge diversities in dialogue rather than domination by one or two decidedly white and Western disciplines. Imagine a lively small group of therapists with backgrounds in indigenous knowledge, African spiritualities, transpersonal psychology, restorative justice, holistic health practices, and the arts gathered together in a more transformative learning mode that is process- as well as structure-focused, that is multimodal and practice-oriented rather than theory-bound and caught in the niceties of diagnostic labeling from a Western medical perspective.

As we saw also in chapter 1, artful inquiry leads to an understanding of s/Self that is fluid, co-constituting, and deeply relational, evolving, and transforming in nested contexts of personal self, family, community, peoples, land, earth and universe (figure 1.1). As a feminist and a community educator in anti-oppression/antiviolence issues as well as an experienced psychotherapist, transformative learning understandings have moved my therapy praxis beyond the individual and psychological, integrating personal, community, and planetary change. In this view transformative learning is more than deconstructing how we have been socialized and how this forms our thinking and our actions. It also implies reconstruction, reclaiming for our own and our community's development, the creative energies previously exploited to benefit those who have dominated us personally and culturally.

In caring for these many distinctive fireplaces, my own and others, I too have been transformed. I have learned to become more indigenous to my own fiery places, that is, to hold dynamic tensions more ecologically and self-compassionately in the moment. It is painful for any of us to sit in the fires of our deepest knowing. I feel it in my bones and muscles, in moments of heart-wrenching grief over what is lost and rage at the awesome glory of Earth life needlessly endangered. At the same time, I have learnt from my own pieces and from the other lanterns that creativity survives longer than an ember deep in ground zero. Tapping into the creativity and knowledge of those surviving extreme circumstances, drawing on the wisdom of those consciously making new meaning out of trauma, offers inspiration and emancipatory hope. In the contexts of women's journeys of personal change and its capacity to hold the tensions between what is joyous and what is painful, artful inquiry illuminates therapy as necessarily a participatory, transformative, embodied, and deeply ecological practice.

Note

1. This article foregrounds the women's community art installation that continues to be a holding matrix for the author's larger doctoral project on self-transformation and raising participatory consciousness. The core of that

project is the Shadow Box, a personal installation that more deeply explores the ways trauma and colonization fragment human participatory consciousness at personal, communal, and planetary levels. This leads to the larger more community interactive Self Transforming installation that addresses the implications for transformative therapy practices and therapist education.

References

Cheney, J. (2002). "The Moral Epistemology of First Nations Stories." *Canadian Journal of Environmental Education* 7 (2), 88–98.

Dirkx, J. (2000). "After the Burning Bush: Transformative Learning as Imaginative Engagement with Everyday Experience." *Proceedings of The Third International Transformative Learning Conference, October 26–28* (pp. 247–252). New York: Teachers College Columbia University.

Einstein, A. (1949). *Out of My Later Years.* New Jersey: The Citadel Press.

Ettling, D. (2000). "I Am Changing: The Praxis of Sustaining Change." *Proceedings of The Third International Transformative Learning Conference, October 26–28* (pp. 99–104). New York: Teachers College Columbia University.

Goodman, Ann. (2003). *Now what? Developing Our Future.* New York: Peter Lang

Heron, J. and Reason, P. (1997). "A Participatory Inquiry Paradigm." *Qualitative Inquiry* 3 (3), 274–294.

hooks, b. (1995). *Art on My Mind: Visual Politics.* New York: The New Press.

Jacks, D. C. (1991). *Silencing the Self.* Cambridge, MA. Harvard University Press.

Jung, C. (1961). *Memories, Dreams and Reflections.* New York: Random House.

Lorde, A. (1984). *Sister Outsider.* New York: Crossing Press.

Macy, J. (1991). *World as Lover, World as Self.* Berkley, CA: Paralax Press.

Margolis, L. and Sagan, D. (2001). "Marvellous Microbes." *Resurgence Magazine* 206, on-line: www.resurgence.org.

McLaren, R. (2001). "Off the Page." In L. Neilsen, A. Cole, and G. Knowles (Eds.), *The Art of Writing Inquiry* (pp. 62–82). Nova Scotia: Backalong Books.

Miller, A. (1990). *Banished Knowledge: Facing Childhood Injuries.* New York: Doubleday.

O'Connor, M. A. (1999). *Women's Creativity: A Relational Perspective.* Unpublished paper.

Stern, Daniel. (1985). *The Interpersonal World of the Infant.* New York: Basic Books.

Tarnas, R. (1991). *The Passion of the Western Mind.* New York: Ballantine Books.

Van der Kolk, Bl. (1988). "The Trauma Spectrum: The Interaction of Biological and Social Events in the Genesis of the Trauma Response." *Journal of Traumatic Stress* 1 (3), 273–290.

CHAPTER 12

From Intersubjective Psychotherapy to Esprit Networking: Mapping a Social Practice

Barbara Dewar and Sandra Campbell

E sprit Networking Practice is a social configuration that both reflects an ecological consciousness and fosters continuous learning toward an ecological consciousness. Through Esprit Publications, we extend the innovations of the intersubjective practice of psychotherapy into the social world and into a social practice. Our practice enacts our recognition of the primacy of inner conscious awareness, engendered intersubjectively, as a causal reality. The intersubjective context facilitates an understanding of diverse differences.

Esprit Association is a community of six women who have been committed to a process of struggling together for greater awareness, by reflecting deeply on our lives for 17 years.[1] The goal of this interactive self-reflective process was to understand how to meet the challenges of our everyday lives and to improve our personal well-being by understanding the context of our personal story. While we have been socialized to function as independent beings, our struggle has led us to a deeper understanding that when we engage a process that supports a safe framework for reciprocal, interdependent exchanges between equals of our personal stories, then we are able to access and converse with the inner self. The relational model as articulated by the authors of contemporary intersubjective psychoanalytic literature supports a similar relational process (Brandhaft, 1983; Beebe and Lachmann, 1992; Stolorow and Atwood, 1992; Buirski and Haglund, 2001).

Not only has this process resulted in expanded personal happiness in our daily lives, but also an embodied knowing of our connection to the web of life. What this means for us is that knowledge derived from a deep awareness of our subjective experience is connected to the unfolding of a wider universe. From this place, we experienced a strong desire to act for positive change in the larger community of the world. Because our process enabled us to see with responsible eyes how to develop a better intuitive connection with unconscious life at a tacit level, we grasped the understanding that the collective unconscious, if not worked with, can operate in ways that are harmful. Interiority and subjectivity can develop into a larger, contexual framework. We chose electronic communications as a means to transfer our intersubjective networking practice into the wider community for interaction and cocreation of ideas.

About Being Human: Esprit Operating Assumptions

Through two years of the Esprit Networking Practice we have defined some of our foundational assumptions, many of which parallel intersubjective principles. The embodied knowledge generated through our practice of intersubjective psychotherapy frames this perspective and its operating assumptions guide our practice. We have discerned the following key elements through this process.

Connection to life is absolutely fundamental to our health and well-being. "Individual experience is inherently embedded in an intersubjective relationship system" (Shaddock, 2002, p. 14). We can survive only in connection and in relationship with others and our biosphere. We breathe in oxygen and breathe out carbon dioxide, which is absorbed by all things greening, and transformed into oxygen again. Our bodies are hard-wired for connection. Our eyes, ears, nose, skin, and tongue bring us into connection with what is outside ourselves through sensate feelings. These sensations inform us about our place in the ecological whole. When our connections operate as reciprocal, interdependent exchanges of equals, as in the dynamics of breathing, we thrive. When we engage in a process of repair, due to ruptured connections, we also thrive. If we remain in a state of disconnection we are isolated from what we need and our survival becomes fragile.

The boundary between conscious and unconscious—the so-called repression barrier—is understood developmentally not only as a fixed intraphysic structure, but as a fluidly shifting property of an ongoing intersubjective system (Buirski and Haglund, 2001, p. xii). What we forget becomes unconscious: a state of not knowing within ourselves, of being unaware. When we forget painful memories our bodies remember tensions associated with this forgetting. We strive to connect to these memories so that we can make meaning of their tensions and frustrations and as we do this we begin to remember our intersubjective personal narratives. Our feelings inform the color and texture of any given narrative. The narratives of each remembered story transform into new meaning in the intersubjective field. To paraphrase Carl Jung (1995), meaning makes a great many things endurable, perhaps everything; meaninglessness inhibits fullness of life and is equivalent to illness.

As we connect to our stories and those of others, we are able to see that we are each a unique being within an ecological system and in being together we see also that we are diverse. This diversity promotes resilience and survival; it enables us to adapt in the face of change. In this knowing we are led to imagine new ways of being that honor very deeply who we are, both in our uniqueness and in our collectivity.

Finally, we dream. As we do, we put flesh on the bones of our longings, frustrations, and understand our inner motivations. Sharing our dreams and stories encourages change in our daily behaviors. And they become part of a larger collective story.

From New Knowledge to New Practice

From this place of our embodied knowledge we shared our longings for a better world, one without the violence and turmoil that disconnects us from each other and ourselves. We initiated a semi-annual electronic publication, Esprit Publications,[2] to offer our own personal narratives as a source of learning in a wider network. Through writing our stories we became increasingly more conscious that everyone's abilities to be more active participants in the development of a healthier world is severely limited by the toxic effects of centuries of inequality—racism and sexism—that are embedded in our everyday interactions. As we wrote we learned how we participated in these cultural practices so that we were at times its victims and at other times its perpetrators. We understood how this diminishes our self-esteem and renders us both angry and helpless. However, as we engaged our narratives and exchanged with others, we learned how to reach beyond these limitations.

Isabel Caceres (2002b) illustrates this story of living the dark consequences of patriarchy, a toxic dynamic of feelings and actions that pulled her into "the revolving door of hate." She tells how, as a victim, she feels "hate, bitterness, jealousy, resentment, and coldness" and often acts from these feelings, which disconnects her from others. She writes that when empathic nonjudgmental listeners witness her victimization feelings, she can engage a struggle to face "the bully inside of me that lies underneath the victim," a more difficult process than the comfort she receives as a victim. It is in engaging with her own dark feelings that she experiences the reward of "extra space for learning, creating, and developing sound connections with others." Isabel unraveled the complex feelings that cause both genders to become "locked in destructive values and behaviors as each is profoundly affected by the intricacy of their hatred." With this shift in awareness comes a new ability for leadership in the world as well. "As long as I keep the bully hidden from myself, I am unable to problem-solve and dialogue with others when there are misunderstandings or discrepancies" (p. 3).

As we became conscious of what limits our abilities to build a better world we began to conceptualize a model that has organically unfolded from our subjective transformations and intersubjective practice. This model is based on a quality of social interaction and the creation of shared meaning. Ursula Franklin (1999) notes that social transactions that support open back and forth flow to the context of others follow "the logic of compassion, or the logic of obligation, the logic of ecological survival or the logic of linkages into nature" (p. 92).

Because our embodied knowledge taught us that the source of our well-being is our understanding of the circumstances of our personal lives, we knew we had to learn how to understand and validate the experiential world of others. For this reason what became fundamental to our model is its requirement to understand personal context and the fact that this understanding leads us inexorably to recognize contextual differences. To achieve this understanding we engaged a process of shared (self-other) communications that we named cocreative dialogue. What is crucial to the process of this dialogue is that we hold the following paradox: as humans we all experience vulnerabilities and in this fact we share sameness, yet, the circumstances that surround these vulnerabilities are unique to the specific context of each individual life and so we are different one from the other.

Cocreative dialogue became our model for understanding connection to living dynamic intersubjective systems in diverse contextual differences. "Any attempt to remove individuals from the history and culture in which they are embedded and to study them as isolated, decontexualized monads is, from a constructionist point of view, a neo-Enlightenment fantasy—it is simply not doable" (Cushman, 1991, p. 1). One of our readers expressed the following fear, "The cautious disclaimers about power and elitism made me a little uncomfortable, like I was witnessing yet another idealistic 'ideology' struggling to be born [they always start out with the purest of intentions]."[3] Barbara Dewar's observation in response was that Esprit essays are a means

Figure 12.1   Cocreative Dialogue.

to understand our unique social practices, in our own local communities. This method of reflecting on our personal stories enables an understanding of difference rather than sameness and reveals ideological principles that might put us in danger. "At bottom we are trying to live more fully in the moment by expressing what the authentic moment is dictating to each one of us individually and reflecting on what this means to ourselves and others."[4]

We began to explore this concept of contexual linking by cocreative dialogue (see figure 12.1) in finer detail.

The Current for Cocreative Dialogue: Social Interactions

In cocreative dialogue, supportive social interactions function like the current in a river. Through the Esprit essays, we share the context of our personal narrative and our reflections on them. Vulnerabilities, uncertainties, and strengths are revealed in our lived experiences. We chose this focus because we assume these are the common ground of all people. From intersubjective psychotherapy we learned, then applied to our writing, the listening quality of an "empathic stance" in which the listener struggles not to judge stories by holding a "fallible" attitude of not knowing (Buirski and Haglund, 2001). The listener maintains this attitude until both parties (self and other) share an understanding. When this understanding occurs both feel a resonance, experienced as a sense of being understood in one's difference. "Recognition is that response from other which makes meaningful the feelings, intentions and actions of the self. It allows the self to realize its agency and authorship in a tangible way. But such recognition can only come from an other whom we, in turn, recognize as a person in his or her own right" (Benjamin, 1988, p. 12).

In her narrative, *Absence into Presence*, Sandra Campbell (2002a) describes how the empathic stance and attunement with her Esprit colleagues led to the development of her own agency and her confidence to establish it. In this essay, she explored the impact of her voluntary absence from an important community event organized by her colleagues. As the event was occurring, she experienced the discomfort of disconnection from her colleagues and felt both longing and frustration. Why had she chosen not to attend? As she shared her reflections on her choice, the story of her beginnings emerged. She was not welcomed at birth and as she shared this story, she felt raw shame. As her expression of this feeling resonated with her colleagues, they filtered her story through their different and unique personal histories of shame. We all cocreated new meanings and yet held an understanding of the circumstances of Sandra's particular feeling of shame. The unconscious inner belief that she did not matter led her to continuously diminish the value of her actions and their effects on others (p. 3). The conclusions that resonated were that each of us matters equally by the presence of our uniqueness.

As we continually engaged in this process, we have learned that conscious awareness of the context of other realities through cocreative dialogue can support positive change in all of us.

Context: Personal Narrative/Feeling Responses

Our narratives focus on the context of our lives. We write to understand the circumstances surrounding individual fears, anger, frustrations and longings, which emerge as we move through our daily lives. As we write on the wave of these feelings, we have a sense of discovery. When we share this information, we give voice to what Susan Griffin (1993) calls, "the not yet spoken." We call these feelings, voices that are newly spoken. Our stories reflect these voices. Jeremy Yunt (2001), an ecopsychologist, believes that in some way or other because we are part of a single "all embracing psyche," disconnection with our inner world has profound consequences for our survival. "For contact with this pre-rational and symbolic dimension of the psyche, it is suggested, helps lead to an experience of one's 'ecological self,' a central ecopsychological concept in which psyche and world are consciously joined through a transformation in psychological perception of both one's self and one's place in the world" (Yunt, 2001, p. 175). The acknowledgment of our responses in our narrative by social support is causally connected to the process of reflection.

Judy Bridges Farquharson's story (2002c) poignantly illustrates how it is important to address inner disconnection in order to enter into relationship. In "Understanding My Split," she tells how she was able to feel the anger, paralysis, and terror that are at its core. As she expressed these feelings, she was led to a moment of being able to conceptualize the two different roads that she travels: the one that she's traveled most of her life is bleak and lacks the consciousness required both to feel and incorporate these feelings into her center so as to be informed by them. The second very different road is "rich in texture and colour" and "peopled with travelers who, knowing their imperfections, work with honest intention towards integration" (p. 10). In "Diary of a Struggle with a Split," Farquharson (2002a) continues to delve into her struggle with her split and with the voice of terror that drives it as it is occurring. "What I have is the ongoing struggle to connect with my terror and to let my feeling responses move through this terror to where I can access them. It truly is a moment to moment experience." As she connects to this terror, she discovers that a "bone-deep fear of humiliation" lies at the core of her authentic self. From this she sees that "there is nothing sweet about the destruction that ensues from being split off from this terror." To prevent this destruction she sees that "Only my capacity to feel my terror of humiliation and my struggle with my split allows me new growth." Then she writes, "I am acutely aware of this feeling as I write. This is raw. It is not perfection and it does not look or feel pretty and neat" (p. 4).

As we see in Judy Bridges Farquharson's essays, if we are not supported to uncover the tensions that are hidden in our unique stories then these unacknowledged parts of ourselves negatively affect our ability to link to the context of the other. When we miss interconnecting links to our inside life, we experience being separate and isolated from the context of others.

Reflections: Creation of New Meanings

Reflections are part of a meaning-making process that leads to a "profound understanding of context," (Franklin, 1999, p. 81). When we write our stories of uncertainties or vulnerabilities for Esprit Publications, we live in our stories and reflect on them together. Then we invite reflections from each other through dialogue. When we publish these stories, we invite our readers to engage this same process. Again, our stance in our reflections is an empathic one: personal experience is unique to the person, and therefore is received without judgment and without prescription. To judge would be to block the storyteller's reflections. An illustration of the generativity of stories came from one of our readers. "I was brought to a place of longing. I am in a desert and you showed me your ocean. Your vast water is a mirage to me in my dry, dry land. I am in luminosity. I miss what I have left and I am curious to find my water. My longing is mistaken for sadness. I have none of what I had, yet I have it all."[5]

When readers write their comments and stories in our website guest book, they share them with all other readers. In this way, all readers and writers are able to engage in a process of reflecting. Stories, thoughts and questions are offered and responses and counterresponses become part of the reflective process. Together, we release new meanings personally and collectively. These new meanings are transformative. We experience the world in a new way.

In "Transforming My Invisibility," Mary Walton-Ball (2002b) reflects on her unspoken story of terror and isolation caused by the cruelty of a relative without conscience. While she struggled to reach out to people and trust, her defense of invisibility plunged her into continuous feelings of poor self-esteem and intense isolation. Her transformation process began as she participated in various therapeutic experiences where she shared and reflected on her story and was heard with compassion and empathy. This profound witnessing enabled her to express her rage at the injustices she had suffered. As she expressed so, she was able to begin to integrate her terror and learn to trust at a deeper level. Mary expresses that as she continues to engage her invisibility, isolation, and terror within the social interaction of the Esprit circle, she has come to a deep, embodied understanding of the nature of conscience (p. 2). Experience and reflection have reframed her perspective and her actions. "It should be experience that leads to a modification of knowledge, rather than abstract knowledge forcing people to perceive their experience as being unreal or wrong" (Franklin, 1999, p. 32).

Safety: New Imaginings and Questions

New questions and imaginings emerge within and among us and these challenge the status quo. Here we often meet resistance due to anxieties aroused by unexplored invisible barriers in ourselves and others. Only when we feel safe can we explore these barriers.

Cocreative dialogue as it is practiced within the Esprit Association supported our safety to imagine and ask questions. We learned to trust the overall nonjudgmental interpersonal connections with each other. Barbara Dewar (2002b) explains that she requires safety for her work as a psychotherapist. "One of the many things Esprit offers me is a place where I can share this (pain) and find support to do the best work that I can do to help with the wounds that I experience in myself and others that I feel are caused by blind injustices." Judy Bridges Farquharson (2002c) shares that Esprit, "calls me personally to new levels of honesty and trust as we define ourselves individually and explore new ideas together." Sandra Campbell (2002b) shares that "the relationships that define Esprit provide an enabling bond that supports me as I navigate the risks and dangers of living the questions." Mary Walton-Ball (2002a) writes, "I challenge my independence, experience interdependence and learn more about connection with each of them, in the moment." Isabel Caceres (2002a) requires safety in order to explore deep spiritual questions. "Esprit is the exploration of the source of all existence and of life principles." We can see that in this environment, Joanne Corbeil (2002b) was able to challenge hierarchical splits. "I have come to believe that it is much more healing to be 'in-step' with my clients, indeed in all my relationships."

Our practice of cocreative dialogue is the template for the creation of safe soil. In this way, Esprit members and our readers have an opportunity together to continue to gain the transformative changes that are needed to inspire imaginings and questions that lead to taking positive actions in life (pp. 1–2).

For example, the safety of Esprit Association enabled Barbara Dewar to imagine a new model of mental health. In her essays, "The Human Side of a Therapist, Personally and Historically (Belly First, theory Later)" (2002d) and "My Speaking Engagement in Belleville" (2002c), she writes of her desire to lift the stigma around mental health and healing; to bust the fantasy of human perfection and to work from a reverence for all our human experiences, all feelings. As she articulates this, she steps outside the safety of the prevailing disease paradigm of mental health practice that posits the therapist as an "expert" who has objective answers, based on scientific truths that lead to prescriptions for what is "right." The client, in this view, is seen as deficient, a person needing to be fixed. Further the client does not have the answers to his or her own deep life-questions and the expert does and will lead them there. This view sets up an unequal relationship that can lead to hierarchical and patriarchal abuses and limit the growth of both parties.

Barbara articulates a paradigm that includes the assumption that the longings, fears, anxieties that push a person to seek help are the spirited tugs of our humanness calling us to greater awareness of who we truly are. These emotionally charged feelings are signals of health, not deficiency. Furthermore, the therapist is not outside the human journey but someone who struggles with her own fears and longings, someone who has taken the therapeutic pathway and continues a self-reflective process on her humanness. On this common ground, therapist and client work together as equal partners in an exchange to sort out issues and challenges. The therapist's tools are cocreative dialogue undertaken through empathic listening and finding attunement with the client. This supports a safe environment for the work at hand. In her editorial, Barbara (2002b) writes that, because of her challenge to the prevailing disease paradigm, she fears the judgment of her peers, "that I am still a kid, not nearly ready for this, and that I should go back to my fox hole and learn some more" (p. 1).

Participatory Action

Our questions lead to actions. "The purpose seems to be that the individual will be led to both assimilate and participate in her or his environment" (Nowak, 2000, p. 28). For example, in "Creative Survival," JoAnne Corbeil (2002a) tells her story of a long-time struggle with learning disabilities, generated by emotional blocks. Through ongoing reflection and cocreative dialogue with Esprit members she engaged the pain of her struggle to give birth to her abilities and intelligence. In this process she came to see how her spirit guided her to take a series of nonconventional steps in continuous self-directed learning that later came together as a solid body of study and experience for her work as a psychotherapist. This awareness led to the birth of new imaginings and questions about how to turn the traditional hierarchical and patriarchal ways of the world of education upside down. She cocreated the school, *Esprite du Training of Psychotherapy Associates*, which is a pioneering psychotherapy-training program based on helping students find their authentic self through a commitment to embodied learning. The school embraces all students, including those who, like JoAnne followed a nonconventional path. Students must meet the challenge of studying psychoanalytical theories not only with their intellects, but also equally with their hearts. The learners are engaged in both academic learning and the exploration of self. In this way, psychoanalytical theories become language that describes the experiential learning. The process of being in, coming from, giving expression to, support a wholeness of self that enables students to work in an embodied way with their clients.

Technology: Connections

One reader wrote, "I realize that you are presenting your readers with an opportunity to get out of their isolation by joining your open format dialogue but I have strong reservations that this can be accomplished by the internet format of Esprit."[6] We live in a "hypertechnical culture," one that reveres technology at the expense of the human spirit (Yunt, 2001, p. 12). Our goal in using technology is to reverse this reverence completely. Implicit in cocreative dialogue whether it occurs in real-time or on-line, is a profound honoring of each human spirit. In our practice, computer technology serves as a tool to extend cocreative dialogue into the social world and into social practice but technology does not drive the process, people do. We are led by Ursula Franklin (1999) who writes about the need to look at technology in "the context of nature and people" (p. 89).

There is a living flow to cocreative dialogue and every part of our model is supported by human interaction. As a parallel to the dual particle wave theory in quantum physics, the computer is a particle that is moved by the wave of human experience. The computer chip is the conduit for the transmissions of our interactions and we experience this movement as alive and vital. Each writer sees the publication of her story as the first step in dialogue with our larger community. That is why each concludes her essay with her personal E-mail address and an invitation for readers to share whatever thoughts, feelings, and reactions that arise within them as they read. Respondents are assured that their correspondence will be considered confidential if that is what they desire. E-mail encourages immediacy of response and we have received many that have challenged us. We are committed to answer each one and as such, we become accountable for our stories. As we engage in the process of cocreative dialogue via E-mail, we respond and counterrespond with the goal that, writer and reader, reach shared understandings. The technology enables us to move in spirals together, back to old information that can be continually transformed into the new. And so we have a tool to support an understanding of the nuances of our experiences of mind, body, and spirit with others within a larger community; to help us reach the unknown in others. In our networking practice, our use of technology reflects a positive response to the challenge of Jeremy Yunt (2001), "Can we not understand that all outward tinkerings and improvements ultimately depends upon whether the man who wields the science and the technics is capable of responsibility or not" (p. 20).

Our website (http://www.espritpublications.ca) offers a unique opportunity to increase reader participation in cocreative dialogue. The site allows access to all editions of Esprit Publications. Most importantly, we have included a guest book that is open for all web visitors, without the complications of a password system. Here people can write their responses, tell their stories, express their challenges, and invite more responses. Dialogues of several people emerge and their content and process are available for any web visitor to read. For us, this kind of dialogue through personal narrative enhances understanding of the context of other lives and is therefore an important step toward increasing the possibility of larger global change. We envision that electronic communications will support a larger thinking together.

Conclusion

At this time, we are among many who recognize that an in-depth understanding of personal story is fundamental for the creation of values that are more suitable for the survival of life. Carol Gilligan (1982) led this understanding when she articulated the necessity to listen to personal experience so that social constructions around morality are based on an accurate conception of how we understand the world. "My interest lies in the interaction of experience and thought, in different voices and the dialogues to which they give rise, in this way we listen to ourselves and others, in the stories we tell about our lives" (p. 2).

The Esprit Association is a grassroots association that has been informed by the intersubjective practice of psychoanalysis "A central organizing concept of intersubjective theory is that our experience of ourselves is fundamental to how we operate in the world" (Buirski and Haglund, 2001, p. 1). The common ground of knowing between Esprit and intersubjective psychotherapy is that our subjective lens and intersubjecive interactions are a meaning-making process. Further, if this process is engaged by specific qualities of social interactions, we participate in the process of personal and collective change. Esprit Networking Practice, with its focus on interiority and subjectivity accomplished through writing our personal narratives, is a process model that leads us to connect our personal experiences to wider and deeper knowledge. Its practice of reflection for meaning-making helped us to define experiential embodied knowledge. This knowledge has in turn helped us to understand the vital necessity to include our inner subjective lens in developing our philosophies of life. Philosopher, Phillip McKenna (2002) reminds us, "What they forget is that the whole discourse about human thought and feeling relies on self-ascription of experiences by living subjects" (p. 16).

Cocreative dialogue continually teaches us how to struggle to achieve an understanding of others' personal context by holding a paradox of knowing and not knowing. Once mutual respect for difference is achieved we are led to participatory actions that are more supportive to collective living. The use of electronic communications in our networking practice enlarges our community with the result that it then becomes even more diverse.

David Bohm (1989) a physicist, continually explored the question of dialogue as a way to developing a coherent understanding of difference and
introduced the concept of "participatory consciousness." As we continue our
Esprit Networking Practice, we are always learning that it is through self-
awareness, shared by our connections to others, that we enter into an ecological consciousness. We are led to the increased possibility, "of transforming
not only the relationships between people, but even more, the very nature of
consciousness in which these relationships arise" (p. 174).

With ecological sight, we move into being change agents, living by values
that support human life in its interdependence on the planet.

Notes

1. Esprit Members are Judy Bridges Farquharson, Isabel Caceres, Sandra Campbell,
   JoAnne Corbeil, Barbara Dewar, and Mary Walton-Ball. Barbara Dewar had
   suggested the formation of the Esprit Association, September 2001, and first articulated the vision of cocreative dialogue.
2. We began our networking practice by distributing the Esprit Publications essays,
   first in hard copy and subsequently, by E-mail. We later designed a web site
   http://www.espritpublications.ca, which includes all the essays and provides
   a guest book for public dialogue.
3. Gwen Nowak's E-mail response to our third publication posed very thoughtful
   questions.
4. Barbara Dewar's E-mail response to Gwen helped push us forward in our understanding of cocreative dialogue.
5. Lauren Little sent an E-mail response to our first Esprit Publication.
6. Gwen Nowak sent this E-mail communication in response to our third publication.

References

Beebe, J. and Lachmann, F. (1992). "A Dydadic Systems View of Communication."
   In N. Skolnick and S. Warshaw (Eds.), *Relational Perspectives in Psychoanalysis*.
   Hillsdale, NJ: The Analytic Press.
Benjamin, J. (1988). *The Bonds of Love: Psychoanalysis, Feminism, and the Problem of
   Domination*. New York: Pantheon Books.
Bohm, D. (1989). "Unfolding Meaning." In R. Burg (Ed.), http://www.muc.de/
   ~heuvel/bohm/html/.com.
Brandchaft, B. (1983). "The Negativism of the Negative Therapeutic Reaction and
   the Psychology of the Self." In A. Goldberg (Ed.), *The Future of Psychoanalysis*.
   Madison, CT: International Universities Press.
Buirski, P. and Haglund, P. (2001). *Making Sense Together: The Intersubjective
   Approach to Psychotherapy*. New Jersey: Book-Mark Press.

Caceres, I. (March 2002a). Editorial. *Esprit Newsletter*. On-line: http://www.espritpublications.ca.

Caceres, I. (Summer 2002b). "Victim or Bully in a Patriarchal Society: The Revolving Door of Hate." *Esprit Publications* 1, 2. On-line: http://www.espritpublications.ca.

Campbell, S. (Summer 2002a). "Absence into Presence." *Esprit Publications* 1, 2. On-line: http://www.espritpublications.ca.

Campbell, S. (March 2002b). Editorial. *Esprit Newsletter*. On-line: http://www.espritpublications.ca.

Corbeil, J. (Summer 2002a). "Creative Survival." *Esprit Publications*, 1, 2. On-line: http://www.espritpublications.ca.

Corbeil, J. (March 2002b). Editorial. *Esprit Newsletter*. On-line: http://www.espritpublications.ca.

Cushman, P. (1991). "Ideology Obscured: Political Uses of the Self in Daniel Stern's Infant." *American Psychologist* 46, 3, 206–219.

Dewar, B. (Fall 2002a). "Co-creative Relationships." *Esprit Publications* 1, 3. On-line: http://www.espritpublications.ca.

Dewar, B. (March 2002b). Editorial. *Esprit Newsletter*. On-line: http://www.espritpublications.ca.

Dewar, B. (Fall 2002c). "My Speaking Engagement in Belleville." *Esprit Publications*, 1, 3. On-line: http://www.espritpublications.ca.

Dewar, B. (Summer 2002d). "The Human Side of a Therapist, Personally and Historically (Belly First, Theory later)." *Esprit Publications* 1, 2. On-line: http://www.espritpublications.ca.

Farquharson, B. J. (Fall 2002a). "Diary of a Struggle with a Split." *Esprit Publications* 1, 3. On-line: http://www.espritpublications.ca.

Farquharson, B. J. (March 2002b). Editorial. *Esprit Newsletter*. On-line: http://www.espritpublications.ca.

Farquharson, B. J. (March 2002c). "Understanding my Split." *Esprit Newsletter*. On-line: http://www.espritpublications.ca.

Franklin, M. U. (1999). *The Real World of Technology*. Toronto: House of Anansi Press Limited.

Gilligan, C. (1982). *In a Different Voice*. Cambridge: Harvard University Press.

Griffin, S. (1993). "Not Yet Spoken." In E. Buchwald, P. Fletcher, and M. Roth (Eds.), *Transforming a Rape Culture* (pp. 445–449). Minneapolis, MI: Milkweed Edition.

Jung, C. (1995). "God in all Worlds." In L. Vardey (Ed.). New York: Random House.

McKenna, T. P. (2002). *The Moral Journey Implicit in Doing Psychotherapy*. Paper presented to International Academy of Law and Mental Health Conference, The Netherlands. On-line: http://www.ctp.net.

Nowak, G. (2000). *Miriam of Nazareth: Who can Find Her?* Toronto: Cortleigh House.

Shaddock, D. (2002). *Contexts and Connections: An Intersubjective Systems Approach to Couples Therapy*. New York: Basic Books.

Stolorow, R. and Atwood, G. (1992). *Context of Being: The Intersubjective Foundations of Psychological Life*. Hillsdale, NJ: The Analytic Press.

Yunt, J. (2001). "Jung's Contribution to an Ecological Psychology." *Journal of Humanistic Psychology* 41, 2.

Walton-Ball, M. (March 2002a). Editorial. *Esprit Newsletter*. On-line: http://esprit-publictons.ca.

Walton-Ball, M. (Summer 2002b). "Transforming my Invisibility." *Esprit Publications* 1, 2. On-line: http://www.espritpublications.ca.

CHAPTER 13

Fostering Ways-of-Giving Within Communities

Valerie Petrie

Introduction

In May 1987 I lay in a hotel room in Montreal, waking to the excitement of my participation in the formation of a Canadian Women's Health Network, a forum of 20 women meeting to establish a national coalition to promote women's health. I would represent the voice of rural women— one voice among 20 talented women, feminists, from across the country. Imbued with the sense of responsibility and opportunity in representing Canadian rural women, I experienced an image arising from my connection to a body that was more than my body; my connection to a mind that was more than my mind. Like an angel embodying the collective potential of women isolated by their geographic context, I was part of (embraced by) an awakening body, a body of political, economic, social, and cultural power that existed in the health, knowledge, willingness, creativity, and generosity of rural women. A focus on efficient use of scarce resources was irrelevant in the emergent force of this massive, abundant potentiality. I experienced an awesome sense of connection that has remained with me ever since. I experienced the embodiment of an awakening prosperity, the potential of including the once marginalized, undervalued, unrecognized, and trivialized, economic value of rural women. I knew my focus needed to remain with the radical and immediate harvest of this ripe potentiality and not be snared by a limiting mind-set that emphasized competition, scarcity, and constraint.

As my work in community development has evolved over the past two decades, the experience of that morning awakening has remained with me, contributing to my identity as an agent of change for rural community and economic development. The abundant richness of this ecological consciousness has the power to lift me out of the constraints of my own limitations. I am able to experience and work with my connection to a larger abundant and generous capacity that I have come to describe as giving agency.

In this chapter I describe how my identity as an agent of change and the ways-of-giving model for agents of change has arisen out of an ecological consciousness that celebrates gifts and giving as having both the theoretical force and practical ability to create abundance. I suggest that the desire to give is embedded deeply within our human-being and that the idea of giving is an essential element of community. I describe the formation of my identity as an agent of change and how this led to the concept of giving agency. I then present the ways-of-giving model for agents of change, describing how this model supports my everyday practice of living and giving as an agent of change as exercised through various roles including citizen, consultant, volunteer, and family member. I hope to encourage social change agents to reflect upon their own giving, what is given, and ways of giving in order to bring a deeper awareness to gifts and giving.

An Agent of Change

The adult education researcher and feminist, Kathleen Loughlin, first introduced me to the concept of women as agents of change in a 1992 report. I resonated with her approach to an understanding of women's emancipatory education. I identified with the women interviewed in her study. My own accomplishments in community development, political action, and advocacy were similar to those of the women she interviewed. I shared with these women the sense of strength and wisdom emerging from my own personal empowerment and the belief not only in the possibility of societal transformation, but that my own personal transformation could be a catalyst for social change.

Loughlin (1992) alerted me to the phrase "agents of change" and I began to hear the phrase throughout popular culture. I heard the Honourable Hillary M. Weston, lieutenant governor of Ontario, praise Ontario hospice workers as agents of change in her keynote speech at the 1998 annual meeting of the Ontario Hospice Association. Similarly, in the exploration of social entrepreneurship, Gregory Dees (1998) claims, "Social entrepreneurs play the role of change agents in the social sector" (p. 4). Margaret McCain, New Brunswick's first woman lieutenant governor, speaking of her active volunteerism emphasizes: "Women not only give with their hearts, they invest their hearts, and get their reward by being agents for change" (cited in Ball, 1999, p. 5).

Having the identity of an agent of change is an understanding that I bring to my professional work. In other words, being an agent of change is not a career choice. It is what I think of as a self-constructed identity, an identity that is self-defined and not imposed by any external social, political, or economic systems. Being a change-agent is cross-sectoral by nature and

> may be facilitated by actions within diverse societal contexts; for example, communications, politics, religion, or education. I understand action for reconstruction in a broad context that extends beyond a definition of political action as the primary means of social structure reconstruction. (Loughlin, 1992, p. 22)

In this sense, being an agent of change is closer to a vocation than a career, because it is what I feel called and compelled to do. As a learner, my calling to be an agent of change includes the call to celebrate my own ongoing learning. Charlene Spretnak (1993) calls for an education that recognizes "the presence of the divine, the face of ultimate mystery in all beings" (p. 188). She postulates:

> What if we were educated to nurture awareness of our inseparable relatedness?... Not only education, but the very nature of work itself would be challenged by a revitalized sense of community that is cosmologically grounded.... The subjectivity of a worker would be appreciated as a gift to be shared. (pp. 188–189)

As an agent of change I am called to work within this cosmologically grounded sense of community as the site of practice for my work (see figure 13.1). The etymology of the word community "is the Latin *munus*, which means the gift, and *cum*, which means together, among each other. So community literally means to give among each other" (Lietaer, 1997, p. 4). Peterson (1996) relates community development to the literal translation of "unwrapping of the condition of fellowship" (p. 142). Putting these concepts together defines community as a place where gifts are given (Lietaer, 1997) and where community developers unwrap the gifts (Peterson, 1996). A concept as potent as giving is deeply embedded in language:

> Old English had a verb meaning "to give." It also had a verb phrase meaning "to trade," which meant, literally "to give with worth"—that is, give

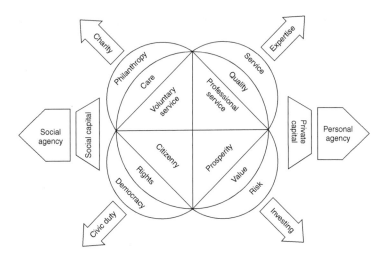

Figure 13.1 Ways-of-Giving Model.

for a price. Our word sell comes from a truncated portion of that phrase for trading, the part literally meaning "give." Time and again, human groups must have differentiated trading from both sharing and seizing.... Old as it is, sharing is still a potent generality.... Economic developments still emerge from it. (Jacobs, 2000, p. 27)

Everyday my attention to the language of gifts and giving enriches my life. Others draw my attention to the way giving is embedded in foreign languages. I met Peter Royal on a flight from Halifax to Toronto as I returned home from the graduation ceremonies for my Master's degree. A gift of fortune seated me next to this retired Professor of French Philosophy who had himself written a paper on the language of gifts and giving. We have continued our dialogue by e-mail since the flight. In a personal communication in May 2001 he wrote: "*There is* in German is either *es ist* or *es gibt* (it is or it gives).... I suppose you know that *gift* in German means *poison*." Through language and as an economic generality, the idea of giving connects us to others. Could *giving* stand under (understand) all human inter-action? I have come to view giving as an antecedent to action and as a fundamental human capacity. It is the human desire to give, to be in relationship with others through giving, that enables communities to develop. It is the spontaneous and mysterious gifts that grace our lives through serendipity and synchronicity that inspires hope and trust in the generous web of life in which our lives are mysteriously embedded.

Giving Agency

My identity as a change-agent led me to explore the way in which contemporary adult educators utilize the concept of agency—a concept inherent in the term agent. For example, Lynne Tirrell (1990) relates how telling stories can develop adult educators' sophistication as moral agents:

It is through the articulation of events, motives and characters that we become moral agents.... In telling stories one develops a sense of self, a sense of self in relation to others, and a capacity to justify one's decisions.... Telling stories may also increase our sophistication as agents. We may begin with rudimentary stories that show a basic grasp of the moral, and sometimes we may eventually develop the thickened judgment that enables one to take control of oneself, one's place in one's community and to have a directed impact on that community. (p. 125)

To explore contemporary use of the concept of *agency* in adult education literature, I conducted a Boolean search in the proceedings of the most recent (year 2000) Adult Education Research Conference. At the conference, the concept of *agency* was applied in a number of ways. In a discussion on the theory of structuration as it relates to teaching practice, John Dirkx (2000) reports, "agency reflects our capacity to act and be acted upon by social forces" (p. 554). Dorothy Lander (2000) speaks of moral agency in critical autobiography:

The narrative form of autobiography situates me as a critically reflective moral agent. In retelling the stories of my family and friends, moral agency intersects my public researcher self and my private selves as sister, daughter, niece, cousin, aunt, friend, and neighbour. Autobiography becomes critically reflexive by virtue of attending to multiple selves. (p. 226)

Spretnak (1993) extends the philosophical concept of agency to include the concept of subjectivity, and brings the concept of agency closer to our discussion of working with ecological consciousness. Following the work of Thomas Berry, who includes subjectivity along with differentiation and communion as basic processes of the universe, she explains the enhanced sense of agency that is contained in Berry's notion of subjectivity:

> Berry's sense of subjectivity extends beyond the philosophical notion of "agency" (the capacity to be an active agent, that is, an initiating and directing subject of action) to include a being's unique interiority, depth, spontaneity, and creativity.... Subjectivity includes spontaneity, in a wriggling amoeba as well as in a human being, and sentience, in the self-regulating dynamics of a coral reef as well as in a mammal. Through subjectivity, manifestations of the universe present the creative unfolding and ultimate mystery of the cosmos. (Spretnak, 1993, p. 29)

Michael J. Mahoney (1996) also enhances the concept of agent. Using constructivism and feminist theory he describes the individual as a proactive agent of change:

> Rather than being a passive and reactive object of manipulations by external forces, the living system is viewed as a proactive *agent* that participates in its own life. Psychologically, this means that the person is both "the changer and the changed" (to borrow from feminist singer and songwriter Chris Williamson). She cocreates the personal realities to which she responds and thereby participates in a reciprocity—not only between her environment and her body, but also with different levels of her own activities. (p. 129)

Mahoney (1996) calls upon the theories of constructivism in explaining that all living systems function to establish a patterned order to their experience, which continues throughout the life span. Much of such ordering of experience happens on an unconscious level. He explains, "Constructivism portrays the individual as an active agent seeking order and meaning in social contexts where her uniquely personal experiences are challenged to continue developing" (p. 131).

I am challenged, as an agent of change, to create the ground that enables the conceptualization of unifying forces—not only to enable my own personal integrity but also to create social and community integrity. Focusing on agency, both personal and social agency, may be a path to such integrity. My stand for personal and social responsibility is consistent with Spretnak's (1993) view. She explains:

> We're trying to reorient human society, including ourselves, to appreciate and live out basic values—ecological wisdom, grassroots democracy,

nonviolence, and so forth. To effect that kind of comprehensive transformation will surely require flexibility and creativity but in a much more grounded sense. (p. 16)

It is my hope that the construction of the Ways-of-Giving model creates new conceptual ground that arises out of my constructivist research. In this way I hope to respond to Spretnak's (1993) challenge when she writes, "If we understood being as participation in an internally related unit, an unfolding whole, we would view our labour as a gift given to the community and the cosmos" (p. 189).

It is in this spirit that I offer giving agency as a theoretical and unifying construct that describes the idealized capacity to integrate and balance the complexities of giving. I use the concept of giving agency as an orientation to agency (rather than the possibility that agency might be given to another). This use responds to the way in which agency has been used within adult education literature. Giving agency provides a perspective that integrates personal and social agency and constructs a new orientation to the idea of agency that transcends both personal and social agency. Giving agency as a theoretical construct presents an opportunity for agents of change to integrate diverse aspects of practice, within diverse communities as sites of practice. An explanation of the Ways-of-Giving model follows that creates the conceptual ground for an understanding of giving agency as a theoretical construct for use in the everyday practice of giving and receiving.

Ways-of-Giving

As I began to examine my own experiences of giving within my practices as a community activist I realized that I had the opportunity to give in four distinct landscapes. Naming these landscapes voluntary service, professional service, citizenry, and prosperity, I recognized that these landscapes existed as distinct socioeconomic contexts in which I had the opportunity to practice. I selected artifacts from my own personal writing that demonstrated the best of my own giving agency in these contexts. The items I selected included letters, a story, a speech, a report, an article, and a press release. These artifacts were evidence of an engaged community life that included activities such as serving as treasurer on the board of a local hospice, fulfilling an appointment to a provincially funded health promotion task force, volunteering for the ministry and personnel committee at my church, acting as an independent consultant to a training board, and managing a case load of clients through my professional practice as a financial planner. The landscapes-of-giving evolved through my self-reflexive study. I realized that the landscapes-of-giving generate four distinct ways-of-giving that I name: charity, expertise, civic duty, and investing.

The Ways-of-Giving model integrates these distinct concepts and fosters discourse that engages in the complexity of giving and being gifted. This discourse constructs new ground that challenges the conflation of giving to a singular concept and creates new conceptual ground for others who hope to enhance their understanding of giving and their capacity to give.

The model encourages us to ask: "Who gives?" "Who fosters giving?" "What is the gift?" "Where is giving?" "How is community a site of practice for giving?" "How am I uniquely gifted?" "What opportunities do I have to give?" "How is an expectation of giving embedded in my various practices as an agent of change?" "How do adult educators, through praxis, reflect on their practice of giving?" "How might an ecological consciousness foster giving agency?"

The Ways-of Giving model responds to the complex and numerous challenges I faced as I endeavored to bring my best intentions to my practice of giving as a generous and involved community member. I experienced challenging conflicts between my desire to give, my need for recognition, and my expectation to have my gifts reciprocated. I was perplexed when I observed my own generous motives devolve into an experience of exploitation and theft as I engaged in various organizational activities. I recognized that my own motivation arose not only out of my own best intention but also out of expectations and structures embedded within the cultural, political, social, and economic realities that shaped my capacity to give. This recognition of the psychological and social complexity of giving led me to see that I needed a more complex tool to analyze and understand how I might transform my experience of giving.

I turned to the mysterious and powerful transformative power of the mandala to bring an ecological consciousness to my study of gifts and giving. The Ways-of-Giving model is presented as a mandalic quaternity, not just as any group of four, but rather a collection that, when placed together, represents a greater whole. The quaternity follows a Jungian tradition that considers the mandala as a symbol for the archetype of wholeness (Bolton, 1994, p. 21). The relationship of each landscape to the other three illuminates an understanding of each. Reflexive insights emerge out of the mirrored reflections refracted between the landscapes-, determinants-, ethics-, and ways-of-giving. The imagery arising out of this mandalic quaternity supports the rich and juicy language of appreciative inquiry described by Gervase R. Bushe (1998) and a mythopoetic perspective of transformative learning described by Dirkx (2000).

Appreciative inquiry (Bushe, 1998; Cooperrider and Srivastva, 1987) holds power as an approach in that it is able to reconcile the seemingly contradictory approaches of constructivism and the mythopoetic. Through the socio-constructivist paradigm (Cunliffe, 1999) I am lifted to an appreciative view, an empathy that fosters my best approach to influence my world. Through the mythopoetic I receive and see the world in new and splendid ways. The two approaches do not stand in opposition to one another, but rather hold the capacity to represent the spiraling circle of my connection to my environment, receiving, through mythopoetic grace, the images that are gifts from my soul's depth and through constructivist agency regifting the images to the world through my ideas and my actions. I dance in life as the changer and the changed, the giver and the gift. Mythopoetic grace connects me to "the best" of my soul's depth, to the gifts that grace my life. Through a generative approach I find my way to wrap these gifts in my own capacity—offering new hope, new images, and new visions to others. I grasp the potential that appreciative inquiry has to transcend the seeming contradictions of my own constructivist agency and my own mythic–poetic grace through a creative tension that is contained in the oscillating dance of the gift received and the gift given.

Ways-of-Giving Model

As agents of change we are both called to give and commanded to give. How do we bring consciousness to this giving? How, and under what authority, do we draw boundaries around our gifts and our giving? Are we agents of knowledge, stewards of the gift of knowing, inherited from our teachers? If so, how do we guard against an unrestrained hubris that, as Jennifer Gore (1992) warns, can be a form of unacknowledged power? In promoting this discussion I do not want to generate an ungrateful discourse: a discourse that inspires reflection on the gift that would "conjure the gift away, refusing its magic or madness in the name of reason, of reducing everything to economic exchange" (Still, 1997, p. 172). My hope is that the Ways-of-Giving model stimulates a discourse that respects the complex and mystical nature of giving and being gifted.

I begin with the landscapes-of-giving: voluntary service, citizenry, professional practice, and prosperity. These distinct economic contexts define where I am able to give. These landscapes are imaginary and idealized. They describe the best contexts for giving, arising out of a socio-rational perspective that demands the creation of the best by imagining the best (Cooperider and Srivastva, 1987). In this sense the landscapes represent a utopian horizon (Lange, 2000) and relate to a feminine economy of abundance, (Canadian Womens Studies, 2002). The Ways-of-Giving model (figure 13.1) demonstrates how the opportunity to give is constructed differently in different landscapes. For each landscape I describe a way-of-giving that is fostered in the landscape yet not confined by the landscape's boundaries. I add factors of ethics-of-giving and determinants-of-giving for each landscape, and I also add ways-of-giving as the outward movement from each landscape. The four landscapes are (a) voluntary service, in which giving as determined by philanthropy, is embedded in an ethic of care, and promotes charity as a way-of-giving; (b) professional practice, in which giving as determined by service, is embedded in an ethic of quality, and promotes expertise as a way-of-giving; (c) prosperity, in which giving as determined by risk, is embedded in an ethic of value, and promotes investing as a way-of-giving; and (d) citizenry, in which giving as determined by democracy, is embedded in an ethic of rights, and promotes civic duty as a way-of-giving.

The model presumes a conscious individual, strong and balanced in the centre of the model, having choice to give in different landscapes. The ethics described do not *belong* to the landscape, but rather, are the ethics that commonly infuse the practice and discourse within each landscape. The determinants-of-giving are preconditions that support the ways-of-giving. The ways-of-giving are not tied to the landscapes but are fostered and promoted in these landscapes and may be deployed in practice beyond the confines of the landscapes. A balance of expertise and investing contributes to personal agency. A balance of civic duty and charity contributes to social agency. A balance of the four ways-of-giving enables giving agency, which holds in creative tension the paradoxes and contradictions of the various ways-of-giving.

Fostering discourse that respects the complexity of giving and being gifted stands against the conflation of giving to a singular concept. The model provides a conceptual frame to consider inherent ethical conflicts in the realm of giving and the paradoxes and challenges of giving that encourages both social and personal agency. This new ground results from the generative capacity of appreciative inquiry (see Bushe, 1998; Cooperrider and Srivastva, 1987). The model I offer is built on a quaternity and assumes that the giving subject is able to integrate and resolve contradictions and paradoxes in a continuing process of action and reaction to changing conditions.

The quaternity reveals meaning through the way in which the four quadrants stand in relationship to one another. Prosperity, which is the landscape that focuses on ownership, mirrors voluntary service, which is about sharing and giving up ownership. Professional practice is about exclusive membership based on knowledge and expertise. This mirrors citizenry that is based on including all. Professional practice and prosperity are linked through a focus on the personal and the development of personal agency. Voluntary service and citizenry are linked through a focus on the community and the development of social agency. Likewise, social capital stands in relation to private capital between these two hemispheres. For agents of change challenged to foster entrepreneurial social infrastructure, as described by Jan Flora (1998), the broader perspective fostered by this model supports an analysis of giving that enables us to see beyond self-interest. It is not only our own self-interest that this understanding enables us to transcend, but also, in understanding the actions and motives of others. Too often, the gifts of community animators are discounted and misconstrued as self-interest. Fear of cooption, hidden agendas, and covert power can lead communities to be suspicious of any and all generosity. I hope that the deeper understanding of giving fostered through this discourse will create the capacity to discern genuine magnanimity as it occurs in communities. In this way the Ways-of-Giving model is ground for a sociological perspective that "includes notions of equality/inequality, inclusion/exclusion, and agency/structure" (Flora, 1998, p. 482), and encourages a less cynical and more positive view of community. The model, therefore, is a new tool for shaping an understanding among those committed to building community capacity (e.g., Kretzmann and McKnight, 1993).

Exploring the phenomenon of my own giving has enabled me to create a deeper understanding of others who act as agents of change. I hope I will have created a gift to help "practitioners deal with ill-defined, unique, emotive and complex issues...to help us cope with more informal, everyday ways of sense making and learning that are the essence of practice" (Cunliffe, 1999, p. 2). My self-reflexive work follows constructionist suppositions, which embrace a belief in my learning as an embodied, relational responsive process in which I am continually struck by new insights and delightfully discover and uncover new ways to think, talk, and be. I hold this in creative tension with the sense of grace that comes from a mythopoetic imagination. I eagerly anticipate the "make sense" conversations I will have with others willing to engage in reflexive dialogue, examining their own ways-of-giving and their own landscapes-of-giving. I hope my model will support others in their struggle with personal, professional, or organizational dilemmas that arise in practice. I intend to work with this model, allowing it to transform and continue to inform my practice as I learn and grow. I hope others will share with me ways in which this model assists them to think through conflicts and ethical dilemmas arising in their practice of giving.

Landscapes-of-Giving

The landscapes represent distinct economic environments or networks where I exercise personal and social agency. Simply, I have a choice of various distinct communities of practice where I exercise my capacity as an agent of change. I will decide whether to work through an organization that is structured as a charity or another organization structured as a business. I will decide whether to present myself as a citizen or as a professional consultant. The landscapes are viewed from my own giving perspective and respond to the questions: "Where will I give?" "Who will welcome my gifts?" My giving agency is exercised by the opportunities that I perceive in these various landscapes and the utopian horizon I imbue with their respective power. I recognize that I rely on social capital expressed as encouragement, opportunity, call, and invitation to stimulate and motivate my giving agency.

Ethics-of-Giving

The four ethics-of-giving (care, rights, quality, and value) are associated with the four landscapes, but not confined to the landscapes. As ethical styles they are more prevalent and embedded in the practice of the landscape with which they are associated. Like the ways-of-giving, the ethics-of-giving are sustained (receive sustenance) from their respective landscape. Yet the ethics-of-giving may be used as powerful influences for conscientization when introduced to dialogue and practice in the corresponding three landscapes. My capacity as an agent of change is often to introduce an ethical perspective that is distinct from the prevailing style associated with the landscape of practice.

Determinants-of-Giving

The determinants-of-giving (service, risk, democracy, and philanthropy) are essential elements that animate each way-of-giving. For example, charity is not possible without *philanthropic* intent. Professional expertise cannot be deployed without an element of *service*. Investing is not possible without a measure of *risk*. Civic duty (freedom) is not possible outside of *democracy*. As an agent of change, I foster attention, knowledge, and development of these determinants-of-giving in order to foster giving agency.

Ways-of-Giving

The ways-of-giving (expertise, investing, civic duty, and charity) supported by the ethics-of-giving and determinants-of-giving, are liberated from the landscapes-of-giving from which they originate to operate in all four landscapes. For example, it is possible to be charitable in the landscape of profit and employ expertise in voluntary organizations. However, in seeking an understanding of the depth and variance of charity as a way-of-giving, one is encouraged to turn to the discourse and the culture of voluntary organizations.

Private/Social Capital

Distinctions between private and social capital rely on issues of ownership. As an agent of change I invest in both private (mine) and social (ours) and recognize that my agency is facilitated or constrained by access to capital. Capital is fuel. Without it, my giving agency is immobilized—not fulfilling my design, purpose, or potential. Capital is not the gift, nor the wrapping, but the energy of giving.

Personal/Social Agency

Personal and social agency is developed distinctly through choices made as to where one gives and ways in which one gives. Giving agency is a transcendent concept that integrates the contradictions and paradoxes between personal and social agency. Giving agency commands a deeper identity than the various roles/identities I construct as I operate within specific landscapes (i.e., consultant, board member, parent, taxpayer), and connects me to a deeper sense of myself and my values. Nevertheless, my capacity to construct these identities and engage within communities of practice through these identities is essential to the exercise of my giving agency.

The Ways-of-Giving model provides an analytical tool for reflecting and engaging in discourse on giving agency. The model fosters an understanding of individual, group, and organizational motives underlying giving and promotes the considerations of how determinants-of-giving and ethics-of-giving are embedded within organizations, communities, and social structures. The Ways-of-Giving model is, therefore, a new tool for community development professionals focused on building community capacity.

For example, I have found the language of giving to be particularly useful when acting as a consultant to community-based organizations and boards. When working with a local training board I was engaged in many conversations with board members (representing labor, business, and specific equity groups) as they created policies for the organization. A contentious policy issue arose regarding wage-loss replacement for board members required to take time off work to attend meetings. Conflicts arose for members as it became apparent that some members would be "paid" for attending meetings while others would not. In many personal conversations, I found I was able to introduce the language that created fine distinctions between philanthropy and civic duty, facilitating a deeper understanding of the personal motivation and reward underlying members' participation on the board. One member, whose self-employment status made her ineligible to access funds through the proposed policy, found that reframing her gift of time and expertise to the board as a form of voluntary taxation enabled her to accept the proposed policy. I determined that setting time aside the day following each board meeting to engage in these reflective conversations was as important a consulting role as attending the meetings themselves.

The model has been equally useful to me in my role as an independent financial planner. Recently I had the opportunity to work with a client who had received an unexpected and sudden inheiritance. Conflicted by the contrary feelings of grief (for the loss of a loved one) and gratitude (for the financial gift), the client sought advice on how to invest the funds. Allowing ample time in our dialogue to move beyond the language of wealth accumulation and risk analysis, I allowed my client time to reflect on the meaning of the gift in his life. Following the language of the landscape of prosperity I asked what risks he faced, what values he held. This led to disclosing his fear of squandering the gift or allowing wealth to corrupt his values. He was determined to foster the values of care and compassion that had arisen through the relationship with his benefactor. As his advisor I challenged him to consider creating his own bequest to a future generation that required him to determine a focus upon the relationships and values (rather than the products and services) in which he would invest.

As a gift to myself and to other agents of change I offer the following recommendations to remind us of the powerful force for change that is located in a gift. These recommendations are summarized as (a) focus on giving; (b) choose giving; (c) foster giving; and (d) locate the giver and the gift.

Focus on Giving

Focusing on giving fosters a profound paradigm shift. To consciously give requires persons to locate the ground of their own giving agency. To give is to make choices in how to give, what to give, where to give, to whom to give, and what is given. A focus on giving fosters empowerment—locating control within the person who chooses to give.

Choose Giving

Agents of change are encouraged to explore the opportunity to give in different landscapes and in different ways. A gift that is frustrated, refused, or thwarted may be welcomed in a different landscape. Yet a change in landscape may not be required. The same gift might be more readily received by importing an ethical frame from a foreign landscape, facilitating a gift that was misunderstood. Challenge others to name the ethical framework that underlies their gifts; challenge others by naming different ethical perspectives underlying their gifts. For example, when the training board member was conflicted by the wage-loss policy proposal, she came to understand her motivation to serve on the board as determined by a commitment to democracy and grounded in the ethics of civil rights. This enabled her to cease thinking of her contribution to the board as pro-bono consulting service and begin thinking of her work as civic duty. The result was a deeper sense of commitment to her work, less conflict with others whose motivations she acknowledged were distinct from hers, and a newly discovered empowering framework to support her ongoing way-of-giving to her remaining term of service.

An unconscious gift is untamed and unfocused power. Learn to cultivate an understanding of the motive and intent behind your gifts. Discard giving that does not enhance your moral and ethical agency. Cultivating giving agency will integrate moral, ethical, social, fiscal, personal, communicative, and community agency.

Foster Giving

An appreciative approach to others fosters giving. Acknowledging giving and expressing gratitude for gifts are the two most powerful ways in which agents of change can foster others' giving. It is important to create opportunities for giving; to call others into the relationships that enable gift giving; and to recognize, acknowledge, and celebrate giving. It is important to resist minimizing others' gifts as mere self-interest. To imagine others' motive and intent imbued with magnanimity and generosity can trigger a perspective transformation. Design curriculum, workshops, group exercises, and programs that foster giving agency. Receive gifts. Build community by creating capacities to receive community gifts. Mobilize groups through collective giving.

Locate the Gift and the Giver

In my everyday practice of living and giving I have found that reflecting on the gift has the transformative power to lift me out of the mundane perspective of problems and conflicts. I ask myself simple questions to reframe many situations, shifting the paradigm to new insights and new opportunities. I ask these questions: (a) What gift is being presented? (b) Who is giving the gift? (c) What is the way or ways-of-giving being deployed? (d) What determinants-of-giving are in force? (e) What is the prevailing ethic(s) influencing the gift? (f) Does the gift foster personal or social agency or both? (g) Can application of the Ways-of-Giving model introduce creative tension between the paradoxes of giving that will foster giving agency?

Conclusion

An ecological consciousness presents a gift to our world. It is the gift of wholeness. Finding our own unique giftedness and way-of-giving challenges us to face the abundance that graces our living as well as the complex web of life to which we are connected. I hope that the Ways-of-Giving model may be useful to social change agents who have experienced a critical incident in their experience of giving. Often such an incident is experienced as theft: the shadow of giving. Through loss and grief, through an experience of betrayal, through the lack of acknowledgment, marginalization or misunderstanding, we experience the theft of our gifts and our giving.

I hope to encourage a sense of respect amongst those who choose to give in different ways and to increase their respect and understanding of others whose ethics, values, and skills in giving may be foreign. This paper promotes an appreciation of giving and especially appreciates the diverse ways of giving by individuals within communities. I celebrate and encourage the potential that exists to foster many ways of giving. I anticipate that a conscious and deeper understanding of giving is knowledge that will be of significance to others who choose to bring an ecological consciousness to their work as agents of change, and especially those who struggle to imbue their social purpose with personal meaning.

References

Ball, C. G. (1999). "Targeting Donors? Target Women." *Front & Centre* 6 (4), 5.

Bolton, V. (1994). *The influence of the mandala and the shadow archetypes in community based organizations.* Unpublished honors thesis, University of Waterloo, Waterloo, ON.

Bushe, G. R. (1998). *Five Theories of Change Embedded in Appreciative Inquiry.* On-line: http://www.bus.sfu.ca/homes/gervase/5theories.html.

Cooperrider, D. L. and Srivastva, S. (1987). "Appreciative Inquiry in Organizational Life." *Research in Organizational Change and Development* 1, 129–169.

Cunliffe, A. (1999). "Critical Pedagogy: Reflexive Dialogical Practice in Management Learning." In C. H. Gilson, I. Arugulis, and H. Willmott (Eds.), *Proceedings of Critical Management Studies Conference.* Manchester School of Management, Management Education Stream. On-line: http://www.mngt.waikato.ac.nz/ejrot/cmsconference/proceedings.htm.

Dees. J. G. (1998). *The Meaning of Social Entrepreneurship.* Stanford University: Kauffman Center for Entrepreneurial Leadership. On-line: http://www.the-ef.org/resources-Dees 103198.html.

Dirkx, J. M. (2000). "Knowing the Self Through Fantasy: Toward a Mytho-Poetic View of Transformative Learning." In T. J. Sork, V. Chapman, and R. St. Clair (Eds.), *Proceedings of the 41st Annual Adult Education Research Conference.* Vancouver: Department of Education, University of British Columbia. On-line: http://www.edst.educ.ubc.ca/aerc/2000/dirkxj&etal-web.htm.

Flora, J. L. (1998). "Social Capital and Communities of Place." *Rural Sociology* 63 (4) 481–506.

Gore, J. (1992). "What We can Do for You!" In C. Luke and J. Gore (Eds.), *Feminisms and Critical Pedagogy* (pp. 54–73). New York: Routledge.

Kretzmann, J. P. and McKnight, J. L. (1993). *Building Communities from the Inside Out: Path toward Finding and Mobilizing a Community's Assets.* Evanston: Center for Urban Affairs and Policy Research.

Lander, D. (2000). "A Critical Autobiography of Moral Learning Across Four Generations of the Women's Christian Temperance Union: A Feminist Genealogy." In T. J. Sork, V. Chapman, and R. St. Clair (Eds.), *Proceedings of the 41st Annual Adult Education Research Conference.* Vancouver: Department of Education, University of British Columbia. On-line: http://www.edst.educ.ubc.ca/aerc/2000/landerd-web.htm.

Lange, E. (2000). "Beyond Transformative Learning: Work, Ethical Space and Adult Education." In T. J. Sork, V. Chapman, and R. St. Clair (Eds.), *Proceedings of the 41st Annual Adult Education Research Conference.* Vancouver: Department of Education, University of British Columbia. On-line: http://www.edst.educ.ubc.ca/aerc/2000/langee-web.htm.

Lietaer, B. (1997). "Beyond Greed & Scarcity. Yes!" *Journal of Positive Futures* 2. On-line: http://hackvan.com/pub/stig/articles/yes-magazine-money-issue/Lietaer. html.

Loughlin, K. A. (1992). *Emancipatory Learning of Change Agents: Context and Description.* New York: U.S. Department of Education, Office of Educational Research and Improvement (ERIC Document Reproduction Service No. ED 373 267).

Mahoney, M. (1996). "Connected Knowing in Constructive Psychotherapy." In N. Goldberger, J. Tarule, B. Clinchy, and M. Belenky (Eds.), *Knowledge, Difference and Power: Essays Inspired by Women's Ways of Knowing* (pp. 126–142). New York: Basic Books.

Peterson, E. A. (Ed.) (1996). *Freedom Road: Adult Education of African Americans.* Malabar, FL: Krieger.

Petrie, V. (2001). *A Ways-of-Giving Model for Agents of Change.* Unpublished Master's Thesis, St. Francis Xavier University, Antigonish, Nova Scotia.

Spretnak, C. (1993). *States of Grace.* New York: HarperCollins.

Still, J. (1997). *Feminine Economies: Thinking Against the Market in the Enlightenment and the Late Twentieth Century.* Manchester, UK: Manchester University Press.

Tirrell, L. (1990). Feminists for a Gift Economy: Statement for a Peaceful World. (2002) *In Canadian Womens Studies, Women, Globalization and International Trade, Spring/Summer,* 21(4), 22(11).

CHAPTER 14

Transformative Rungs on Wisdom's Ladder

Merriam F. Bleyl with Patricia Boverie

> The pursuit of wisdom forces the true lover of knowledge to continually overcome the narrow worldview that selfish interests illuminate in order to climb to the higher perspective that wisdom seeks.
>
> Csikszentmihalyi and Rathunde (1990, p. 40)

Of all the pursuits in our modern, technologically advanced Western cultures, pursuing wisdom has not been one of them. In fact, (as seen in the Introduction) the present technological era [in which everything (including human beings) is compared to machines] effectively undermines the credibility of a concept like wisdom (Marcel, 1955). It is possible, however, that a clearer understanding of wisdom's role in individual and communal life has the potential to enhance survival, stimulate growth, and deepen human experience (Bleyl, 2000). Anciently, wisdom held a universally important and significant role in the development of individuals as well as in maintaining the healthy continuance of communities (Assmannn, 1994). Moreover, even today in most non-Western societies throughout the world, those people who are considered "wise"—the sages, elders, shaman, medicine men and women, and so on—are highly respected and revered.

Although the acknowledgment of those who are wise is not apparent in Western societies, this situation may gradually be changing. More and more, individuals from Western cultures are seeking the advice and counsel of the "wise ones" from other cultures. This may be prompted by an awareness of a "turbulent environment" (see chapter 1) wherein people realize that the knowledge and technological expertise of our activities within the earth's biosphere cannot be predicted with assurance, as was once assumed. Slowly, many are realizing that we can be informed through other ways of knowing and different forms of information. Furthermore, some are beginning to believe that those individuals who respect and revere life and the earth in a holistic way may possess a wisdom or an insight sorely needed by the rest of us. Books on native or non-Western cultural wisdom, written by "outsiders" who sense that traditional knowledge and wisdom can assist humankind in recognizing the "big picture," are becoming abundant (e.g., *Black Elk Speaks* (Neihardt, 1961), and *Wisdom of the Elders* (Suzuki and Knudtson, 1992)). As Pagels (1988) stated: "Science shows what exists but not what to do about it."

The ideas presented in this chapter coalesce from information gathered by a relatively small qualitative research study (Bleyl, 2000), where life history interviews were conducted with 20 individuals (five women and fifteen men) deemed to be "wise" by their peers. The participants represented five different cultural groups—Navajo, Japanese, Saami-Norwegian, Kenyan, and Western (Austrian/French/German), and the interviews were conducted in their respective home communities. Although the cultures, skills, knowledge bases, economic levels, and occupations of the study participants varied greatly, the experiences, attitudes, habits of mind, and perspectives held by these "wise ones" were remarkably consistent and similar.

As the life histories of the 20 "wise" participants were compiled, it became evident that their life stories bore a remarkable similarity to descriptions reported in the transformational learning literature with regard to individuals who have undergone perspective transformations or transformational learning experiences (Mezirow, 1991, 1998; Daloz, 1999). Somehow these 20 individuals were able "to negotiate and act on [their] own purposes, values, feelings, and meanings" (Mezirow, 2000, p. 8). They did not automatically and uncritically adopt the assumptions of the culture surrounding them. For the most part, the participants lived balanced lives of service to others. They exhibited a deep and broad understanding of their lives and their roles within their communities. They were socially responsible and clear thinkers. They also seemed to understand that the "deep structure of [human] needs is ultimately embedded in the wider processes of the earth and extend further to the universe itself" (O'Sullivan, 1999, p. 239). Thus, the findings of this study hint that wisdom is probably achieved through some normal, universal human developmental (transformational) process.

If wisdom is a universally achievable human condition, then recognizing those who are wise and understanding the process(es) whereby wisdom is attained can facilitate our knowing "what is best for humankind" (Csikszentimihalyi, 1995, p. 133). Indeed, if ever humankind needed the knowledge and advice of wise individuals, it is now. Yet, can the life histories and viewpoints of ordinary individuals, wise or not, really inform us about the relationship of transformational changes, human development, and wisdom? Laurent A. Daloz (1999) stated that life histories may help link transformational theory to the real world experiences of adults. He stressed the importance of life narratives: "For each of us writes with his or her life, the story of our species, and in those tales of transformation can be found the maps by which we guide our own lives—and the lives of those for whom we care" (Daloz, 1999, p. xvii).

Is wisdom related to perspective transformation? If so, how? Within this chapter, a brief discussion of what is meant by wisdom and its possible connection to theories of human development and perspective transformation is followed by a comparison of those common principles of perspective transformation that seem to also be observable in the qualities and traits of the 20 "wise" study participants. This comparison is presented metaphorically as a ladder. The final portion of the chapter discusses the possible implications from such a comparison.

Wisdom

Wisdom has been defined in multiple ways. It is a type of specific knowledge that serves as a relatively untapped "potential" in each individual and a "guiding principle" in some societies (Clayton and Birren, 1980, p. 131). It has been described as "integrated thought" and the ultimate goal of adulthood (Labouvie-Veif, 1990). Not only does wisdom represent an important aspect of the human condition (Erikson, 1982; Csikszentmihalyi, 1995); but also, it represents, among other things, a type of knowledge manifest in the ability to make sound moral and ethical judgments (Marcel, 1955). Terming it "wholesome knowledge," Aleida Assmannn (1994) described wisdom as "a type of knowledge that is age-old and, for all we know, intimately connected with human aspirations and endeavours of all times and places" (p. 188). Robert J. Sternberg (2000) related wisdom to practical intelligence, values, and tacit knowledge (the core of wisdom):

> In particular, wisdom is defined as the application of tacit knowledge as mediated by values toward the goal of achieving a common good through a balance among multiple...interests [intrapersonal, interpersonal, and extrapersonal] in order to achieve a balance among...responses to environmental contexts. (p. 637)

Thus, wisdom is a superior, universally admired, highly respected human attribute, trait, or state of mind that, as a human potential, is desired and encouraged by societies throughout the world.

Like the phenomena of courage or love, wisdom has been difficult to study empirically (Sternberg, 1990, 1998; Csikszentmihalyi and Rathunde, 1990; Assmann, 1994; Csikszentmihalyi, 1995). In the modern Western world, inquiry into wisdom has taken place over the past 30 years—primarily in the domain of psychological (life span development) research. In her studies on cognition, Vivian P. Clayton (1982), a psychologist and an early investigator of wisdom, noted that developmental progress in humans seemed headed toward wisdom. James E. Birren and Laurel M. Fisher (1990) wrote: "Wisdom is not simply for wise people or curious psychologists; it is for all people and the future of the world" (p. 332). However, in spite of that allegation, wisdom appears to be a phenomenon that today is most readily identified only in individuals from non-Western cultures (Assmann, 1994; Bleyl, 2000).

Human Development and Wisdom

It appears that only one researcher *directly* linked wisdom to a universal developmental model for human beings. More than fifty years ago, Erik H. Erikson, in his epic work, *Childhood and Society* (1950/1982), delineated eight possible developmental stages in the life span of man. He stated that each age (or more accurately, each psychosocial stage) of life contained a basic virtue to be mastered. According to Erikson, the basic virtues were achieved by resolving the inevitable personal crises that occurred at each developmental life stage. The final stage of integrity, rarely reached, represented the basic virtue of wisdom—which Erikson explained as "ripened 'wits,' . . . accumulated knowledge, mature judgment, and inclusive understanding" (1982, p. 140). He considered wisdom the culmination of human social–emotional development, coming near the end of an individual's life and consisting of a balance between knowing and doubting.

Erikson felt that the eight developmental stages were universal among all human beings, regardless of culture:

> Each individual, to become a mature adult, must to a sufficient degree develop all the ego qualities mentioned, so that a wise Indian, a true gentleman, and a mature peasant share and recognize in one another the final stage of integrity. (p. 274)

Others (Piaget, 1970; Kohlberg, 1973; Fowler, 1981; Gilligan, 1982; and Kegan, 1982, 1994—to name a few) have expanded on Erikson's theories.

Developmental *stages* have given way to developmental *processes*; but no other human development researcher appears to have used the term "wisdom" to describe the culminating stage of development.

Transformation and Wisdom

In the transformative learning literature, on the other hand, human wisdom does not appear to have been addressed directly at all. Many researchers have noted perspective transformation as an important process of development in adulthood. Perspective transformation leads "developmentally toward a more inclusive, differentiated, permeable, and integrated perspective and that, insofar as it is possible, we all naturally move toward such an orientation" (Mezirow, 1991, p. 155). Transformative learning is described as "experiencing a deep, structural shift in the basic premises of thought, feeling, and actions. It is a shift in consciousness that dramatically alters our ways of being in the world" (O'Sullivan, 2000, p. 29). Mezirow (1991) also stated that transformative learning involves "a shift in perspective."

Robert Kegan (1982, 1994) described the transformational process as a shift in consciousness through five different orders (levels) that are both developmental and cultural. Consciousness represents the complexity in various ways of knowing. For most of us, these shifts in consciousness rarely extend beyond the fourth level (Kegan, 1994). Most people function at the third level. However, those individuals who function at the highest level (Kegan's fifth order) have characteristics that seem similar to those who are "wise." Furthermore, perspective transformation "occurs between thirty-five and fifty-five years [of age], and its duration may extend from five to twenty years" (Labouvie-Vief, 1984, p. 179)—similar to folk beliefs about wisdom.

Thus, although the connections to wisdom in the transformational literature are almost nonexistent, there appear to be similarities in the characteristics of the "wise" and the "transformed." The "wise ones" interviewed possessed the characteristics of individuals who had experienced significant transformational change—in attitudes, in learning strategies, in sensitivity to the needs and feelings of others, and in a deep appreciation for the earth's environment. For instance, Hiroshi Shimoguchi, a "wise" Japanese study participant, spoke of transformations in his life as he related his life's story. As a 15-year-old college student, he was conscripted into the Japanese army and sent to Mongolia to fight in the brutal China War (1931–1945).

What I experienced there in China was different than I had ever imagined.... Thinking power was not important for Japanese soldiers. It was only their physical strength that was wanted. They didn't want the soldiers to think; they just wanted you to work. So, in that environment, knowledge or wisdom, etc., were denied or nonexistent. Everything that I had developed—all the thinking etc.—over fifteen years up until that time was denied me. The only thing that they taught me was what is the appropriate way to die. They did not teach me how to live at all. When those things [thinking, knowledge, wisdom] aren't valued, it is just like you have died already.... I feel that the person I had been died with the war.

After the war, Shimoguchisan returned to an ecologically devastated and economically struggling Japan with a new perspective. He stated that he felt that he *needed* to live a "new life" for his friends—those less fortunate than he—who died in the war.

For me, I think that my life already ended once—before 1945. Now I am living a second life. Everything since [1945] is just a surplus.... The good life for those in my generation is not honor or wealth. It is as portrayed in the following poem:

Tomo no himei ni ware ha naku,   I cry with a friend's adversity
Ware no yorokoi ni tomo ha naru   A friend rejoices in my happiness.

Shimoguchisan then said, "I want to be surrounded by these types of people."

Transformative Rungs Toward Wisdom

Assuming that wisdom represents the culminating "stage" of human development, one might imagine a metaphorical ladder leading to wisdom (figure 14.1). Undoubtedly, a ladder is not the most accurate image to employ, since transformational changes probably occur through a spiraling *process* rather than steps or levels (Kegan, 1994); however, for purposes of comparison, the ladder analogy may be helpful. Each rung on the ladder represents a principle of transformative learning as described by Jack Mezirow (1991, 2000), Edward E. Taylor (2000), Daloz (1999), and others. Each principle was exhibited in the lives of the study participants. Moreover, starting at the bottom, each rung seems to lead to the next. A description of the principles represented by the rungs follows:

Rung 1. Adversity

It is in the winter of our discontent that transformation can most readily take place.

Daloz (1999, p. vxii)

Figure 14.1 Transformative Rungs on Wisdom's Ladder. The Rungs on the Ladder Depict the Qualities of the Wise that Appear Similar to Those Involved in Perspective Transformation.

The first transformative principle—the bottom rung of the ladder, if you will—relating to a characteristic of the wise participants appeared to be the prevalence of adversity in their lives. What we are terming "adversity" can be thought of as being similar to Mezirow's (2000) "disorienting dilemma." In transformative theory, this triggering event, challenge or dilemma (usually representing an experience not willfully chosen) is often cited as the catalyst that begins the process of an individual's transformation.

For the participants in this wisdom study, the "adversities" reported were often severe. Their dilemmas included war (as soldiers and victims), deaths of family members, physical and mental abuse, poverty, starvation, losses (including finances, jobs, and relationships), illness, and discrimination. Often, these kinds of events were multiple, occurring frequently throughout an individual's life. Even so, the study participants did not actually say or even indicate in any way that they had personally experienced adversities in their lives. The adverse events of their lives were so labelled by the interviewer (Bleyl, 2000).

Psychological research into wisdom by Birren and Fisher (1990) questioned "whether there are not crucial experiences in life and critical periods that might further the development of wisdom. This alludes to the often-expressed view that tragedy is a substrate of experiences from which wisdom can arise" (p. 323). Although most participants in the study had experienced great difficulties in their lives, somehow they were able to integrate these sometimes-terrible life events, changing and transforming their life's course when necessary, to eventually emerge as valuable, wise, and respected members in their communities.

Rung 2. Reflective Assessment

Reflection and contemplation are often cited as actions of those who are wise (Assmannn, 1994). Reflective learning is a significant part of transformational theory (Mezirow, 1991). That critical reflection limits external distractions, produces optimal attention to a stimulus, and leads to expanded awareness has been advocated since the time of John Dewey (Dewey, 1933; Mezirow, 1990, 1991). The practice of self-reflection helped the study's wise participants to become aware of who they were as people—as well as to solidify their opinions and beliefs about things going on about them.

Twelve participants spoke directly of their personal practice of reflection, especially when faced with difficult situations. Philmer Bluehouse, a Navajo Peacemaker, spoke of the process whereby he learned how to proceed with a new job. For Bluehouse, reflection was similar to being mentored:

> When I started with Peacemaking... I had to ask myself, "Where do I find this information about peacemaking?" So, for whatever reason, I was compelled to go behind Window Rock—the actual rock itself.... Back there, I spent at least a month and a half every day at noontime. And I would just select a spot—I called it "my place"—and I would sit. I would listen. I would look. I would smell. I'd use all the senses. And I think, reaching back to nature, that those are the teachers that taught me in that little ten-by-ten foot area.... It's not like we can hear right now. It's a different level—the esoteric level. It's a holy level of understanding.

All study participants mentioned the importance of those periods of time in their lives when they questioned and searched reflectively on life's meaning.

Rung 3. Self-Awareness and Self-Reliance

We learn from transformational theory that self-awareness and self-reliance are the products of reflection. Each of the wise ones interviewed was well aware of and took seriously their responsibilities. They did not wait for others to solve their problems or to care for their needs. They took action. They did "whatever it took" to survive—and they especially worked to help others survive and grow.

This principle is dramatically illustrated by events in the life of Kristian Kristensen, for whom survival was an ever-present challenge. Born in the far-northern area of Norway above the Arctic Circle known as Finnmark, Kristian, a Norwegian, learned from his father and his Saami friends how to survive and even thrive in that frigid northern land—by living in balance with nature. When Germany invaded and occupied Norway during World War II, the occupying Nazis hastily built a camp for housing Russian Prisoners-of-War next to the Kristensen home in Alta, Norway. Kristensen described times of cold, hunger, and unconscionable treatment of the prisoners, but he and his family, by befriending the guards and their prisoners, found the means to slip extra food to the prisoners whenever they could. Near the end of the war, the German army, retreating southward, devastated the land and burned the forests, leaving no bridges, homes, or buildings standing in Finnmark. The local population, including the Kristensen family, was evacuated as the German and Austrian troops fled south from the approaching Russian army.

Kristian was among the first to return to rebuild homes and livelihoods in the wasteland left of his community. When Alta, Norway, was restored, Kristian went out to sea to earn a living harvesting seals, but following a shipwreck (where he was marooned for a time on an Iceland sheep ranch), he decided to raise mink—only to have the fur market plummet in the 1970s—bringing him close to the edge of financial ruin. He recalled his plight with humor:

> I didn't know exactly what I should do after I stopped raising mink. The last payment I got was so little money that I thought I was going to lose everything. I had to do something. But I thought, at least I have my shirt—they can't take that away. I get to keep the shirt. And that's enough! It went better than I thought. I just worked and worked and worked. I began with farming and I invested small amounts.

Finally, in the land of the midnight sun, the aurora borealis, and an extremely short growing season, Kristensen became a self-reliant, creative, and successful farmer. He was able to look at his circumstances, critically assess the situation, and institute change when needed. To this day, he relishes learning new skills. His confidence in himself, his optimism, his faith, and his sense of humor undoubtedly help him thrive.

Rung 4. An Empowered Sense of Self

As Daloz (1999) points out, "...development is more than simply change. The word implies direction" (p. 23). This view, in terms of Mezirow's (1991) transformative theory, would represent the ability to reflectively assess one's premises, discern what the implications would be, make a judgment, and take an appropriate action. For the wise participants, this empowered sense of self was not one of self-centeredness, but involved, rather, a "forgetting of the self" to some extent. The participants of this study had confidence in their abilities to do whatever was necessary and did it.

As one example, a charming 78-year-old woman from Wakayama Prefecture, northeast of Osaka, Japan, is popular not only with her immediate neighbors, but with everyone who knows of her. This compassionate woman has been nearly blind since she was ten years old. Coming from a life of poverty and loss, she is, nevertheless, well known for her generosity, her skills, and her faith. She is a healer—helping people through massage, prayers, herbs, and practical advice. She has only one wish in life: to make the world a better place in which to live. Men, women, and children line up outside of her old-style Japanese house, waiting their turn to have her "treat" their hurts and diseases, to ease their burdens, and to seek her wise advice for their problems. Her life's work, for which she accepts no payment, is important to her. When she speaks, her voice is strong and melodic:

> Even though I had a bad eye, I found some purpose or object in my life through my work. Through my work, I was able to help other people. I am proud of my work. People must be proud of what they do.

When asked how she developed her ability to heal people, she humbly replied, "I think it is something God has given me, *but action is also necessary!*"

Rung 5. Socially Unobtrusive and Open

The participants in the study were socially unobtrusive (or humble) and open to different ideas. They did not attribute their often-respected positions in their cultures as having anything to do with being earned by them. Respectful to those around them, they listened to and valued the views of all individuals—even those who disagreed with them.

Ole Henrik Magga, a Saami participant, humbly exhibits a style of leadership that is truly exemplary. He was actively involved in helping the Saami people address grievances with the government (such as the attempted elimination of the Saami language, dress, and lifestyle). Magga opened a dialogue with the Norwegian government (and other Scandinavian governments) and was instrumental in establishing a Saami Parliament so that the rights of the indigenous peoples in Finnmark and the environment of their lands (which was slowly being destroyed) could be protected. Elected as the first President of the Saami Parliament, Magga called himself "an activist," yet his attitude toward others showed great tolerance, patience, and understanding. In discussing what characteristic is most important in being a leader, he stated:

It's a kind of basic belief in other people—even with people who disagree with you. You should not seriously doubt their motives. Their motives can be good—as good as yours. That means there is not only one truth in this world. There can be many truths and you have to respect that. Therefore, you shouldn't define your opponents as evil people.

Magga is a man who truly cares about others—his people (the Saami) and even the church and government leaders with whom he negotiated about Saami rights. He is open and respectful to everyone—even those who oppose him. He now heads a UN committee on the rights of indigenous people worldwide.

The "wise ones" interviewed were respected by their peers—that is, they were regarded with honor and with esteem. This respect did not stem from their power, prestige, fame, or wealth (or lack of it). It appeared to be from their genuine openness to others and their consistent respectful treatment of others. They were conscious of the effects that their actions had on other people and on the environment.

Rung 6. Focused on the Common Good

Transformative learning often helps individuals choose pathways that lead toward helping not only themselves, but others as well. The work of Paolo Friere (1970) and others—to help individuals recognize and actualize themselves, improving themselves and others—is cited continually in the transformational literature. Similarly, the "common good" is an attribute that has been associated with wisdom since the time of Socrates. Gisela Labouvie-Vief (1990) has stated, "Wisdom consists, so to say, in one's ability to see through and beyond individual uniqueness and specialization into those structures that relate us in our common humanity" (p. 78).

The "common good"—for all people, life forms, and for the earth itself—seemed paramount in the thoughts and actions of the wise ones in this study. They focused on serving and helping others achieve their own worthy goals. For instance, Bethwell Kiplagat (Kenyan) is taking action for the common good of humanity as well as earth's environment. Although retired, Kiplagat now works almost around the clock to try to resolve the serious problems that face Kenya—and Africa as a whole. (He has recently been appointed as Special Envoy to the Somalia Peace Process.) The solution to Africa's problems, Kiplagat said, is of a spiritual nature:

> Presently, I am going through a change—a shift—in my life.... What I am saying today, is that Africa needs to relook at its inner life. Africa needs to look to put an emphasis on its—I call it *the spirit*—rather than just knowledge. We need to go back to the spirit.... And, therefore, what I would like to do with the remaining part of my life is to put an emphasis on this area. To say what is important is not the money or the time that you [speaking of loans requested of the World Bank] give us; but, first and foremost, it is to rebuild the broken spirit of our people. Because if your spirit is weak and broken, then really it doesn't matter what people do to you. You will not overcome whatever the problem is. But if that spirit is strengthened, then anything that comes, you face it—because the inner— the inside—is true. You face this problem, and you look at it and say, "Now what can I do?"

Many participants spoke of a spiritual influence in their lives; however, not all participants were "religious" per se. Some were agnostic; some were atheists; some were devout Christians; some were Buddhist; some followed their native beliefs. However, most referred to the spiritual strength of the human being, and many spoke to the power of the Creator and the need for balance in life.

Along with their concern and respect for humanity, the "wise ones" were especially conscious of the earth's environment, and the balance needed to sustain life. In fact, 17 participants expressed great concern for the environment. Leading by example, they served as mentors to those about them in helping to bring attention to environmental problems.

Wangari Maathai, a Kenyan environmentalist who has garnered many awards, including the Global 500 Award, spoke eloquently and passionately of the earth's environment and the role it plays in sustaining life. Maathai, recently (December 2002) overwhelmingly elected to Parliament, now serves as Kenya's Assistant Minister for Environment, Natural Resources and Wildlife. "Professor Maathai," as the Kenyan people affectionately call her, has dedicated her life to humanitarian and environmental causes. She has actively worked from her sense of the "common good" and her work has not always been easily accomplished. The first woman in East Africa to obtain her doctorate, Maathai founded the Green Belt Movement in Kenya, an organization that has multiple purposes—one of which is to safeguard and even restore the Kenyan landscape, and another of which is to help people help themselves out of poverty and despair. Physically beaten, hospitalized, jailed, defamed, and berated by those whose self-interests were threatened by her appeals to treat the Kenyan people (especially women and children) and the environment with respect, Maathai explained:

> I try to teach adults about how to take care of their environment, and how to take care of themselves, how to make decisions and be in charge of [their own lives]—because partly when you don't do that, then you destroy the environment.... I try to say that, in our environment today, we have a lot of problems. We are poor; we are over-mining the environment; we are consuming pesticides and herbicides; we are killing the soil with all these chemicals; and we are polluting our water, our air. And I say we are in the wrong bus, and we are walking toward the wrong destination. Because if you step in the wrong bus, and if you walk toward the wrong destination, you will surely get into a lot of problems.

So, Maathai and the Green Belt Movement encourage Kenyans to "get out of the wrong bus" and to change their assumptions. Although the Green Belt Movement began with encouraging women to become "foresters without diplomas" by replanting Kenyan forests that had been destroyed and to combat desertification, it has expanded to encouraging people to plant mixed crops of vegetation native to Kenya. Individuals are also encouraged to assume civic responsibilities. Maathai mentors thousands of Kenyans and is revered as a "wise" and courageous woman.

Bethwell Kiplagat, mentioned earlier, is also keenly aware of the environmental conditions in Kenya that are destroying that beautiful land. He, like Maathai, not only recognizes the problems, but proposes solutions—solutions that he personally implements in his own life. For instance, one of the problems in Kenya that Kiplagat personally addresses is that of the ubiquitous trash (primarily plastic bags, etc.) scattered along the road and countrysides of Kenya. Kiplagat elaborated:

> Plastic is a big problem with us.... So, every shop I go to, if they give me plastic [bags], I say, "No! No! No! Please! I don't use plastic. Do you know

the dangers of plastic?" And they say, "Why?" And then I explain. And now when I go to those shops, I will find [bags made from] degradable materials.

The "wise ones" of this study were leaders of similar character, who led by not only talking about wise actions, but also by having the personal integrity to *act* for the common good—be it in their own self-interest or not.

Discussion

> The citizens of the earth are faced with complex problems—and it
> is this area where wisdom is needed.
>
> Pagels (1988)

This chapter compares the similarities between the characteristics of those known as "wise" in their communities and those whose levels of consciousness have changed or transformed through a process of normal development or through the guidance and encouragement of a mentor. Principles of perspective transformation seem to lead to a level of consciousness that has the qualities of wisdom. Although not definitively answered in the study considered here, we suggest that wisdom, although rarely attained, may represent the highest consciousness level in the process of transformational human development (or growth).

Whether or not wisdom is reached through the processes associated with transformative change and growth may not be the important message of this chapter, however. In spite of Western civilization's apparent devaluation of wisdom, it seems that wise individuals do exist and are living in all cultures of the world. Not only do they exist, but also their "wisdom"—their outlooks, thoughts, and deeds—has much in common. The actions taken by the study's "wise ones" were courageous, ethical, caring, and admirable. As leaders in their respective cultures, they inspired those about them, giving freely and humbly of their time and talents to others—regardless of social or fiscal status. As mentors, they led by example, and were able to help the people with whom they interrelated feel empowered. Despite the ravages of war, poverty, or social and environmental degradation, these individuals were able to transcend their problems and transform their thinking—resulting in what might be considered a high level of social and ecological consciousness (as defined in chapter 1). (These adverse conditions actually may have facilitated that growth.)

It is possible that the study of those known to be wise may provide a "guide" or a framework for the development of a heightened consciousness— one that transcends culture, nation, politics, and religion. Using the metaphor of the ladder of transformation, perhaps we as educators can begin to develop purposeful experiences that move individuals along the developmental continuum. Of course, we can't actually put individuals in the path of adversity; however, our modern lives naturally provide us with dilemmas that can trigger transformative growth (for instance, illness, divorce, death, discrimination, war, threats of terrorism, etc.). Perhaps what most of us need in order to transform and increase our levels of consciousness are "wise" mentors who purposefully promote healthy human growth and understanding based on example and curricula that includes much reflection and analysis.

It also seems crucial that humankind renew its pursuit of wisdom (especially in Western societies). That we have much to learn from one another seems evident. As Daloz (1999) explains:

> It seems that the more entranced we become with the amplification and distraction made possible by high technology, the more fiercely we must simultaneously burrow back down to the truth that we know through our immediate experience, to our direct encounters as embodied human beings with one another and with the earth. (p. xxvi)

This type of direct interchange helps us become aware of each other and to educate and "transform" our thoughts.

As noted in the first chapter of this volume, the benefits derived from technological advancement and the materialism that threatens our world must not be allowed to threaten the existence of any portion of humanity. The following wise words from study participant Wangari Maathai challenge us to consider the importance of the wisdom that exists in every community around the globe:

> Every community in this world—no matter how large, no matter how small—has wisdom. And wisdom, to me, is the experiences that people go through.... So their wisdom, their successful experiences, was "coded" into a culture that became a tradition—that became a way of life. And so I like to persuade all people—especially communities that are marginalized and have been subdued and oppressed and exploited, and have been persuaded that their culture is not worth it—to appreciate that. Whatever it is—however trivial it may appear—it is wisdom! We ought to be really grateful that those who experienced it passed it on to us. And we should not be persuaded by anybody to throw it away at this time. As a human race, as a people, we are so much better off with all these bits and pieces of culture.... We need *all* that wisdom!

Human wisdom, although rare, is universal. As the "wise" among us reflect on the complex problems facing humanity, they may, after all, be able to *teach* the rest of us something about taking appropriate action when action is necessary, about tolerance and respect for all peoples, about the importance of honing our own and our collective levels of consciousness (socially and environmentally), and about what it takes to be "wise" and act wisely.

References

Assmann, A. (1994). "Wholesome Knowledge: Concepts of Wisdom." In D. L. Featherman, R. M. Lerner, and M. Perlmutter (Eds.), *Life-Span Development and Behavior* (pp. 187–224). Hillsdale, NJ: Lawrence Erlbaum Associates, Publishers.

Birren, J. E. and Fisher, L. M. (1990). "The Elements of Wisdom: Overview and Integration." In R. J. Sternberg (Ed.), *Wisdom: Its Nature, Origins, and Development*. New York: Cambridge University Press.

Bleyl, M. (2000). *The Wise Ones: A Multi-Cultural Perspective*. Unpublished Ph.D. dissertation, University of New Mexico, Albuquerque, New Mexico.

Clayton (1982). "Wisdom and Intelligence. The Nature and Function of Knowledge in the Later Years." *International Journal of Ageing and Human Development* 15, 315–321.

Clayton, V. P. and Birren, J. E. (1980). "The Development of Wisdom Across the Life-Span: A Reexamination of an Ancient Topic." In P. B. Baltes and O. G. Brim, Jr. (Eds.), *Life-Span Development and Behavior* (Vol. 3) (pp. 103–135). New York: Academic Press.

Csikszentmihalyi, M. (1995). "Toward an Evolutionary Hermeneutics: The Case of Wisdom." In R. F. Goodman and W. R. Fisher (Eds.), *Rethinking Knowledge: Reflections Across the Disciplines* (pp. 123–143). Albany, NY: State University of New York Press.

Csikszentmihalyi, M. and Rathunde, K. (1990). "The Psychology of Wisdom: an Evolutionary Interpretation." In R. J. Sternberg (Ed.), *Wisdom: Its Nature, Origins, and Development*. New York: Cambridge University Press.

Daloz, L. A. (1999). *Mentor: Guiding the Journey of Adult Learners* (2nd ed.). San Francisco: Jossey-Bass Publishers.

Dewey, J. (1983). *How we Think: A Restatement of the Relation of Reflective Thinking to Educational Process*. Chicago: University of Illinois Press.

Erikson, E. H. (1950) [1982]. *Childhood and Society*. New York: W. W. Norton.

Fowler, J. W. (1981). *Stages of Faith: The Psychological of Human Development and the Quest for Meaning*. New York: HarperCollins Publisher.

Friere, P. (1970). *Pedagogy of the Oppressed*. New York: Herter and Herter.

Gilligan, C. (1982). *In a Different Voice: Psychological Theory and Women's Development*. Cambridge, MA: Harvard University Press.

Kegan, R. (1982). *The Evolving Self: Problem and Process in Human Development*. Cambridge, MA: Harvard University Press.

Kegan, R. (1994). *In Over Our Heads: The Mental Demands of Modern Life.* Cambridge, MA: Harvard University Press.

Kohlberg, L. (1973). "Stages and Aging in Moral Development: Some Speculations." *Gerontologist* 5 (13), 497–502.

Labouvie-Vief, G. (1984). "Logic and Self-Regulation from Youth to Maturity: A Model." In M. L. Commons, F. A. Richards, and C. Armon (Eds.), *Beyond Formal Operations: Comparisons and Applications of Adolescent and Adult Development Models* (Vol. 2) (pp. 153–180). New York: Praeger.

Labouvie-Vief, G. (1990). "Wisdom as Integrated Thought: Historical and Developmental Perspectives." In R. J. Sternberg (Ed.), *Wisdom: Its Nature, Origins, and Development* (pp. 52–83). New York: Cambridge University Press.

Marcel, G. (1955). *The Decline of Wisdom.* London: Harvill Press.

Mezirow, J. (1991). *Transformative Dimensions of Adult Learning.* San Francisco: Jossey-Bass Publishing.

Mezirow, J. (1998). "On Critical Reflection." *Adult Education Quarterly* 48 (1), 60–62.

Mezirow, J. (2000). "Learning to Think Like an Adult: Core Concepts of Transformation Theory." In J. Mezirow (Ed.), *Learning as Transformation: Critical Perspectives on a Theory in Progress* (pp. 3–33). San Francisco: Jossey-Bass Publishing.

Mezirow, J. and Associates (1990). *Fostering Critical Reflection in Adulthood: A Guide to Transformative and Emancipatory Learning.* San Francisco: Jossey-Bass.

Neihardt, J. G. (1961) [1932]. *Black Elk Speaks.* Lincoln, NE: University of Nebraska Press.

O'Sullivan, E. (1999). *Transformative Learning: Educational Vision for the 21st century.* London: Zed Books.

O'Sullivan, E. (2000). "Integral Education: A Vision of Transformative Learning in a Planetary Context." In *Proceedings of the Third International Transformative Learning Conference. Challenges of Practice: Transformative Learning in Action* (pp. 29–34). New York: Teacher's College Columbia University.

Pagels, H. F. (1988). *The Dreams of Reason: The Computer and the Rise of the Sciences of Complexity.* New York: Simon and Schuster.

Piaget, J. (1970). *Structuralism.* New York: Basic Books.

Sternberg, R. J. (2000). "Intelligence and Wisdom." In R. J. Sternberg (Ed.), *Handbook of Intelligence* (pp. 631–649). New York: Cambridge University Press.

Suzuki, D. and Knudtson, P. (1992). *Wisdom of the Elders: Honoring Sacred Native Visions of Nature.* New York: Bantam Books.

Notes on Contributors

Merriam F. Bleyl is an independent academic researcher and Adjunct Professor at the University of New Mexico, Albuquerque, New Mexico. Her research interests include learning and cognition, culture, human development and wisdom. She received her Ph.D. in Organizational Learning and Instructional Technologies from the University of New Mexico in 2000.

Patricia E. Boverie is Associate Professor of Organizational Learning and Instructional Technologies (OLIT) in the College of Education at the University of New Mexico. She teaches classes in adult learning theory, group processes in learning, team development and training, critical thinking, learning to learn, school/business partnerships, delivering effective presentations, organization development, consulting theory and practice, and transformational learning. In addition to teaching at the university, Patricia co-owns Boverie, Kroth & Associates, a private consulting firm specializing in personal and organizational transformation.

Gregory A. Cajete is Director of Native American Studies and Associate Professor in the College of Education, Division of Language, Literacy and Sociocultural Studies at the University of New Mexico.

Sandra Campbell (www.gettingtonormal.com) is a writer and community educator who lives and works in Toronto, Canada. The primary focus of her work is learning and the imagination. Her first novel, *Getting to Normal*, Stoddart, 2001, explores issues of health through the eyes of a seven-year-old child. *A Due: A Memoir*, is an exploration of blood and belonging, memory and perception, the arts and transformation and will be published in 2004.

Laurent A. Parks Daloz is Associate Director and faculty of the Whidbey Institute for Earth, Spirit, and the Human Future in Clinton, Washington. He is author of the award-winning book, *Effective Teaching and Mentoring* (second edition entitled *Mentor: Guiding the Journey of Adult Learners*), and coauthor with Sharon Daloz Parks and Cheryl and Jim Keen, of *Common*

Fire: Leading Lives of Commitment in a Complex World (Beacon Press, 1997), a study of how people come to care for the common good. He has published widely in adult education and holds an honorary doctorate from the University of New Hampshire.

Don W. de Guerre is Assistant Professor at Concordia University in Montréal where he teaches in the graduate program in Human Systems Intervention. From 1989 to 1999 he was Manager Organization Effectiveness, Syncrude Canada Ltd., where he completed a total organization participative redesign process. Earlier Dr. de Guerre worked internationally on organization consulting in both the public and private sectors.

Barbara Dewar is a member of The Esprit Association and cocreator, with JoAnne Corbeil, of the Espritedu Training of Psychotherapy Associates. She is a clinical member of the Ontario Society of Psychotherapists (OSP). She has had a psychotherapy practice for 20 years and her practice is in Toronto, St. Catharines, and the Niagara region. She is passionate about the challenge to honor her authentic self and those of others. She believes that when those moments are achieved there is no divisional split between her inner self and the world.

John M. Dirkx is Associate Professor of Higher, Adult, and Lifelong Education at Michigan State University, and the Co-director of the Michigan Center for Career and Technical Education at MSU. He has worked extensively in education for the professions, continuing education, and professional development of educators of adults. Among his research interests are transformative education and learning, dynamics and developmental processes of small learning groups, workplace learning, and education of academically underprepared adults. He is the author of *A Guide for Planning and Implementing Instruction for Adults: A Theme-based Approach*, which describes an integrated model for teaching adult learners. He is currently working on a book that explores transformation and deep change from a mytho-poetic and depth psychology perspective.

Dorothy Ettling is an educator, consultant, and researcher working in the university and in community settings. She is Associate Professor in the doctoral concentration on Organizational Leadership at the University of the Incarnate Word in San Antonio, Texas. She is founder of Interconnections, a community-based network for education and research and Director of Women's Global Connection, a virtual gathering place for promoting transformative learning and exchange of resources among women around the world. Her research interests are transformative change processes, in individuals, groups, and organizations, and the role of spirituality in transformative change.

Lulesa Guilian has been studying a process called transformative training for five years. She is the creator of the program the Achievement System, which prescribes a method of taking people from poverty consciousness to affluence thinking. She is presently developing a nonprofit agency in the San Francisco Bay area that is based on the principles of her research. In addition, she is currently the Director of Human Resources for the California Institute of Integral Studies in San Francisco.

Stuart B. Hill is Foundation Chair of Social Ecology at the University of Western Sydney. Prior to 1996 he was at McGill University, in Montreal, where in 1974 he established Ecological Agriculture Projects, Canada's leading resource center for sustainable agriculture (www.eap.mcgill.ca). He has published over 300 papers and reports. His latest book (with Martin Mulligan) is *Ecological Pioneers: A Social History of Australian Ecological Thought and Action* (Cambridge University Press, 2001). He is currently on the editorial board of four refereed journals and represents professional environmental educators on the NSW Council on Environmental Education. He has worked internationally in chemical engineering, ecology, soil biology, entomology, agriculture, psychotherapy, education, policy development and international development.

Jessica T. Kovan is currently a nonprofit organization consultant. She completed her doctorate at Michigan State University in 2001 in Higher, Adult and Lifelong Education with an emphasis in nonformal education and social activism. Her dissertation was entitled, *Sustaining Passion: The Experience of Being an Environmentalist in a Small Nonprofit Organization*. Jessica has worked for many years in the environmental movement, including working as a program director for the Kellogg Foundation, leading their Water Resources programming area, and serving on the Board of Directors and as Executive Director of the Mid-Michigan Environmental Action Council. Her research, consulting, and volunteer interests emphasize helping to empower youth and adults working to improve the world we live in.

Michael Kroth has developed and administered corporate-level leadership development and succession planning programs, has been the administrator of a corporate foundation, and has served as a director of corporate community affairs. Michael co-owns Boverie, Kroth & Associates, a private consulting firm specializing in personal and organizational transformation. In addition to BK&A, he is Adjunct Professor at the University of New Mexico in the Organizational Learning and Instructional Technologies program. He teaches classes in adult learning theory, team development, delivering effective presentations, organization development, consulting theory and practice, and transformational learning.

Marilyn E. Laiken is Professor of Adult Education in the Workplace Learning and Change specialization at OISE, University of Toronto, and Director of the OISE/UT Certificate Program in Adult Training and Development. She is also Principal of Laiken Associates, a Toronto consulting firm, which, since 1975, has served over 150 clients in the public, private, and not-for-profit sectors. Marilyn combines an interest in adult education and organizational change through research, teaching, and field development in such areas as organizational learning and renewal, system redesign, work-team development, participative leadership, and experiential, transformative adult education. She speaks internationally and has published widely in all of these areas. Her book, entitled *The Anatomy of High Performing Teams: A Leader's Handbook* (University of Toronto Press, 1998, 3rd edition), focuses on work-team facilitation concepts and skills.

Eimear O'Neill is a psychotherapist, community activist, and educator in Toronto, Canada. She is affiliated with the Transformative Learning Centre at the Ontario Institute for Studies in Education of the University of Toronto where she is completing her Ph.D., which uses artful inquiry to reveal the processes of decolonization and healing of trauma at multiple levels as central to women's and to communities' self transformation. She is currently developing courses in transformative psychotherapies for healers from diverse communities: these are artful, multidisciplinary, and intended to develop community and peer supervision across agencies. Her most recent publicaion is "Transforming the Ecology of Violence" with Ed O'Sullivan in *Expanding the Boundaries of Transformative Learning* (Palgrave, 2002). As someone Celtic-identified, her current workshop focus is on working with indigenous scholars in learning circles for women becoming indigenous to their bodies, peoples, and place.

Edmund V. O'Sullivan is Professor of Education at the Ontario Institute for Studies in Education at the University of Toronto. Currently, he is the Director of the Transformative Learning Centre. His latest books are *Critical Psychology and Critical Pedagogy* (Univeristy of Toronto Press, 1990), *Transformative Learning: Educational Vision for the 21st Century* (London: Zed Press, 1999), and most recently, *Expanding the Boundaries of Transformative Learning* (New York: Palgrave Press, 2002) and *Learning Toward Ecological Consciousnesses: Selected Transformative Practices* (New York: Palgrave, 2003). His E-mail and website are: eosullivan@oise.utoronto.ca; www.tlcentre.org.

Yuka Takahashi is currently pursuing her Ph.D. at Ontario Institute for Studies in Education (OISE) of the University of Toronto. She had previously worked for an environmental NGO in Tokyo, promoting environmental education in Japan and in the Asia Pacific region. She then went to Toronto to study at OISE/UT. After obtaining her M.A. from OISE/UT, she took a post as Associate Expert for United Nations Educational, Scientific and Cultural Organization (UNESCO). Based in Bangkok, she worked on inclusive education and environmental education projects around the Asian region for two years. Back at OISE/UT, she continues to be involved in a community education project in India as a consultant for UNESCO.

Marilyn M. Taylor is cofounder the Canadian Institute for Research and Education in Human Systems, Adjunct Professor at the Ontario Institute for Studies in Education/University of Toronto's Transformative Learning Centre, part-time professor at the Professional School of Psychology in Sacramento, and Professor Emeritus of Concordia University in Montréal. She is a designer of innovative programs for systemic leadership education and is widely recognized for her process model of transformative learning.

Valerie Petrie lives in the town of Goderich and brings 20 years of living and working in Huron County to her research into community and economic development. Valerie completed a Bachelor of Independent Studies from the University of Waterloo in 1994 and a Masters of Adult Education from St. Francis Xavier University in 2001.

Kevin Watson is Lecturer in science, technology, and environmental education in the School of Social Ecology and Lifelong Learning at the University of Western Sydney, Australia. He is interested in environmental attitudes, learning, and the strategies that are employed to facilitate learning. He has a variety of research interests that explore "best practice" in science education and how these can be incorporated and sustained in diverse learning environments. Other research interests include perspectives on environments that recognize and respond to human cultural diversity within broad ecological frameworks.

Steve Wilson is Head of the School of Social Ecology and Lifelong Learning at the University of Western Sydney, Australia. He is interested in lifelong learning as a construct that helps us to understand learning methodologies that can lead to personal empowerment and transformation, social engagement, and employment. He currently researches and writes about "responsive curriculum" in secondary schools, particularly as it relates to student participation. He also researches the effective delivery of nonformal education through "integrated, community-based education."

Made in the USA
San Bernardino, CA
24 September 2017